Second World War RAF Pilot

Philip Hermolle

6th March 1920 – 4th January 1944

Letters

FROM A GOOD MAN AT WAR

'I had not read through Philip's letters since the time when I received them, but some points have always stood out in my mind. On re-reading them I am confirmed in recollection of him as being a young man of deep faith and holiness and of having a wisdom above his years . . . His idea of the standard which a priest should set himself makes me feel very humble now. Had he lived he would have been an inspiration to us all in whatever vocation he found his own.'

FATHER JOHN GARVEY PARISH PRIEST,
CHURCH OF ST. BIRINUS,
DORCHESTER ON THAMES, OXFORD, 1979

Second World War RAF Pilot

Philip Hermolle

6th March 1920 – 4th January 1944

Letters

FROM A GOOD MAN AT WAR

COMPILED BY SUE HESSEL

DEDICATION

*I am indebted to Philip's sisters, Monica and Kathleen Hermolle,
for their help with documentation as well as their faith, encouragement and
safe care of all the letters during these past seventy years.*

*Most of all, this is written in debt to Philip who, alongside his generation,
offered up his life for ours.*

In Memoriam

First published in Great Britain in 2016
by SMT Hessel Publishing

Copyright @ Sue Hessel 2016

Hardback ISBN 978-1-5272-0080-7
Paperback ISBN 978-1-5272-0319-8

SMT Hessel Publishing
9 Haslemere Rd
London N8 9QP

suehessel@hotmail.com

EDITOR'S NOTE

Philip's parents, Gerald and Norah Hermolle, met and married in Birmingham. Norah came from Ireland as a baby. Although Gerald's parents were from Germany, he was born in England, and as a British citizen he served on the front line in the Royal Army Medical Corps in the First World War.

Philip was the eldest of their six children, and began his Second World War service in the RAF from July 1940. In 1942 their eldest daughter Mary was also called up, and worked on secret and innovative work as a radar operator, identifying and tracking enemy aircraft.

Their other four children, Gerald (12), Kathleen (10), Lorna (7) and Monica (4) were evacuated after war broke out.

CONTENTS

INTRODUCTION

We used to say what a shame it was that we never knew Uncle Philip 'who died in the war'.

Philip Hermolle was just twenty years old when he was called up, and twenty–three when he was killed in the aftermath of the Battle of Ortona, Italy.

One of the nicest things about reading these letters has been getting to know this kind man and his family who, even during the stresses of nightly bombing, never faltered in love. I feel I know my Grandparents much more now than I ever did as I grew up (I was eighteen when Grandpa died; Grandma died nearly three years later). It has been the greatest privilege to have worked on the letters, and I have delighted in their innocence and natural charm. Philip's values of family love, obedience and gentleness shine throughout, and are testimony to his Catholic life and values in the early 1940s.

His letters begin, light–hearted, in Blackpool. Blackpool is his phoney war: 'I am still here at the seaside having the longest holiday I have ever had,' he writes. While there are air raids in Blackpool, he greets them with the carefree nature of youth: 'All this week we must have had nearly an average of four each day, and on Thursday last we had six! Bombs are rarely dropped however though planes hover overhead' (10 November 1940).

But only too soon the tone darkens and letters are sent and received against a backdrop of almost nightly air raids in Birmingham. By Christmas 1940 the family had been bombed out of their home, with the four younger children evacuated for their own safety and his parents temporarily rehoused. It is an unbearably sad and anxious time. 'I cannot help thinking very often how hard it must be for you remaining at home with five of your family spread about all over the country.' We feel a palpable anxiety beneath the surface. 'It seems a very long time since I heard anything from you, and I am eagerly awaiting some news. I see that Birmingham has just had two raids but I trust all is perfectly well and normal' (7 July 1941). I suspect Philip kept the worst of the war from his mother and father. The letters are anyhow censored, and he cannot say what he is doing for the war: 'It is rather unfortunate really that some of the highlights have to remain obscure, but it will not matter much,' he writes at the end, almost sensing the imminence of death, but with faith that truth endures.

What strikes most in these letters is their immense courage, unfailing courtesy and tenderness. 'You must have felt it very much indeed on Christmas Day, however

I expect that we all thought of and prayed for each other with the hope that next Christmas Day may perhaps see us all once again reunited.' In fact the last time the family was all together was in the summer of 1939.

With the hindsight of seventy years these letters can be seen to reveal themselves not only as a record of the war, but a documentary of how people lived – of a simplicity and family life that was retained from the 1930s. Philip's warm and self–deprecating descriptions of the organised dances and social life in Blackpool sound so pure and hearty compared to the antics of today! When Philip describes watching the sea at Blackpool (16 Nov 1940), with amazement we have to remind ourselves that in the 1930s seaside holidays were a great luxury. Coming from Birmingham, he had rarely even seen the sea.

Philip's later account of his journey to Canada (indeed all his trips abroad) is particularly interesting, the more so because he would have gone there wide–eyed. Unlike our generation there would not have been much prior knowledge of what other countries were like. There was no television or internet, and not much overseas travel, and the letters treat us to illuminating accounts of his experiences.

Philip was an ordinary yet extraordinary young man, with deep human qualities; his letters are written when he is still in his early twenties but radiating through them all is a maturity and a wisdom beyond his years. His secondary school years had been spent as a boarder at Cotton, a seminary for the priesthood. Over the duration he becomes firm in his decision that he would not become a priest – though he would have made a good one – but his spirituality remains profound, and the letters reveal an unfaltering faith. In the Appendix I also enclose some moving correspondence with his parents and his friend, affectionately named Gargoil (later ordained as Father John Garvey) that expresses his path towards this decision. The discipline of Catholics was stricter seventy years ago. Some of the attitudes which prevailed then seem curiously archaic and partisan to the modern reader, but they document the thinking of the time and may even seem rather endearing.

When the letters ceased I felt a deep sadness. By the time I reached the last letter I felt I really knew and loved this generous and faithful young man. It was a tragedy for all that he was only given twenty–three years. We lost a good man.

SUE HESSEL

CHAPTER ONE

BLACKPOOL

'I am still here at the seaside having the longest holiday I have ever had'
(10 November 1940)

38 Banks Street
Blackpool
16th July 1940

My Dear Mother and Father,

Well we have arrived here without undue mishap, but the wind is quite coldish and it looks as though there is rain about and I have not my coat. Still it is not worth sending it on, but there is my missal in the pocket for which I would be grateful. We have had this whole afternoon and evening to ourselves and have been watching angry sergeant majors swearing lustily at thousands of poor victims in blue. There must be literally tens of thousands of R.A.F. chaps here and you cannot look upwards without seeing spitfires and various brands of bombers flying no higher than the tower. There are also some hundreds of both Poles and French (airmen).

Well I'll give you more news later, and meantime everything looks as though we're going to have a good time. So best love and wishes to you all,

From Your Most loving Son
Philip

P.S. This above address is my billet (not half a minute from front!)

38 Banks Street
Blackpool
Thursday, 18th July 1940

My Dear Mother and Father,

Thanks for your letter and parcel received this morning, but as yet I've had no post card.

Yesterday was a pretty awful day I must admit, for we had to go from one place to another for different reasons but most of the time was spent in simply waiting in the open, and I'm afraid I must agree with you that the wind does blow with relentless persistency here in Blackpool, though they try and persuade us here that we must have brought the weather with us. But what made it worse was that in the morning we were vaccinated (four fainted) and in the afternoon inoculated against typhoid with the result that we had to go about very carefully protecting our left arms and it was quite a feat of endurance when at night we had to take our collars and ties off. They are still quite sore and swollen but a little easier than last night.

There is however one distinct advantage I have over yesterday, viz. that we now have full kit and uniform, and I am in it as I write and with the help of a vest I feel quite warm. Incidentally, we seem to be rigged out very well and have two pairs of pants, vests, trousers, shirts and boots, three pairs of good thick woollen socks, two towels, one pair of gloves and one scarf, sewing outfit, a good serviceable pen–knife, a gas mask with its bag to carry it in, another grey rucksack with more little bags inside, together with frying pans, water bottles and what not, and a good big oilskin cape and sou'wester. There is only one thing about all this and that is that it is all very cumbersome to carry about. It must all cost a great deal of money, because the bare uniform would run into some pounds if bought from a shop. I'm already finding the polishing up of buttons a major curse, and just think I've to do this for two or three years.

According to an estimate I have heard there are 20,000 R.A.F. in Blackpool alone, not to mention fragments of the army stationed up here and the considerable number of Poles and French. Some of these Poles look fine men and it can only make one wonder when Hitler says that they are an inferior race to the Germans. The French have not a very inspiring uniform, they wear black berets on their heads and the rest of their uniform is similar to that of the A.F.S.[1] men.

Was the 'Winter Gardens' here when you were last here? Or the Olympia? At any rate both these are now taken over by the R.A.F. for staff work, and St. John's Market Hall is the centre where they issue the uniforms and kit. In fact most of the places here are now under Government control in one form or another. The Tower is one notable exception; the Pleasure Beach is now almost deserted, but I believe it goes into full swing during weekends.

The crowd with whom I am billeted (eleven of them) could certainly be much worse, so in that respect I am lucky. The corporal and sergeant seem to be better than some others we've seen but on the whole they all seem more human than one is wont to imagine.

I have not seen any relatives yet as I haven't had time (and last night I think I must have had a touch of typhoid fever and therefore stopped in) but I will probably have a go tonight.

Well I will now close for the time being, and so with all my best love and wishes I am

Your Most Loving Son
Philip

P.S. Could you look in the cupboard in my room for that form for my holiday pay from Hercules[2] and send it on please? Also that Ebenezer Record Membership card?

---

1. Auxiliary Fire Service
2. Since leaving Cotton College had been working for firm called Hercules Bicycles before called up

---

38 Banks Street
Blackpool
22nd July 1940

My Dear Mother and Father,

I will get this letter off so that you will be able to expect after this a letter every Monday morning.

The weather has now definitely made a turn for the better which is something to be thankful for. Today i.e. Monday we went to school for the first time and had our first lectures on morse and receiving and transmitting messages. There were earphones to each one together with the little gadgets for sending the morse, and most of the time was spent in learning the alphabet by sound so that one day it will become second nature to us. Then from 1.30 until 4.30 we had parade on the front; our squadron has been put under a new corporal, and he certainly put us through our paces. All the R.A.F. has its parades along the front and if you were to walk during any part of the day time from the Pleasure Beach and go into the direction of Fleetwood for a good mile past the tower you would see the R.A.F. chaps being put through it every part of the way. When we have school in the morning we have our drill in the afternoon and the next day is vice–versa.

If you would like to know where Bank Street is, it is the next but one street to Talbot Street in the direction of Fleetwood, so you see I am only 200 yards or so from the Sacred Heart Church which is an extremely stately one in my opinion, and has a life–size white marble statue of St. Theresa placed on an ornate and elaborate stand also in marble.

Last night (Sunday) I passed a very pleasant evening listening to the North Pier Orchestra. I got into conversation with another chap who says he goes there most nights and he was leading violinist in a Scottish Orchestra and also deputy conductor. He certainly was extremely enthusiastic for he told me how he had spent nearly a whole night trying to thrash out a hard movement of Mendelssohn's something or other, and he is doing his best to get an R.A.F. orchestra started up here. I don't know how long he will last though, since he is training for a flight rear gunner which is generally regarded as a suicide squad up here. Talking about that sergeant, this morning they told us we were being trained for wireless ops.[1] and gunners (not rear gunners, at least I hope not).

This reminds me too that I was told in that letter you posted on to me, that a Cottonian, Johnny Byatt, in my form at school for my first four years there, was killed in action as a rear gunner. R.I.P.

I have not visited the Tower yet, but I went and saw Uncle Arthur[2] last Saturday night, and though I didn't see her, Auntie Mailey[3] lives there now. They were all out except Uncle Arthur, a young boy about ten, and Margaret who was only a few months old when last I saw her. He was very interested to see me and asked many questions about you all and has told me to go down as often as I wish, and to come again quickly to see the rest of the family, which he assured me was a very considerable one, especially as it had been only recently augmented by the arrival of twins to a daughter who is also stopping there now. It is a very big and nice house.

Well I will finish for the time being, sending you my very best love and wishes

From Your Most Affectionate Son
Philip

P.S. If you want know how I like the life, I can only answer that it suits me fine and is a hundred times better than being at the 'Hercules'.

---

1. Wireless operators
2. His father's brother
3. His Uncle Arthur's sister

38 Banks Street
Blackpool
24th July 1940

(Thanks for letter last Tuesday)

My Dear Mother,

Apart from wishing you the happiest of birthdays and many returns I will not dwell further on your anniversary which generally seems to be a sore point with you. I am sorry I won't be home though because I had planned to buy you a record of Myra Hess and had already made enquiries to that end, but that pleasure will I fear have to be postponed some weeks, and then I suppose there will be three birthdays to see to.

    This morning we went to school at 8 o'clock which means a good quarter of an hour's march beforehand, and then this afternoon during drill the C.O.[1] paid our squadron the compliment of telling us we were the smartest on the prom. Indeed we did attract a large, colourful and appreciative audience who always seem to find a great source of amusement in the aside remarks of the sergeant, and who are never slow in making great mirth at such mistakes as are occasionally made. This afternoon for instance we had to do the front salute (practice for taking a message up to an officer with the appropriate salutes) and of course the first time we did it I suppose it DID look rather funny, but one does feel a fool when one can only hear peals of laughter from above, behind and in front! It was also extremely hot work this afternoon but still very enjoyable – I am now getting used to my boots. I think we will be about ten weeks in Blackpool whence we proceed to somewhere near Swindon I believe.

    Well here's wishing you a very happy time and so with my very best love and wishes,

I am Your Most loving Son
Philip

---

1. Commanding Officer

My Dear Mother and Father,

This letter will I trust find you all in the very best of health and spirits, as it leaves me. For me however the horizon is not entirely cloudless since we have another inoculation coming off this week and they say that the second proves even worse than the first; in addition to this I can see that my vaccination has not taken, so that is another pleasure in store.

Last Tuesday after paying a visit to the church I noticed a card with a statement to the effect that there was a Catholic Club open to members of H.M. forces in Queen Street. I was very pleased and went straight along and found it a very large house with a large comfortable lounge in which was a radio, armchairs, a piano and periodicals; next came another room with tables for eating and drinking, brightened by the voice of McCormack on the gramophone! (They were nearly all Irish in there). Further along still was the canteen (cups of tea one penny, sandwiches one penny and cakes one penny). Upstairs was the R.A.F. Chaplain's room, a billiard room, then a games room (darts, bagatelle etc.) Upstairs again there were three rooms, one of which was for table tennis and another a study for writing and reading. I have been there most nights since and the night before last met a chap by the name of Hope[1] who is in our Squad and is the friend you told me Molly Smith[2] mentioned. I also met there another who works with Arthur Laughton.[3]

Last night when there I had the pleasure of playing both a French and a Polish airman at table tennis. The French beat me by two games to one and the Pole also beat me in only one game. It was however very amusing trying to make each other understand the score.

They say that the 10a.m. Mass to which all the Poles parade and which is exclusively for soldiers is a sight one would never forget. The Poles sing Polish hymns throughout and are said to have exceptionally nice voices. I did hear them singing once when on the march which was in striking contrast to the whistling of 'Roll out the Barrel' by most of our squads. Everywhere we march we do it whistling, and our signature tune is 'Happy is the day, when the airman gets his pay'.

Yesterday morning we had physical exercises on the sands and finished up with a game of all–in rugger played with a slipper. The one team took off their shirts and only had their trousers on, we kept our shirts on, the sergeant (the Leeds United centre half) played on the other side and I had the rare pleasure of making the only decent tackle of the game and it was on him. In fact I did it so well that he came down with a terrific thud (he is six foot one inch) and was put out of action for the rest of the day. In fact he could not take us on our march to school in the afternoon. However I'm a little anxious about the future as rumour has it that he does not intend to allow that event to pass by unavenged!

Well from all I'm telling you, you will be wondering what our armed forces are coming to nowadays. Still there are the worse periods as for example four continuous hours of morse each day and all these inoculations etc. As for the drill and marching I quite enjoy that, but of course it would not be as strenuous or as tiresome as army drill – we have never marched more than three miles at a stretch. Blackpool is getting very crowded now.

Well, this is all for now, so my very best love

Your Most Affectionate Son
Philip

---

1. Paddy or Tom
2. Friend from Handsworth, Birmingham
3. Son of neighbour in Farnham Road, (family home)

---

38 Banks Street
Blackpool
4th August 1940

My Dear Mother and Father,

Thanks for your last letter which I received on Tuesday last, but I hope you have not forgotten about that record card from the Ebenezer! I also received your postcard last Wednesday as to whether you should send on my coat!

This morning I saw Mr. Duffy[1] at the 7 o'clock Mass. He'd had to sleep on the prom all night. But if you are anxious at all on my score you can rest assured I am getting along very well, with good food (there could be more variety about it) and as a matter of fact everything is pretty good. The weather is at the moment royal; far too royal for marching and rifle drill. We get to the baths (the most modern I've seen) twice a week; the shower baths provide ample opportunity for bodily cleanliness, and so my head is quite all right now. In fact it has been better ever since I came here.

You will be able to visualise what Blackpool is like today; I went to 7 o'clock Mass this morning as we had pay parade at 8, and that Mass was very well attended; but for all the subsequent Masses long queues were waiting outside and all down Talbot Road until the 12 o'clock Mass. The 10 o'clock Mass was crowded out with Polish airmen of all ranks, and their singing of the hymns and especially their national anthem at the end was most striking. I did see one or two women waiting outside who were in tears; but the only thing is that it does not take much to put some people in tears, so you wouldn't have to take too much notice of that. Still it is rather touching when you think of them all miles away from their homes and not knowing what has become of their own dear ones and not even able to make any contact whatsoever. I always imagine that they must feel rather isolated in such a place for pleasure as Blackpool; I notice they go in large numbers to the orchestra on the pier, but apart from that I don't think they go to many places of entertainment.

I went to Uncle Arthur's for the second time last Wednesday, and again they were all out except Margaret (whom they call Peggy) and Tony and his wife. The other daughter with the twins has gone back again I believe. Tony is taking me and a pal I've made up here to a C.Y.M.S.[2] meeting tomorrow but he assures me that practically the whole meeting is taken up in games etc. However I have been very pleasantly surprised by the whole family, who seem very happy and courteous with each other, and as far as I can see they are all quite good and active Catholics. Tony's wife also seems a very good sort. Tony registered in February last and still has not heard, and he tells me he is not on important work at all. I have not seen Auntie Mailie at all yet.

I am signing that voluntary allotment of pay today and I will let you know when it takes effect. By the way, I have got over the second inoculation which sent me into a high fever on Monday night and all the next day, but, though with the second vaccination he tried to make sure and nearly scratched my arm off, I see now that even this one is not taking!

Well it's about time I ended again so here goes, sending you all my best love,

I am Your Most Loving Son
Philip

---

1. He served in WW1 and kept in contact with lads in forces, also a member of CYMS at St. Augustine's, the family church.
2. Catholic Young Men's Society

38 Banks Street
Blackpool
Saturday, 9th August 1940

My Dear Mother and Father,

I received your letter yesterday for which I convey my thanks. The main questions in it were I believe as to how the record book affected my financial position. Well I can soon put you at ease on that score as my financial position is quite sound, and talking about that reminds me that next month brings me a rise of three shillings six pence per week (which is a better one than Hercules were ever good enough to give me) and since (as yet) I have not taken up either smoking or drinking it will be quite a nice little help.

Talking about Hercules also brings to mind the fact that you should have received my holiday money from there within the last two or three days; have you? I hope you will pardon this further sudden remembering on my part, but you should also have received the attache case with my 'civs'[1] inside over a fortnight ago; you have not mentioned anything but I presume it's all O.K.

And now to get to more personal matters, how are you doing for air raids lately? I know you had at least one on Wednesday or Thursday and that Sutton was the unfortunate target, but I hope that they are not becoming a regular nightly affair. As yet we have escaped, but I cannot imagine that we will remain unscathed as the Germans are sure to know something of it all.

I can assure you however that as regards defence works for countering invasion, even Blackpool is seeing great activity. There are very strongly built barriers across even the main roads and there is only sufficient room for one vehicle to get through at a time; while all the entrances onto the Prom from the beach are completely barred to everything that goes on wheels. During the night from dusk onwards they are continually guarded, and no one may pass through without presenting his or her identity card.

Last Monday I went out with Tony (i.e. Uncle Arthur's) and had quite a good time. I was also with Bernard – the proud father of the twins – and we played billiards, ping pong etc. and of course darts at which I am sadly below standard. At any rate I made a point of getting to know something more about these twins entirely for your benefit; well here are the fruits of my labour:

1. I was introduced to his wife (I forget her name now). She too seems a very good sort.
2. She showed me the twins in the pram and asked me what I thought of them. Of course I replied that I thought they were delightfully charming and bonny. You of course will understand that they may be quite skinny and bony for all that I

know as I am by no means a connoisseur in that department – however for babies they looked quite all right and they made a very good impression on me because neither of them was awake and hence were not crying.

3. I went on to ask their age and then whether they were boys or girls or both. They were then (Monday) five weeks old, and so will be six weeks old when you get this letter; they also turned out to be one boy and one girl. I think that is all I managed to glean from them. You will think all this sounds rather heartless on my part, but I am not quite so disinterested as the above would paint me; I simply want to persuade you that you must come and see them for yourself if you do not want a distortion of the real facts!

Tomorrow (Sunday) I am again going out with Tony and Bernard after dinner, but I don't know where. Bernard by the way asked me to remember him and his family to you all! Aunty May[2] also asked me to do the same.

Next Monday (18th) the London Philharmonic Orchestra are up here at the Winter Gardens and both my pal and I are going. There are two others from my billets also going, which makes that at least three out of the ten at our house are, or intend, going.

Last night down here at the club, I heard a Polish Air Force Captain tell a group of us in quite good French how he had taken the statue of Our Lady of Victories, which he had before us in a very elaborate oak case, from a church in Warsaw while bombs were falling all round. He tucked it under his arm and has hardly lost sight of it since. He is exceptionally proud as he believes that it is the only one of four in Poland that will have escaped. He said that it went even in his fighter aircraft when in Poland and in France when he has actually come to grips with the enemy. He has carried it about everywhere, when he escaped from Poland into Romania, through Italy, into France and finally to England. He also immersed it in the stream at Lourdes while there. It is his intention he says 'Quand Hitler est fini' – here there was an appropriate gesticulation as he passed his hand across his throat – to reinstate it in Warsaw as a thanks offering to Our Lady of Victories. I could have almost laughed the way he spoke, as though ultimate victory was simply a matter of course – not that I doubt it – but he simply took it for granted that a year or two would see him carrying this statue back to Warsaw in triumph. Yet with all that confidence it was as plain as punch that he derived it not from any worldly source at all, but as he said 'Divine Justice' would ensure it in the last degree. I think he was a rather well–to–do Pole and from a rather good family, but he was certainly a very earnest Catholic.

Well I hope I have not bored you too much with this rather long epistle which after all does not leave you much wiser; however you will not always be so (un) fortunate to get nearly four full sheets like this, so I am sure you can put up with it for this once.

So now wishing you all the best of wishes and sending you my very best love I am

Your Most Loving Son
Philip

P.S. There might be a chance of a short week and pass one of these times but do not bank on it, as it is doubtful.

P.P.S. Don't tell me too much of these unappreciated puddings – my tongue nearly drops out of my throat!

---

1. Civilian clothes
2. Uncle Arthur's wife

---

38 Banks Street
Blackpool
Saturday, 16th August 1940

My Dear Mother and Father,

I received your letter last Tuesday and the Ebenezer's greetings. Thanks very much. I have written to the latter myself giving them instructions which I have received from here.

My first duty is to send to you my sincere felicitations on that wonderful concert which you produced with such stupendous and remarkable success. I can assure you that had I been there I would have been delighted with it. It is a little ironic that my next duty is to convey my deep sympathy in your new troubles with this cursed plague harassing you to such an extent during the dark hours of the night. I hear that the guns have now been in action and that Hitler's bombs also have started to fall; well I don't envy you one little bit but I cannot help feeling a little anxious now that things are beginning to move in your direction. I hope you will all hold your spirit high and remain in very good cheer, and that the children will not cause undue trouble.

Last Monday we went on the rifle range where I learnt pretty conclusively that whatever my vocation is, it is not to go about killing people. The rat–tat of the rifle and the smell of the fire sent a rather sinister feeling down my back and I thought what a terrible thing it seemed when you were practising to aim straight to kill another human being. Rather soft hearted I suppose, but none the less true; at any rate I did very badly for apart from two bulls eyes I only had five on the target out of five rounds from 200 yards range – in fact the C.O. informed me that I belonged to the awkward squad, which if it was not gladly received, was to the point. However I am going to improve in this sphere, distasteful though it is.

I am looking forward to the London Philharmonic concert tomorrow (Sunday) conducted by Malcolm Sargent, which you will hear on the wireless after the 9 o'clock news – so when you hear the clapping, my hands will also be helping to swell the applause. It will be a very good programme but you will be very surprised when you know that 'Rhapsody in Blue' is one of the pieces and apparently it is a classic of its type. In fact in a paper up here it says that in structure it has much in common with a symphony.

These four or five weeks of life up here have seen a great change in my character in some ways. I well remember sneaking out of my bedroom to go to Sunday Mass the first week, but since then I am pleased to record that I am nothing like so reticent about my principles or what I do in the way of going to church. The chaps in the billet are quite a good sort in most ways, but the conversation often drops to a very degenerating level and I find it best at such times to be completely absorbed in a book of G.K. Chesterton which I have taken from the library up here. Of course they think it the height of madness to lose an hour's sleep on Sunday morning by getting up for the 7 o'clock Mass when pay parade is at eight, but what they think matters far less to me now than what I thought they might be thinking when I first came. In spite of this spiritual tension as it were, I get on very well with them all, and I am convinced that they think none the less of me for it.

But in any case for all I have to go through in my billets and at meal times etc. I am well compensated by such friends as I have met at the club; there are some really excellent Catholics there who, for their impressive characters, put me to shame. There is one in particular who hails from Walsall – who is extremely fond of classical music and is going to the concert with me tomorrow; he is already in the stage of converting two very anti–Catholic airmen he has come across. On Wednesday night coming out of church a young man who had only come that day to join up asked me if I could give him any help about the next day which was a Holiday of Obligation; well I got talking to him and discovered that he was only home from Spain three years ago where he had been training for the priesthood. He was just as pleased to meet me as I to meet him. Then there is Tony[1] who is also a Catholic before anything else; he is one of exceptionally few men that I have seen wear that R.C. badge. He is very well liked, as is Bernard, by the priests of the parish.

So in some ways the army life (a very opposite life) has done more for me in five weeks than Cotton did in six years which is an exceedingly strange thing when you come to look at it.

I am enclosing some photos of myself which make me look much too fat.

These cost me 2/6 (six of them) and an enlargement is 6/6. If you want an enlargement I'll get it done, but if you are disappointed with the photos (which you may well be) I shall just leave those and wait for another time, perhaps when in Birmingham. I particularly want to give one to Kathleen in gratitude for her chocolate the day I left home, a gesture that, far from forgetting, I still cherish and mean to reward.

Well, I hope this has not bored you too much – I must write awful tripe at times – and now I will bid you goodbye and jolly good luck, and so with my very best love and wishes I am

Your Most Affectionate Son
Philip

P.S. Tonight Jim (my pal)[2] and I have been having a very interesting conversation with a Polish airman who escaped to England via Romania, Italy and France. Their confidence in victory is simply astounding, he told us that even if England loses, they (the Poles) will go somewhere else and fight until it is won!

P.P.S. Should you be writing to Auntie Kathleen[3] perhaps you would enclose one of these photos and also one of the small ones I had taken in town. I wrote to her about two weeks ago.

---

1. Cousin
2. Jim Gough, later Fr. James Gough
3. Mother's sister in New Zealand

There is a chap up here from Portsmouth and he receives all his letters from home like this:

1. I am now in an air raid shelter so am taking advantage to write to you – All clear.
2. In the shelter again, so will continue letter.
3. Third air raid, so will write a little more, etc. etc.

His last letter was written in five such stages!

My dear Mother and Father,

Thanks for your letter of Friday, and for Kathleen's[1] and Aunty Kathleen's. Yes I dare say I hear as much about the air raids as you do by the time I hear little odds and ends from the numerous letters that come from Birmingham. I bet you would like to be up here for a night or two, to be able to sleep in peace. I have just heard from the 9 o'clock news that the Midlands had its longest air raid of the war last night. The passive resistance which you and the rest of the population puts up seems to me to be magnificent, and I hope it will not get you down in any way at all.

I will not be quite so quick to laugh at Daddy about that big gun making him jump since I jumped considerably with a mere rifle shot when on the range. We were all flat on the ground taking aim to fire our first round when the chap next to me let go; needless to say I had to commence the little operation all over again.

In my last letter I forgot to tell you that Uncle Arthur wished to know why you couldn't come up here to see me and then see them at the same time. He said there was no excuse as Uncle Walter had a car! Actually I do not see too much of Uncle Arthur, I do not know whether he is working or not but Auntie May works, and I do not see too much of her.

By the way about my training up here for a W.Op. I have let myself in for a great deal more than I imagined! It means that I have got to settle down to REAL work and more swotting! It is certainly quite a highly skilled job, and as a matter of fact it seems to me that all the ordinary Air Force jobs demand a great deal of brainwork and swotting. There is my pal Jim, training as a flight mechanic; he is at school all day and though there is a fair degree of practical work, he has exercise books full of notes on Scientific principles and laws which he has to assimilate. Then at the end of each stage there is a proper written examination which MUST be passed if you are to get through for the particular job for which you then get substantially better pay. Should you fail and then fail again and even a third time you then get put on general duties, which means that you are little better than a mere labourer.

Thanks for telling me all about Schubert's 'Unfinished' Symphony which I heard in peaceful tranquility at the Catholic Club last night as well as Grieg's 'Anitra's Dance' and Wagner's 'Faust'. There would not have been a chance at the billets of hearing it. Mrs. Harrison[2] is left completely cold by some really cheerful light music, so you can guess how Symphony affects her. The London Philharmonic was really excellent; there was a record attendance at the Winter Gardens of over 4000 which included a large proportion of Air Force blue and some khaki. Beethoven's symphony was easily the most enjoyable and appreciated of the night. The Halle Orchestra is making a visit soon and I hope to be here for that whenever it is.

Well I shall now finish hoping that this letter finds you all well and in high spirits; and I often remember you in my prayers so you ought to be okay! Well here is my very best love and wishes to all

From Your Most Affectionate Son
Philip

P.S. If you find little time to write, or feel tired do not bother, so long as you are all right I will not mind waiting a fortnight or even longer.

---

1. His second eldest sister
2. His Blackpool landlady

---

38 Banks Street
Blackpool
31st August 1940

My Dear Mother and Father,

Thank you for your last letter and news. I was not surprised to see Leslie[1] on Thursday evening, as I have been keeping my eye open for a week or two to see if I could see him amongst any new recruits. The funny part was that he was by our house looking for me amongst the various squads as they marched up to be dismissed and he did not see me, in spite of the fact that I did my best to attract his notice. I have now shown him round the club and have played him at ping–pong. (He told me he was no good at this, but he gave me a fright with his first shot which left me fairly standing). Tomorrow we, together with Jim, are going to a social at St. Cuthbert's and expect to have a good time. Some Polish airmen are doing choral singing.

But I was very astounded this morning when I came in from church and found a note waiting for me from Bernard Hall[2] who had called round! He too is now posted up here and I am anxious to see him this afternoon, although I have already arranged to go out with Leslie and Jim. The funny part was that I wrote to him this week to his home address, which came to him in Blackpool (from where it started)!

This morning being the anniversary of the invasion of Poland I went to the Polish soldiers' Mass and the singing was very stirring as usual, but you ought to have heard a tenor solo of 'Ave Maria' (your Mother's favourite one). He had one of the very best voices I have heard, and gave a wonderful rendering.

Yesterday being Saturday, all our squad had to undergo a medical exam for Air Crew. The remark on my form was 'Fit for A.C. wireless operator and Air Gunner'. So it looks as though I will one day be roaring across the calm countryside of Germany. There were a large proportion who failed mostly because of eyes and heart.

Well I'm still having a fine old time up here and the weather has been fine this last one or two days. Actually bombs fell on Blackpool the very first night Leslie was here, so he thinks they are following him about (special orders from Hitler to get Les Hartley!) No damage and no casualties however and I slept through it all. Jerry has come over here the last two or three nights but we have had no sirens; I get to know this from the aerodrome.

I am glad to know you are getting along okay and adapting yourselves to your new circumstances! Well I will now conclude sending you all my very best love and wishes

From Your Most Affectionate Son
Philip

P.S. Leslie looks jolly smart in his uniform, and he assures me that Mary[3] would be uneasy if she could see him now, for he says that it is obvious that all the other girls recognise it as well! However he has said quite a lot about Mary so she need not worry. He has, he says, warned her that if she paints her face he will grow a moustache!

---

1. His eldest sister Mary's boyfriend, later husband
2. Friend from junior school
3. His eldest sister

38 Banks Street
Blackpool
14th September 1940

My Dear Mother and Father,

Did you hear of a thickly populated working class district of a North West coastal town being bombed with high explosive bombs on Friday's news? Well I might tell you I heard the bombs all night which landed not more than 300 yards from our billets demolishing eight of these rather poor houses just on the other side of North Station. In fact one or two bombs fell on the station but did no substantial damage; there were a number of fatalities that have been extricated from the ruins, and there are still more missing I believe. The funny part of it was that this aeroplane circled all round Blackpool about three times so low that we could see it plainly although it was nearly eleven o'clock. In fact I was watching it and rather imagining it to be British, but not being quite certain (as no sirens had gone) when all of a sudden just before he was directly above our house a terrific scream or rather howling began to penetrate the air. Why, in that split second the visions that came into by head; and the prayers for happy death I would have gladly said, for I thought it was coming straight for us. Anyway I'm still here, so is Leslie and it couldn't have landed more than a hundred yards from him and he slept all through it! What he was aiming for seems a mystery, for there was not much point in hitting that station which is of pretty well no strategic importance and is only a mere terminus. There was an important training centre near at hand but everything to do with that is an official R.A.F. secret, so I will not say more of that.

Well now that I have that story off my chest I will proceed a little more normally. Yes I returned back O.K. and much to the relief of us all nothing was found out about our breaking away early. I arrived in at exactly eleven o'clock, and found the wind strong as ever. On the train I discovered that a number of the soldiers had been recalled from leave; incidentally I was very fortunate for the next day Monday an order was read out that there should be no more applications for weekend passes as they were to be temporarily stopped except for a very important reason. So it looks as though that might be expecting something doesn't it? Well I cannot promise when I will come and see you all again, the only thing is that I cannot possibly come every weekend; and it might be some weeks before I get another chance. In fact it is more than likely that it will be as things are now. By the way they are asking both the army and the R.A.F. for volunteers for parachutists, and you get 8/6d. per day straight away. Shall I volunteer? Well not to keep you in suspense, I have no idea of volunteering: and I'm certain the thought of 8/6d. per day does not appeal to me all that forcefully, and in any case if I pass out all right I will get 7/6d. per day as it is.

The other night at the club we had some Catholic airmen in there giving us accounts of their experiences when bombing Germany or in contact with the enemy. Someone asked a fighter pilot whether the figures given for enemy losses were really reliable, to which he answered that the intelligence officers had to be absolutely foolproof and another witness before they would accept a raider as down. He said that he was himself absolutely positive of bringing one down, that a large patch of oil and wreckage was on the sea for well over a day, and still he was not given credit for it. In fact they all testified very strongly as to the reliability of our reports and figures; although one wireless opp. and rear gunner (who had been over the Ruhr over twenty times) did admit that sometimes individual pilots perhaps exaggerated damage done in night raids. But even these were substantially true when he had compared our papers to what he had seen. At Essen he said, they left a terrific mess on one of their raids, one that he could never forget. It was also generally emphasised how strict the intelligence people were and pilots too, that they should hit only military objectives. All those were up here convalescing for one reason or another.

Well I certainly did enjoy being home last weekend though it was for so short a time; I did feel momentarily depressed as we drew out of New Street[1] as though "what was the good of life?" but that very quickly passed, for one thing I suppressed those kind of thoughts and deliberately got into conversation with some other chaps. So I was soon my old self; and now wishing you all my love

I am, Your Most Loving Son
Philip

P.S. I hope you won't mind if I only send one photo of myself as Mrs. Harrison seems keen on having one of each of us for herself. I will get some more done.

---

1. Birmingham rail station

38 Banks Street
Blackpool
21st September 1940

My Dear Mother and Father,

Well it has been a very hectic week since last I wrote in more senses than one. I don't mean that anything much has happened to me, for it has not, but what with the weather and the growing intensity of the war and what not, it seems an almost remarkable week to me. I don't know whether you will believe me when I tell you that the wind in two or three points along the front on Tuesday was literally blowing people right off their feet; I saw one poor old lady who was just crossing the road blown right over and then sent rolling over and over until the kerb stopped all further progress. I myself was all but whipped off my feet in one unprepared moment, and even then I was sent running down this street, along which I did not want to go, and found I could not stop myself until I caught onto a piece of wall protruding from a shop. And although it caused great mirth and merriment, it was something I would never have believed possible. And then there was the sea itself, which although it was not Blackpool at its best was certainly sufficient for us to see why Hitler's invasion would have to wait. And yet last night Saturday, the sea was as calm as a lake, and there was not a breath of wind; but what was most striking was the wonderful colour scheme at sunset, when the sea was simply a plain glass surface of bright yellow and pale blue streaks. Leslie was quite as struck about it as I, and thought he was looking on a picture of fairyland.

Well how are you getting on with the organ nowadays; I don't suppose that you are finding much trouble in it and putting the old organist in the shade[1]. And about the air raids, are they causing you much trouble nowadays? Actually we have had three air raid sirens in Blackpool this week, one of which was in the afternoon, so you see things are beginning to look up even up here. Last night there was a good firework display down in Preston direction, but the sirens had not gone while that was in progress.

I think that it will be alright if you write next week although it is possible that we will have gone from here by Saturday but I think most improbable. At any rate I will get a postcard off just before we go, and you will then understand if you don't hear for a day or two.

I find I have to put these wretched photos into another envelope as there will not be room to put in both letter and photos. I say get wretched photos because they almost frightened me when I first looked at them, and I can only hope and pray that they do not affect you as they did me.

We had our science exam yesterday and I think I got on O.K. in that.

One thing, I do know a little about wireless now, so next time I come home you will have to be prepared to allow me to fish out all the various valves, transformers, condensers etc., etc! I find morse a little difficult however, more so than most chaps here.

By the way, did you hear that concert on the wireless last Wednesday (the Polish Relief Concert). It was most enjoyable, but that Beethoven *Symphony in C minor* was the one we heard the London Philharmonic play and I like it very much.

Well will now finish, wishing you all my most sincere love and wishes

From Your Most Affectionate Son
Philip

---

1. His mother was now organist at St. Augustine's Church
as the previous organist had been called up

---

38 Banks Street
Blackpool
Saturday, 28th September 1940

My Dear Mother and Father,

Thanks very much for your letter of Wednesday last. I did not think that you would like those photos somehow, so it is in no way disappointing to me that you didn't.

Well I hear that Mary is coming up here today, and she will certainly find the weather very nice to what it can be in Blackpool, in fact the sun shines in a clear blue sky. I've seen Leslie this morning who is obviously very excited but also on the point of madness because he cannot escape bathing parade at 7.30 this evening.

I am still in ignorance as to when we are due to leave Blackpool; our squad will leave sometime late this coming week I think, but it is possible that my stay at Blackpool will be extended a little since I am not up to the sufficient standard in morse – not of course that I mind in the least, 'there's method in my madness'. Still all this is conjecture, but I feel sure that if you try and get a letter in here by Wednesday I shall be here; on the other hand don't rush yourself unduly, because I will not mind if you leave it over for a period. I have not seen Bernard since last Sunday so I have a feeling he must have gone from here – he is not a W.Opp. and so would not be conversant with the various parts of a wireless. Neither would Leslie as a matter of fact for he has not started his science course yet.

Well we are certainly taking pretty hefty bites from Hitler's 'Luftworte' or whatever you call his air force, which is a pretty good job considering his new burst of diplomatic activity. One thing I'm glad it's the R.A.F. I'm in, and not the German air force, if only for reasons of self– preservation.

Yes, I did hear the King's speech which was quite a good one. The 'all clear' signal which came through caused many people to think that there was an air raid on Blackpool, and I must confess that I myself was a little mystified at hearing the 'all clear' siren when we had been given no 'alert'.

From reports we get here, from sources from Liverpool, they are having a very rough time down there, but they all say that of real damage to the docks and military targets, there is practically none. Down in Preston direction too we see a wonderful display of 'fireworks' about 8.30 every night, and recently it appears to have become far more intense, with very bright and vivid flashes from the ground occasionally, whether from bombs or not, I could not say.

There are some number of poor chaps up here who have received telegrams from the War Office saying that their houses in London have been smashed or some of their relations killed. One chap from Liverpool has had his whole family killed except for one sister; a chap in our very billets has had his next door neighbour killed in Portsmouth and another chap in our billets has had his grandfather killed in London. London must be a terrible mess judging from what I have read in an Irish (Dublin) paper, which however has the highest praise for the efficiency of the A.R.P.[1] services which have kept casualties so comparatively small.

Well it is all a terrible thing but I hope it will be a better England after this war – if so it will have been well worth all our present troubles.

Well I will now conclude wishing you all my very best love and wishes

From Your Most Affectionate Son
Philip

P.S. Yes tell both Lorna[2] and Monica[3] I was very pleased to receive their wonderful little letters. (In fact I will endeavour to enclose one for them.)

---

1. Air Raid Precaution
2. Second youngest sister
3. Youngest sister

My Dear Mother and Father,

Well the weekend is here again, and still I am here as are the whole squad. I am afraid that I still do not know much about when we are going except that it must be soon next week, but even then as to whether I will be kept back or not is a matter for the future to tell.

How are things looking at home now? Are the air raids still as frequent and intensive as ever? And how do they affect your daily life and routine? Last Monday I met a rather young lady who had seen me kneeling before the statue of St. Therese, and being herself a great devotee of the Little Flower started to speak to me on her. She had just that day been compelled to evacuate London, and she reckoned that no words could describe what those people were suffering. She said that the land mines dropped by parachute did terrific damage, wrecking whole streets of houses at a time.

She had herself been bombed out of her home, and then out of another house, and said that the last month seemed like twelve. There are now quite a large number of people up here that have come from London and judging by the tales that come in from one source or another they have certainly had a very bad time.

Last Tuesday Jim roped me off to a dance for members of the Forces that the Children of Mary of St. Cuthbert's were arranging. Price was threepence including refreshments! And I reckon we had at least four penny worth of things to eat so we did not do so bad, did we? The evening was one of the most amusing I have had for some time, however, as I discovered that Jim was almost as bad, if not worse, than I am at these social affairs. He cannot dance for which he was extremely sorry as there was one girl who had properly taken his fancy. The peak came however during the last dance when with a sudden burst of courage he stood up determined to ask her if she would give him a 'trial run' as it were, but when he almost got there his nerve cracked up and after he had hesitated he went and asked someone else.

There were two dances (some kind of novelty things) which were so easy that I joined in them; actually the one was not a dance but more after the style of musical chairs, for if one together with one's partner were caught on the mat when the music ceased you were out. Jim was very thankful that Leslie was not there that night because he knew that had he been, Leslie for pure spite, or what Leslie would call fun, would have teased him by making a point of having one or two dances with her 'just to rub it in'. Anyway both Jim and I culminated the night by escorting this girl and her friend home, which nearly brought us both seven days

C.B.[1] as they lived in the wrong direction and made us a quarter of an hour late in that night. We have now to be in at 10.30 at night.

Last Thursday I went to a C.E.G.[2] class at St. John Vianney school which I found very interesting and instructive. They continue every week for nine weeks and it is a pity that I will not be here much longer to go to them. The priest, Fr. Baron, is very good and clever and has asked me to bring along as many other members of the forces as I can and I have got five or six who have already a promised to go along next week. Did I tell you that I had also been getting to morning Mass sometimes? Well I was able to for one short spell but now they have made us parade earlier and so it is impossible. I cannot complain too much though because the church here is extremely handy and open all the day until about 7 o'clock in the evening which is an advantage we certainly shall not have when on a station. I had a letter from Doyle[3] the other day who sent me one of those Cardinal's crosses especially for members of the Forces. I do not know how he obtained it for our Padre has been waiting a long time for a large number of these, and he says they are very hard to get. At any rate I am the only one up at the club who has one.

Well I don't know how you will go on about writing to me; I will leave Auntie – that's what we call Mrs. Harrison – your address if anything happens, just in case. But on the other hand I will not worry at not hearing from you so if you like to leave it over until something is definite I don't mind.

Did Mary enjoy herself up here? I did not see too much of her but of course Leslie was her host rather than me and so that is rather natural in a way. Leslie complained that the number of officers he met while out walking with her was scandalous, and just for spite when seeing an officer arm in arm with another young lady, he went out of his way to salute him! Well I will now conclude if you don't mind and I hope that you are quite as happy and on top or the world as I am. It sounds impossible these days but still I do manage to feel extremely happy in spite of it all.

Well with my very best love and wishes to you all, I am

Your Most Loving Son
Philip

---

1. Confined to barracks
2. Catholic Evidence Guild
3. Father Colin Doyle, parish priest at Market Drayton

My Dear Mother and Father,

Your letter last week was received just after I had posted my letter to you so you will understand why I made no mention of it.

Well this week that is now drawing to a close has been the laziest I have had for a long time. We have done precisely nothing at all except parade about four times a day when we have been promptly dismissed. There is some re–mustering of squads and wings going on and nobody seems to know where anybody is, except that most of our squad went to Yatesbury or Compton Basset last Friday.

It is a jolly good job that the weather is so wonderful now for otherwise life would tend to become rather tedious, but as it is I have been able to go for some long walks which have been very much appreciated after being tied down to more or less the same spot.

Bombs were again dropped in Blackpool, this time in the same street Bernard lives in (who has not gone after all). There was, however, little damage and no casualties. A number of incendiary bombs fell on South Pier but as it was simply pouring down with rain, they did no damage at all. The Jerry in question also dropped a flare which lit up the whole of Blackpool and made my quick walking pace develop into a steady run.

Richard Tauber in 'The Land of Smiles' has been at the Opera House (Winter Gardens) this week, and of course I went to see and thoroughly enjoyed it. 'You are my Heart's Delight' was encored four times. I also see that the Halle Orchestra under Sir Henry Wood will be up here a fortnight today, and I sincerely hope that I will still be up here for that.

How small is this world, is it not? At least judging from the number of chaps of whom I know or others who know other chaps I know (e.g. I have met someone here from Reading who knows Bernard Coakley[1] quite well – Bernard C. is now in the R.A.F.) that I have come across up here. Last Tuesday quite by accident down at St. Cuthbert's I met a chap whom I used to kneel next to every day at St. Chad's midday Benediction but to whom I had never spoken. I asked him if he recognised me or had seen me before, but he could not remember until I reminded him where. At any rate it turned out very fortunate for he was not feeling his best, as he knew nobody and had only come up the day before. It turns out that he knows several Cottonians, was in the Birmingham C.E.G. and his name is Philip![2] He was therefore very pleased to come to the C.E.G. meeting at St. John Vianney's along with two others I had brought.

I received your letter via Leslie this dinner time, and I am glad that you do not find the air raids too disturbing. I will see what I can do as regards that voluntary allowance, perhaps I will be able to change the name to Mrs. Hermolle but I cannot see them before 6p.m. on Friday and even then I don't think it takes effect until a fortnight later.

As to your query on leave I don't see that there is any likelihood until the end of my training, though if they cannot absorb us quickly at these different stations they might send us home for a week – but that is something which I cannot promise. On the other hand I hope to get home for a few weekends which I think will be a little more frequent on a station.

Well I will have to come to a finish now and so until next week I will send you all my most sincere love and wishes

From Your Most Affectionate Son
Philip

---

1. Coakley family lived in and went to school in Handsworth
2. Later went on to become Fr. Philip Garrett.

---

38 Banks Street
Blackpool
18th October1940

Dear Mother and Father,

Today it is Friday but the week so far has been spent much the same as last, and for want of something else to do I am making a start on this next week's letter.

I am now the only one of the original lot from 38, Banks Street. The house is now full of other new 'rookies' all from London but still they seem quite a good set of chaps. The way things are going on, Leslie will pass out of Blackpool before me for they have not yet re–squadded me, and by the time they do it will be possible that Leslie will have got ahead of me. I don't mind however at all for there is so much in Blackpool to keep me occupied that I'm in no hurry whatever to leave.

There is for instance a new 'study circle' formed at our club and our chaplain is exceptionally enthusiastic on that sort of thing as well as C.E.G. work. I am going to ask him if arrangements could not be made for early daily Communions every morning for the benefit of members of the R.A.F. of whom a number would be pleased to come. Then again there are those C.E.G. classes at St. John Vianney's with Fr. Baron whom I like very much. I have been the source of much merriment when he has gone to great pains to explain some argument to me, and then asked me if I understood only to be answered with a calm 'No'. He has asked us few R.A.F. chaps to join in a game of soccer next Saturday but I am afraid that I could not very well as I have not played for some long time now. However I am going up to watch the others and will also see how Tony plays as he is very keen about it.

Tomorrow there is a British–Polish concert at the Jubilee Hall, price only 3d. and from what I see about it, it seems that it ought to be really good. Then on Monday there is the final of a choral societies' competition in the Tower Ballroom. On Saturday the Halle Orchestra under Sir Henry Wood is the greatest attraction of all, but I am a little doubtful as to whether I will be able to get there, I only hope with all my heart that I will.

Last Sunday I heard two hours of Reginald Dixon and the Tower Ballroom was simply packed. But still it was well worth going to hear and I only wish I had known of these Sunday recitals before. The programme was of course very mixed and included one or two modern tunes, a fair number of older songs, some light classics such as Strauss 'Waltzes' and then one or two real good pieces like 'Hungarian Rhapsody No.2'.

Now all this time I have been speaking of myself or things related to me, and now what of you? How have you survived those two bad air raids which I can only presume applied to Birmingham on Tuesday and Monday nights. I am afraid that up here we hardly realise that there is a war on, apart from a few alerts which fortunately never materialise into raids. Of course there is the spectacle of a large number of little children who are now playing on the sands, who are up from London with their mothers; for the weather is very mild now.

It is now about 5pm and I have just received your letter. Well I will try and see to that voluntary allowance of which you speak. Yes, I can quite imagine you have had one or two rough nights with the Jerries about on their mission of destruction and death, but I hope you found the anti–aircraft guns very consoling and that they did sterling work. However I think that Birmingham will acquit itself as nobly as London and Liverpool in these bombardments – the people of whom are wonderful from what I hear. In fact one chap told me when fifteen incendiary bombs were dropped on his street, the whole lot of the residents simply flocked out together with buckets of sand, stirrup pumps, water, mud and anything of use, in spite of falling debris, splinters and even bombs – and finally put each bomb out of action within five minutes!

Leslie and I are two out of five airmen who are taking up a challenge at ping pong to play a team of five Children of Mary from St. John's on Tuesday next so we are going to have a bit more fun. Jim won't be there, he has gone on a week's leave – still I think he deserves it for he has not so much as seen home since April last – and I'm afraid that he fears he will be sent out to Egypt after this, which certainly seems a great probability at the present time. Regarding your query about Tony I still see him, in fact it was only last night that I was playing him at ping pong, however about having meals there, I have had very few since we always go out to this club at St. John Vianney's.

Well I don't think there is very much else I can say, and so I hope you will not mind if I bring this short epistle to a close. Here, then, are my very best love and wishes for your safety and health,

From Your Most Affectionate Son
Philip

P.S. Bernard came up to see me last week while I was out, and as I have seen nothing of him since, I presume he had come to tell me he had been posted! (His billet was a good two miles from mine, right down South Shore).

This letter contained a programme of the above mentioned Polish concert, on the back of which was written: "This concert was very good. The choir and the Revellers especially were greatly applauded and all were Polish airmen. The Polish folk dances in their national costumes were also very quaint and graceful. Incidentally an air raid alarm went at 6.45pm while it was on, nor did it end until 12.10pm – quite long for Blackpool wasn't it? Bombs were again dropped in Blackpool but with what damage and casualties I don't know."

38 Banks Street
Blackpool
21st October 1940

My dear Mother and Father,

Your letter and one from Michael arrived for me last night, and thanks for both. Yes I know full well that Birmingham is now undergoing a good part of the blitz and I only hope and pray all remain safe and unharmed through this terrible time. How are the children taking it? And do they still go to school as usual? I would not mind betting that I would be quite a baby if I went to Birmingham now, for though air raids are now a very regular occurrence even here, and though we hear quite a deal of machines above us, as yet we have had no serious attack which is just as well as we are (I think) entirely undefended. Last night the air raid siren went at 7.15p.m. and ended sometime after midnight, and in the meantime several aeroplanes were flying very low but fortunately nothing materialised.

Leslie has told Mary something about my being a pilot I believe, but I don't know whether he gave the facts correctly. Well, here they are. All the Wireless Opp. Air gunners not yet posted were called down before the Selection Board and were told that there was a radical change in policy, and that we would be given the exceptional chance of applying for a pilot. There were fifty three of us and only seven of us passed the Selection Board as recommended; I was one of these, largely because I had attained a good standard at rugger and cricket I think. Then I went off up for a medical examination and five of us passed that; it was a tougher one than any of the others I have had. I have now the CO's signature to the recommendation and am awaiting events. However this is only the first step of the ladder, and all this preliminary examination merely sets me as fit to appear before No. 1 Board at Padgate which is THE medical board for pilot airmen. Well I never thought that such an opportunity would ever come my way, yet it has done just when I thought it was least likely. The questions asked by the selection board were mainly of a general knowledge character and general observation such as 'what countries border on Egypt?' and 'What are the names of four B.B.C. announcers?' Just in case you may be wondering what I am going and letting myself in for I can assure you that it is certainly no more dangerous than W.Opp Air Gunner which is reckoned the most dangerous job in the R.A.F.

I will enclose the programme of the Halle Orchestra. I enjoyed it immensely and thought it really magnificent. What was my joy when I saw they were going to play that *Fifth Symphony in C minor* of Beethoven, which is the one I have told you of before, and was played by the London Philharmonic Orchestra. It is the most wonderful piece of music I think I have ever come across, and there is one run in the second movement, that is taken in turn on all the strings, which simply thrills me through and through. Four members of the Orchestra were in uniform, (three army and one R.A.F.)

Well I will now conclude sending you all my very best love and wishes and prayers too (for you'll need them)

From Your Most Loving Son
Philip

P.S. Today at our own request a party of about thirty of us from the club are having a day retreat from our Padre. He is also going to fix those 7 o'clock Communions about which I asked him.

14 Clevedon Road
Blackpool
Saturday, 3rd Nov. 1940

My Dear Mother and Father,

Please note my new address to which I have moved today. I was about to tell you a tale of woe about this new place because the food is far more limited and not nearly so good as the last place, while they are far more particular here on certain details as for instance meals; they will not serve meals until all are in together. There was another big drawback, that breakfast is at 7 o'clock prompt every morning which of course would prevent me from going to Holy Communion. However by a stroke of good luck when I mentioned about going to church and that consequently I would not be quite early for breakfast (for I had determined to go on Sundays even at the risk of missing breakfast) I found out that the people here are Catholics, and they seemed very pleased to have a Catholic airman in the house, and are already showing me some little consideration. So now I will avail myself of the first opportunity to ask her if she will not mind my having breakfast later every morning.

Mrs. Harrison was very sorry to have me go but I have promised to go and see her before I leave Blackpool. In any case I shall have to call round early every day to see what 'post' there may be for me. Except for you I will not bother about telling others of the change of address since I don't expect to be in Blackpool long.

I was thankful to receive your letter last Thursday. We all look for news from home far more eagerly while such places like Birmingham are having it as badly as they are. I still hope and pray for the safety of you all both mind and body. Arthur Laughton is distinctly fortunate in having leave so early, we have asked time and time again and can make no headway at all. At the moment there is little possibility of even 'French leave' since we are all awaiting various lists and postings to come through, and if they did and we were not there, then we would be in the soup. Besides I would have to hitch–hike for you cannot get a ticket on the station without producing a pass, and hitch–hiking is a very worrying business these dark nights, especially trying to get back to Blackpool. Actually there is a slight chance that I might get a leave if I get posted for training as a pilot, especially if they take us off to Canada. This is all hypothesis and only conjecture however so we had just better wait and see.

The Halle Orchestra is making a return visit to Blackpool on November 16th, a fortnight's time. I should like to be here for that, but somehow I doubt whether I will. I have as yet been able to do nothing about that voluntary allowance scheme; I have been to our own Station H.Qs and to the Accounts Office, and at neither place have they a form which must be filled in and duly signed before they attempt to go any further into the business. However I will take the first opportunity when it comes along.

I heard from Bernard Hall the other day and he appears to be rather bored with life in general, saying that they have nothing special to do apart from different odd jobs throughout the day.

Well I will now conclude hoping that this letter will find you all safe and in excellent spirits, then with my best love and sincerest wishes I am

Your Most Affectionate Son
Philip

---

14 Clevedon Road
Blackpool
10th November 1940

My dear Mother and Father,

I am still here at the seaside having the longest holiday I have ever had! What an inefficient lot these R.A.F. people seem; they do not seem to know what to do with us, or even who we are, or what we are supposed to be doing. In short we are doing nothing special save for odd jobs that want doing, such as in stores, or equipment or laundry. While we sometimes have to help with the laundry (not washing of course!) we cannot even have our own washing sent there with the result that for the last six or seven weeks I have had to wash all my own shirts, vests, socks etc. and by the time I have finished ironing my shirt it is invariably dirtier than when I began to wash it! Neither can we send our boots to be repaired, and the one pair have become so bad that I had to have them done privately – they are real clod–hoppers now with thick iron tips on the heels, studs on the soles!

I do hope with all my heart that they leave us here until next Saturday for then the Halle Orchestra under Sir Henry Wood is paying a return visit to the Tower Ballroom. There will be Beethoven's Symphony no. 8 (I don't know it by name), and 'Polonia' (Elgar), 'Casse Noissette' (Tchaikovsky) and Schubert's 'Unfinished' Symphony! In fact it all appears very inviting, so as I say I hope I will still be here.

So far this morning we have not had an alert which is very peculiar indeed. All this week we must have had nearly an average of four each day, and on Thursday last we had six! Bombs are rarely dropped however though planes hover overhead.

These alerts would have a very different effect on me I suppose if I were in Birmingham.

This week I have managed to get to Mass and Holy Communion every morning as the tenants here make an exception of the breakfast rule for me; in fact they treat me like a lord! On Monday our Chaplain (R.A.F.) went to his altar without a server so I immediately went up to serve him, he thanked me and said he would offer the Mass up for my intentions, so as part of my intentions I embraced those of you as well. I serve him every day now and he calls me 'Pip' or 'Pipsqueak'.

Tomorrow I am speaking at that C.E.G. meeting on my old subject of 'Infallibility'. I have no books to help me to get the subject up but I hope I will be all right. Anyhow Fr. Baron will not mind I do not think, for I think I have sufficient of it to speak off hand; he is a wonderful priest and we have had some wonderful arguments!

I have just heard that poor old Neville Chamberlain is dead, what a pity.

Yes, I did receive that Cardinal's Cross from Joseph Baggot, but I gave it to another airman here who badly needed one. I have had a Cardinal's Cross for a long time now sent by Doyle.

The sea this morning is really worth watching, and great mounds of water towering up to crash against the beach walls causing terrific spray. It is peculiar but I think I could go on watching the sea for hours at a time, and especially as it is.

Well I will now conclude wishing you all my best love and prayers for your continued safety.

From Your Most Affectionate Son
Philip

---

14 Clevedon Road
Blackpool
Friday, 16th November 1940

My Dear Mother and Father,

Believe it or not but as I write this letter there is an air raid on! At least we have had an alert and I have a shrewd suspicion I have heard a Jerry plane and also some machine gun fire. However it is possible that it was only a British trainer plane having some gunning practice so I cannot be at all sure. Actually though I feel so unconcerned about this 'raid', I cannot help feeling a little concerned at the news this (Friday) dinner time which spoke of the Midlands being the centre of last night's activity, and saying that a special announcement would be made later. It sounds really bad and it rather makes me half ashamed when I consider that I am in the forces and am supposed to be ready to give my life for this great cause yet, not withstanding, I enjoy comparative safety and ease, while all you at home are having such an anxious and perilous existence.

However I do my best by praying for you all and today especially I remembered you all during the lunch–time Exposition of the Blessed Sacrament. The children from the school always come in and sing for the concluding benediction and I often think how nice it would be to see Lorna and Monica trotting up the aisle with them; there must be a fair proportion of evacuees amongst them, at least there seems to be a number of cockney accents mingled with all the shouting and shrieking that issues from a school playground.

I was slightly disappointed this morning for four of us had got our corporal to get us a 'pass form' each. This he had managed (for he had instructions that under no circumstances could he give them out) and our hopes ran high as we filled them in and thought of spending the weekend at home, but alas, this morning all were handed back with a thick 'blue pencil' line across the middle. Nevertheless I shall persevere, and one day I hope my patience will be rewarded. There will be one advantage of remaining at Blackpool till Christmas – I am beginning to give up hopes of going now and Fr. Oldham tells me I'm a fixture for the duration! – and that will be that. I would at least be able to spend Christmas day and Boxing day round the old fireside (if it will still be there). I think that it would be almost certain that we could get away from Blackpool then, so in a way I almost hope now that I shall be able to hang on another six or seven weeks .

The first part of this week I spent most of my time running round the streets of Blackpool picking up people's hats for them – that was of course when I was not running after my own! At night time I do not risk wearing it, preferring to carry it, or if the wind were to suddenly whip it off in the blackout, I would be in a way wouldn't I? It was very funny on Monday (for the onlooker) when a stout old gentleman was walking up the street and his bowler hat was suddenly whipped straight off his head and blown straight up into the air to rest on top of the Odeon Cinema – and I can assure you it is a very high building. In fact for those two days hats were being blown off people's heads as the leaves fall off the trees in autumn, and the more experienced womenfolk of the town all come out with scarves tied round their heads. Talking about these winds, Fr. Oldham told us the other night that last year a policeman who was on point duty was literally carried away through a sudden gust and blown through a shop window! He sustained fairly severe injuries and had to be pensioned off the force!

The sea too has been a wonderful sight this week, and looking out you can just see a series of great white tossing, mounting and falling waves, and when full tide is in they hurl themselves at the stone work with an almost frightening ferocity and thunderous roar causing large explosions (for so they appear) of white foam. It is a spectacle, I think, that cannot fail to bring home to anyone how strong and powerful is the hand that causes it, and that though men are exploiting their destructive powers to the full there is nothing they can bring forward that can compare with the irresistible might of the sea. You will wonder whether I am turning into a philosopher when you read this, but they are thoughts which ever assail my imagination and they do, I think, help one to put the temporary horrors of this war into their true perspective.

I spoke at last Monday's C.E.G. meeting and Fr. Baron made some criticisms, but said it was quite good on the whole; he has got me to speak again this Monday, and if I don't watch out he will have me speaking on the sands!

The Halle Orchestra tomorrow! and I'm certainly looking forward to it. There will also be the Blackpool Symphony Orchestra on Sunday but unfortunately it clashes with Benediction so I'm afraid it will not be honoured with my presence.

I have not heard from you so far this week but will do probably tomorrow so for the present sending you my most sincere love and best wishes

I am Your Most Affectionate Son
Philip

P.S. This will be rather a long P.S. for it is in answer to your letter of this morning. Leslie says he is almost sure to be going home this weekend (lucky chap) and I will endeavour to let him have it for this afternoon. Some chaps do send their washing home, others to the laundry, others again wash it, and others I regret to say, prefer wearing dirty shirts for weeks on end. Well as you know I am not too rushed for time! Therefore I feel that I am well able to do my own washing which is certainly the cheapest way. To send it home would only give you more work that I am well able to do for myself, and in addition there would be the cost in stamps both ways apart from the extra worry of getting it dispatched at each end. This week however, I took my washing down to hang on the line and the next day as I was breakfasting by myself as I always do now, the landlady came in and whispered 'Ssh! I've ironed your washing for you!' She bade me not to tell the other chaps in the billet, so this week I am quite okay and perhaps will be in the future. I'm afraid that being a Catholic they are rather spoiling me, and allow me many a privilege they deny the others. It would not be quite fair to ask the landlady to do any washing either, I don't think, for she must have all her work cut out cooking and washing for thirteen hungry airmen.

Fancy Bernard having seven days! (leave I mean of course). I really do not know how some of these chaps do it. There are several in Blackpool who are distinctly worse off than I, and it is not for any want of trying on their part.

Yes I heard with a certain amount of relief that it was Coventry that took the brunt of it – it sounds rather selfish doesn't it? But still I pray for all those people as well, and cannot help feeling very sorry for them. It is marvellous to hear of your attitude to these raids but it almost makes me fear to go home for if I were caught in a bad raid I think that I would be a bit of a baby amongst you experienced veterans. I suppose it is all a question of resignation to the inevitable, for I have the same feeling that I am prepared to take the worst in aerial combat if necessary.

I will not be able to tell you of the Halle concert before this letter goes out but I will include a card with the programme on, and I can assure you that when you do read this letter I shall have participated at an extremely entertaining and enjoyable concert.

I am glad Lorna and Monica have settled down all right in Leicester[1]; were they ever much trouble? I shall have to go and see them when (and if) I come home on leave. Could you let me have their address and I will perhaps be able to send them a letter. I think it is 38 or 35 Berners St. but I could not be certain. Bernard's (Aunty May's son) twins are progressing fine I believe. Tony who registered in February and is not exempt, is still here in civilian clothes wondering whether the war office has forgotten all about him.

What do you think of the latest phase of the war? I am simply perplexed by Italy and cannot understand the position at all. I often wonder if she has not something up her sleeve. At any rate we have been putting in some good work and making the best use of our opportunities, haven't we?

Well I will now bring this postscript to an end and once again sending you all my best love and wishes,

Your Most Affectionate Son
Philip

P.P.S. 1 have been here four months today, 16th. November

---

1. Four younger siblings by now evacuated: Lorna and Monica to
Aunt Celestine in Leicester, Kitty (aka Kathleen) and Gerald to Herefordshire

14 Clevedon Road
Blackpool
December 1940

Dear Mother and Father and All,

This is just a short letter in which I want to wish you all that is implied in the sending of this Christmas Card with all my heart. I'm afraid it looks as though after all I will not be able to be home with you, as there is not a chance for anybody even N.C.O.s[1] during the time between December 21st. and January 1st. because they want to lighten the burden on the railways! Will you please forward the enclosed Christmas card on to Kitty, Lorna and Monica (I presume and hope they will be all together) also to Gerald. I will leave them open for you to see.

I arrived back in Blackpool okay, but I got a fright on Central Station when a number of S.P.s[2] lined all Army and Air Force chaps to file out single file. I prepared to show them an old "pass" form I had on me, but it appeared they were more anxious to see the railway tickets, for some reason or other. Anyway I got back to the billets at 12.15 a.m. without further incident save that the people left the wrong key in the door and I reluctantly had to wake them up.

Well I will now finish with very best love and wishes to you all

From Your Most Loving Son
Philip

Tomorrow (Tuesday) I'm going to Padgate for a day or two where we have a final medical exam for pilot. Will return to Blackpool after.

---

1. Non Commissioned Officers
2. Special Police

CHAPTER TWO

STRATFORD-UPON-AVON

Family bombed out of home

For the first time letter sent to Lansdowne Road and not Farnham Road, after family bombed out of home.

1354399 AC/2 P.J.Hermolle
1 /4 FLIGHT
No 2 Section
R.A.F. Stratford on Avon.
24th December 1940

Dear Mother and Father,

Well here I am now down at Stratford after being so long in Blackpool. We had to rise at 5a.m. yesterday to parade at 6.10a.m. down by the Winter Gardens, and we caught the 7.05a.m. train and arrived in Birmingham at 4.30 p.m! Nine and a half hours! We had then to march round to Snow Hill where we waited fifteen minutes as the Flight Sergeant told us. I asked if I could slip round the corner for a couple of minutes to Pitts[1] and he said no. So I went down the back way out of the station and asked the porter to allow me to pass out for a minute or two (that would be just after 5p.m.) which he did. Well I simply rushed up to Pitts (with full kit on) and almost kicked the door down but I could make no one come, though machinery was going upstairs. They had also left the office so after two or three minutes I had to rush back the same way I had got out.

I was exceptionally sorry in a way to leave Blackpool as I have been treated so well there, and had made so many friends. I was to have had my official test for C.E.G. that Monday night as well.

When I went to say goodbye to Fr. Hanford, our Padre, he said 'Thank you for your excellent example to your fellows' which cheered me up very much, considering that my greatest fear before joining up was that I should miserably fail to live up to my standards in face of such difficulties. Of course I will not now be able to continue Mass and Communion – one of many reasons why I regret leaving Blackpool.

I have done my utmost to try and get a leave or pass from here but they say there is nothing doing as we will soon be going elsewhere. This is only a receiving centre.

I have missed a jolly good week at Blackpool for they had arranged some jolly good things in connection with the Catholic Services Club (a good free supper on Christmas Day, and a social and supper on Boxing Day etc.) In fact I actually did go to one social and dance arranged for the airmen and the girl helpers in the canteen there. You will no doubt be surprised to know I cast all caution to the winds and danced! I asked Evelyn (whom I have mentioned to you before) if she would mind my practising on her, promising of course that I would pay the highest respect to her toes and do my best not to tread on them too often! Anyway I did not hear her squeal and she said afterwards that they were all right so I could not have been too bad. It is surprising the number of airmen you see there who will not risk dancing, though there were one or two peculiar dances where you have to wind under various people's arms that nearly all joined in. The greatest fun was in trying to disentangle oneself from all the alien numbers who had also become caught in the morass.

I will tell you more later about my present dump at Stratford – it is not nearly as good as it sounds – but the food is good and there is plenty of it.

Well, tomorrow Christmas day I will remember you all individually and pray for you, and especially Lorna and Monica who must miss Christmas at home very much.

So for now here is wishing you all the very best of love and wishes

From Your Most Loving Son
Philip

P.S. I would like to thank Mary very much for the Christmas card. Other mail might have been sent and I will have it forwarded from Blackpool.

---

1. Pitts was his father's employment. His father worked very long hours here as an engraver here until his retirement

---

(Postcard)

Stratford
27th December 1940

My Dear Mother and Father,

As leaving Stratford tomorrow (Saturday) and we think we are off to Scarborough but do not know for certain. Will write you as soon as possible and meantime hope that all the family are well and happy. So very best love to you all

From Your Affectionate Son
Philip

CHAPTER THREE

SCARBOROUGH

'My Christmas Day was really rotten' (29th December 1940)

4 Flight 2 Squadron, RAF
Grand Hotel
Scarborough.
29th December 1940

My Dear Mother and Father,

 Well what do you think or my being at Scarborough now? It is proper barrack life for us now but in the grand hotel which must have been one of' the biggest and poshest in the place in peace time. Our course starts tomorrow, but it will be nearly like being back at school again from what I can see of it.

I did not have a chance at all to do anything when I passed through Birmingham the second time, not even get on the phone. I have not heard from you now for a little time so I hope you are still quite all right and well and happy, and that Jerry is not causing too much trouble. I could hear him regularly at Stratford those nights he came, but I think he was on the way to Manchester. I think we are settled here for eight to ten weeks now (if I pass the Maths which I ought to with a little work). I must say that it is rather nice to be back at the seaside again even though it is on the east coast. The sea looks very calm, and the wind certainly is not comparable to that of Blackpool. We are some of the first airmen to arrive here, otherwise the place is mostly occupied by men in khaki as you might well imagine.

I am not fully settled down yet so I hope you do not mind this letter being scrappy and short. My Christmas was not the happiest I have had, but I hope that under the circumstances yours was as happy as could possibly have been. At the moment I have a very bad cough and cold (a result of cold and damp at Stratford I think) but my spirits are all right and I think I will be all right here, but I could do with a bit of leave.

Well I will now finish sending you my very best love and wishes

From Your Most Loving Son
Philip

My Dear Mother and Father,

As I write now it is only Monday but I hope to leave myself more time to write in greater leisure for next week. By the way I think there is a slight addition in the above address from that which I gave you before.

We are really hard at work now on the pilot's course which will be quite a stiff one as I can see. However it is far more varied and interesting than that of W.Op, which I was taking. At the moment we have lectures on signalling, Vickers guns, military law, mathematics (quite a lot on these) and aircraft recognition. Besides these we have physical training, and drill while there is every prospect of organised games in which case I shall probably be sending an S.O.S. for my rugger togs.

The hotel which we occupy, though devoid of all its peace time conveniences must be the most fashionable in Scarborough and is very warm, which is quite a luxury after our short stay at Stratford. The sea here is very different to that of Blackpool, as it is not nearly so rough and the water is far cleaner. I have also found a Catholic club here for the services, but when I got there I discovered that I was the only airman, the others were all soldiers. It is not in the least comparable with that at Blackpool; I could however hardly expect that, for the one at Blackpool was exceptionally good. Unlike Blackpool, Scarborough is almost empty, and great large hotels and houses have big notices on 'To be let' – that is if they have not already been commandeered by the army as a great number have.

We will not do any flying here at all. Our course is supposed to finish in about 8 or 10 weeks and if we pass out we go on to an E.F.T.S.[1] I sincerely hope that I do pass out OK. The discipline here is very strict compared with that at Blackpool; now we have always to be on the alert, to be quick in the mornings, and have our buttons gleaming and faces cleanly shaven. The food is quite good, but needless to say I could do with ten times the amount!

Did I ever tell you that I had been on twenty four hour guard duties at Blackpool just before I came away; yes with tin hat on, all the ceremonial webbing on, and a gleaming bayonet point at my side, with plenty of ammunition in the rifle; it is very peculiar how strong one feels when done up like that. It was half past four in the morning that I had to challenge an officer who came round; not until he produced his identity card could I let him pass. I had never before had visions of being able to halt an officer. However, I do not want any more of these duties than I can help. How is Leslie getting on at Compton Basset? Does he know whether be will be flying yet, or has he done any yet?

For some reason or other it is very hard for me to get news of any kind these days, and I'm afraid I do not know whether Birmingham has come in for much of the blitz this last few nights. I hope not. How is the new house looking now? There must even yet be a great deal of work to be done, and it must feel very quiet and empty. I cannot help thinking very often how hard it must be for you remaining at home with five of your family spread about all over the country; you must have felt it very much indeed on Christmas Day, however I expect that we all thought of and prayed for each other with the hope that next Christmas Day may perhaps see us all once again reunited.

Today is Thursday. I have just received your letter for which I thank you very much. I see I have anticipated your feelings of the Christmas, but still we can only live and hope for better times to come. I'm extremely sorry about the wireless – I mean of course from your point of view because these are just the days when you could do with it more. I am a little annoyed too, because I almost reminded you, but I thought Daddy would be sure to think of that. My Christmas Day was really rotten as well, they didn't even do anything to make it jolly for us; I had no breakfast because I went to Communion and there was nowhere open to get even a bar of chocolate or a cup of tea. I went for two walks during the day, and early to bed. There was literally nothing to do or occupy us on that day, and the Firs Hotel was extremely cold and lacked every convenience. Had I realised early on that the roll call at mid–day would not have been called, I should most certainly have bolted home.

Please do not worry about me and my future, because Pilot is certainly no more dangerous than any other air crew job; while its course is the longest, most varied and intelligent of them all. In fact myself I feel very sceptical as to whether I shall be able to pass out or not, and I am certainly not considering myself already 'growing my wings' as many others seem to take for granted. The discipline is very strict, and they expect a far higher degree of efficiency and smartness for Under Training Pilots than any other branch of the Air Force. Many of the present subjects and lectures we have because it embraces part of the training for officers. To those who finally pass out they will give a certain percentage commission according to the impression made while on the course. So if you might not desire my commission if in the army, there is no reason why you should not in the R.A.F. However I am very far from all that now, and for my own part give little thought to it since I prefer to get on with the job of the moment and let the future look after itself.

Nowadays we get very little free time and though I have been in Scarborough for well over a week I have really seen very little of it. It seemed a very long journey here so I cannot get home for weekends. In any case we have been told definitely by the C.O. that no weekend passes will be issued while we are here; on the other hand he said that when we have passed out up here, we will probably have to wait around for a fortnight or so, because the next station will not be ready to take us, as flying training is held up by bad weather this time of the year. In that case he says that many of us, especially the more deserving ones, will probably have some leave; so I hope that I may be able to spend a few days with you in a few weeks time.

Do you know that we have two hours on maths every day and in addition we have what they have the cheek to call maths 'home–work' which is quite a good amount, I would however certainly welcome it if we could go home to do it.

By the way, will you thank Gerald, Kitty, Lorna and Monica for their Christmas cards and I do hope that they will soon be back home again.

As you remarked in your letter, Italy is only getting all she deserves and it is a pity we still have not the help of France to 'rub it in'. Anyway I hope the war will be over this year, and somehow I have a presentiment that it will. 1940 was a year of the most outstanding unpleasant surprises and there is no reason why 1941 should not be a year of equally stupendous and equally agreeable surprises. I often wonder whether Germany is developing her air force to the extent that Britain is. If Germany is not, then woe betide her, for it seems to me that, especially when reinforced with the R.A.F. out East, we shall have a colossal Air Force. In fact I cannot help feeling that all our adverts for men for flying duties and stressing of the difficulties owing to inferior numbers is one big piece of bluff to lull Germany, or conceal from her the full strength of our potential Air Force. Certainly the R.A.F.'s strength out East must have been a bitter pill to poor old 'Musso'[2] don't you think?

Well I will now conclude sending you all my very best love and wishes and hoping that all your present troubles will soon vanish into the joys of the home–coming of your prodigal children, when all the bells will once again ring out their glad tidings that peace has come to replace blood and strife.

From Your Most Affectionate Son
Philip

---

1. Elementary Training Flying School
2. Mussolini

R.A.F. Grand Hotel
Scarborough
12th January 1941

My Dear Mother and Father,

Thanks ever so much for the very pleasant and unexpected surprise you had in store for me! I never bother to wait for the list of parcels so you can imagine my delight when I heard from the distance my name at the head of the list! I am very grateful indeed because with all the present troubles you have on your hands and with so many other absent children to think of, I did not really expect you to bother much about me, especially as you are under such a financial strain at the moment. Anyway again I say thanks very much.

I was going to write to you immediately on Thursday, but I found I had not time before the post and now the letter has had to wait until today, Sunday. As a matter of fact our time is very full here, we rise now at 6a.m. and are 'going to it' until 6.30 p.m. every day. At 7 p.m. there is supper and after that we have still our maths 'homework' to do. However this week we have our maths exam, which if we pass we start navigation, while if we fail we get slung out and have to go back to W.Op. They certainly believe in putting us through it here; last Sunday and Monday we had to plough through fairly thick snow on two long route marches at a fairly brisk pace; and since then we have had drill two hours each day, and I can honestly say that we put more into two hours drill here than we did in a week's drill at Blackpool. In fact Blackpool was less than child's play compared to this. At the moment my whole body is stiff and aching, though in fairness I will have to admit that it is in part due to the rugger, and in part to the physical training.

However there is some consolation in knowing that you are being thoroughly trained even if it is very rigorous and in spite of it all I must say that I am enjoying myself. I think I can now definitely recognise some aircraft at any rate and there are one or two things that I am glad to be learning. Morse is again proving to be an obstacle; if I could only pass now at twelve words a minute I would be through with it for the whole course, but morse is a thing that one cannot 'drive home'.

It is very interesting being on the East coast here, though I must say I was very disappointed in what I have NOT seen. There is not half so much military activity as I expected and I have not seen any big guns and not even any small pill–boxes as were frequent at Blackpool. Still no doubt the Military Authorities know what they are up to, and in any case there is probably quite a lot here that is hidden from view. The only thing is that as soon as an alert goes (the ships at sea give it out first) we generally get near a place to take shelter, as planes have been known to swoop out of the sky and start machine–gunning soldiers on the beach and there have, I believe, been one or two casualties. Then again, big large convoys of thirty or more ships are a common sight, and I can now recognise warships. The other day we were reading the flash signals a destroyer was sending to a coastal command aeroplane which was zig–zagging in and out of the convey, but the message was of course in code.

By the way I received a letter you had sent to Blackpool last Monday, thanks very much. I have not heard from you this week, but I shall always assume that no news is good news and I realise that it is more urgent that you write to Kathleen, Lorna, Monica and Gerald.

As I am a little pressed for time at the moment I hope you will not mind me bringing this letter to a conclusion and here's sending you all my very best love and wishes

From Your Most Affectionate Son
Philip

P.S. VERY Important: Could you please include a note in your next letter to the effect that you give me full permission to cease making that voluntary allowance – it has already been held up for that.

P.S.2. thanks especially for those woollen goods you sent me. That head covering piece looks a masterpiece of knitting and it ought to be very welcome during long night watches. Tonight I am hoping to see '*The Great Dictator*'

Enclosed: Post Card from Scarborough:

You will be able to judge for yourself what sort of place the Grand Hotel is and what an excellent view we can get from our room, which is marked by a little arrow I have put in. There is one big disadvantage, namely that there are so many steps to climb to get there. There are some gun emplacements now, on part of this view but perhaps I had better say no more.

N.B. you do not see people on the beach like this now.

My Dear Mother and Father,

As I write now I can hear the strains of Schubert's 'Ave Maria' voluntary of Sunday Morning service on the radio which has just been put on in our reading room. I do not suppose that I would be left in such peace but for the fact that pretty well all the rest of the squadron are on church parade; of course I have been and come back.

What a day it is and what a night it has been! The wind at present vying with that at Blackpool, but even now it is not quite so bad as I have seen it there. The sea too is exceptionally rough at the moment, easily the worst I have seen it here at Scarborough, but it is very peculiar how very different it is from Blackpool; there the sea gets tossed about madly in every direction – here the waves come regularly in great long powerful sweeps and crash with a terrific roar over the jetty, throwing fine white spray into the air. Since it is simply blinding snow outside I have been watching this scene from our room window; when I went to church this morning there were great snow drifts and it was fairly thick everywhere, so I am wondering what it will be like in Birmingham, whether it will be anything like last year.

Fancy you, Mother, having a job; I cannot help feeling very sorry that circumstances should have so compelled you to change your whole mode of life, but I hope that you will be as happy in it as the times allow. What a blessing it will be when this war is over and done with! I often wonder whether there was anything so earnestly desired by so many masses of people, and yet so far away. It all seems incredible to me when I start to think about it. Won't it be nice when we all meet again as I hope we all will?

I have now had one or two games of rugger and have played for the squadron. It is peculiar in what a high way everyone talks about the game and themselves here, and boasts of the teams for which they have played, and yet except for one or two notable exceptions none of them are very good. I am positive that I could play for the wing team before many of those who have simply talked their way in; however I shall play my way in, a far more dignified and permanent method, but one which will take some time.

The work here is still fairly hard but we have had an easier week as regards drill because of the weather, but they see to it that we get plenty of exercise either through P.T. runs or route marches. I can see too that there will be plenty of swotting before I have finished here. We had our mathematics exam last Wednesday, the papers went to Reading to be corrected and so we have not the results yet. I don't like prophesying generally, but I think I ought to have topped the 60% mark easily enough ; for comparing answers I think I had those nearly all right that I did, if not all, but there was one problem that I could not do for the life of me. Anyway in the meantime we have started navigation which is proving very interesting indeed, it seems to be a combination of maths, geometry and geography, and infallible rules that one learnt at school as for instance that there are 180 degrees in a triangle fall flat to the ground when applied to the spherical earth.

No wonder they said it costs £10,000 to train every pilot – why, I would like to bet that the preliminary maps we have for our navigational work run into five shillings each and we have two each; and then there are several items like that. There is a cinematograph installed with talkie apparatus simply to demonstrate principles of air flow, and flights and aircraft recognition. And we are supposed to be poorly equipped as an Initial Training Wing for pilots because we have only just started. I believe that if and when we pass out here we get our Leading Aircraftsman badge (L.A.C.) and get about five shillings odd per day; actually I think that pay is supposed to be starting now but that we will not draw it until then.

I am very glad Birmingham has had a short respite lately because it will need to have a good rest. I only hope that the next big onslaught will be by day, and then perhaps he will not get all his own way and it will not be nearly so terrifying.

As you see I shall include Auntie Kathleen's letter to which I have already replied; and I heard from Tony this week, and as you see he has some news and perhaps you will be able to tell Auntie Celestine first this time! I have also heard from Leslie this week and I wondered whether he was just as frank in telling Mary what he thought of her as he was in telling me! Anyway I think we can both give and take hand blows in that respect!

Well I shall now finish wishing you all, not forgetting Gerald, Kathleen, Lorna and Monica my very best love,

From Your Most Affectionate Son
Philip

P.S. I am writing to Gerald this week and will try and get one to Kathleen and others a bit later.

R.A.F. Grand Hotel
Scarborough
26th January 1941

My Dear Mother and Father,

Thanks for your letter which I received on Friday together with that of P. Coman[1] who tells me he is now in the R.A.F and on the point of going to Blackpool! What a pity he was not a few months earlier.

I received a letter also from Gerald who appears to have been down with a cold or something similar; however I shall include it for you to read.

Yes it has certainly been very bad weather this week, but the snow could not have been so bad here as you had it, though it was bitterly cold and there was a biting wind. I have kept very well myself in spite of the fact that we have been continually sent out in all the rigours for P.T. or runs or drill. The food seems very inadequate here – at least for our appetites; they tell us that it is quite enough to keep one going in normal health, and it is quite a good diet – we all however suffer from perpetual hunger and I have spent a very good portion of my money this last fortnight in making up the deficiency. Of course we might tend to feel it more at the moment on account of the excessive cold.

Anyway I have good news about leave; it seems almost certain that we will have a week's leave at the end of this I.T.W.[2] course which ought to be in four or five weeks. I am almost going mad at the thought of it, for it seems it cannot be true.

I have more confidence too because I passed the maths exam with 82%! and in the meantime I have actually passed the morse at twelve words per minute which has taken a load off my mind. That means that all being well we will not have to bother any more officially with morse on the whole of this Pilot's course, although I shall have to see that I do not lose what I now have.

Meantime I made a bad slip in armaments in an unofficial test which we had on the Vickers gas operated gun – I am afraid that I have not a mechanical kind of mind and find it difficult to follow how breach blocks and rear catch springs dash backwards and forwards and knock each other about at the same time picking up new bullets and extracting old cases; however if I get down to it, it should not prove beyond me, and in any case it is not vital like maths and navigation and signals.

Yes I still find the navigation most interesting indeed, and it involves quite a lot of scale drawing and plotting of positions and such other things that are concerned with maps which I like very much. The whole reason for navigation is because what appears to be a straight line from London to Berlin on the map is not one in practice, and would bring an aircraft to Danzig or some such place, owing to the spherical nature of the earth; in addition there are of course such things as wind velocities and bearings that have to be taken into account, because an aeroplane's speed is taken by the number of miles per hour through the air, and if there is a 60 mph. wind in the opposite direction, it makes no difference to the aeroplane's speed but only to its ground speed, that is, the speed it takes to go over the ground. Well anyway you will see that it is all most interesting, and I am very glad that I am having this course even if I am not ultimately successful.

I am very glad that you are having some respite from the air raids lately. We had a daylight raid in the neighbourhood the other day, and there was an air battle going on high above, but I could not see anything. You possibly heard that bombs were dropped in East Riding. I do not know what is the big attraction round these parts; no doubt Jerry knows what he is after.

I was talking to a crippled lady in a shop the other day and she was telling me that her malady was the result of the bombardment of Scarborough in the last war. Looking at the map however it looks to be one on the safest places on the east coast i.e. most distant from German controlled shores. There seems to be a lot of talk about invasion and terrible things this spring doesn't there, people do not blind themselves this winter like they did last. One thing, I should hate to be a German soldier who will have this job, because no matter how ingenious they will be – as I daresay they will – they have certainly a big job to do if they want to get a firm footing here.

Well I will now conclude if you do not mind wishing you a very peaceful week to come and hoping you all enjoy good health. Here is wishing you all my love and best wishes

From Your Most Loving Son
Philip

---

1. Paul Coman, friend from Bradford, an old Cottonian
2. Initial Training Wings

R.A.F. Grand Hotel
Scarborough
2nd February 1941

My Dear Mother and Father,

Thanks for the letter received on Thursday. I'm sorry to hear of mother being down with a bad cold like that but hope that she will soon be better.

I had to go to the M.O.[1] this morning, but that was the result of yesterday's game of rugger in which I had my knee rather badly twisted when I was playing for the squadron; it is rather painful but has its compensations for I can get off drill and P.T. and walk up to Navigation lectures at my leisure. I have to go again to him tomorrow and as I have noticed that this neck gland of mine is causing a bit of trouble again; I shall just mention that as well. Apart from this however I am still perfectly well and having a good time.

At the moment all our Flight are confined to camp. For some reason or other we cannot hit it off with our C.O. who never fails to jump on No.4 Flight whenever he can. No one can understand why because we are certainly no worse than the other flights except that being the last flight we are often at certain disadvantages which we cannot avoid, and which are worse for us to put up with than for the C.O. to witness! Anyway today a Group Captain turned up from somewhere and made an inspection of the rooms, and for some reason or other we were the only flight who were not warned, with the result that one or two of the rooms laid open to the Group Captain and our C.O. were a trifle chaotic (ours was NOT one by the way!) and it is now through our flight that the C.O. got 'the worst ticking off he has ever had' from this G. Captain. Of course we are all highly pleased about that but realise that the C.O. will not be any more affectionate towards us because of it, and he unfortunately has the last word. However all being in it together we manage to laugh at it all which is really the most sensible thing to do.

Yes I am certainly looking forward to a spot of leave and am only hoping that 'due to the international situation all leave will be cancelled' will not prevent me from going home. I doubt if, even when at Cotton I ever looked forward so much to coming home; had I thought in those days that I could only go home for a week I would have been most dissatisfied but somehow even a mere seven days seems wonderful now.

Gerald answered me in that last letter of his, for I had told him with quite a touch of pride that we had to recognise 88 types of aircraft – that seems a terrific number to me – and then he has the calm cheek to retort 'is that all?' even going on to say that there are many more etc. etc.! Well I could not say how many types I know now; I know most of' the British, a few American, a fair number of German but as yet I have not seriously commenced on any Italian at all; and already it has taken me quite a long time to learn all I have , because as you might well imagine many of them are very similar, and you can easily get mixed up with the different details especially with the different numbers of the aircraft such as Junkers 90, 89, 88, 87, 86, or 52 to mention only one type. So as you see I have still a great number to learn only to complete 88 types! The Italians are some of the hardest to learn because they are all very similar to each other, though in most cases it is very easy to distinguish Italian from either German or English. The latter two kinds seem very near to one another, while the Italians appear to be behind in everything.

When I mentioned about the food here of course I realised that we are treated like lords compared to what was apparently served up in the 1914–18 war, because I should think that that branch of the service has been vastly improved. I was rather talking in a comparative way; the army here seem to fare better than us in that respect, but of course once they get on to real active service they will not do so well.

By the way I have just heard of Colonel Knox saying from America that the Germans will most likely use gas on a very large scale if they make an invasion. Well I can add that they are taking big precautions regarding us here; we have now very strict gas drill and many instructions regarding it, special signals etc., and I notice that the army on most of their training manoeuvres are carrying their gas masks at the alert if not actually wearing them. It is a good thing that our anti–gas equipment is exceptionally good, and regarding the forces they seem to be taking no chances. I do not want to cause you any alarm at all, but I hope you won't mind if this could be a little warning to you if you do not now carry your gas mask. Of course there may not be much in it, but it seems rather significant to me and I notice too that one or two daily papers have drawn notice to the fact that very few people carry their gas masks with them. Well as I say, I cannot help feeling that this sudden preparation is not without some reason, and I will feel more satisfied if I can give you a quiet warning, because forewarned is forearmed and it may be that the government do not wish to make an official statement about it.

On a route march the other day I did see a little more of the extreme forward defences around here which appeared to be protecting a good road which leads up from the shore to somewhere or other, and I must say they did appear pretty formidable and at least I cannot see how any tanks could penetrate, but of course being no military expert I would not know.

You asked me whether I was still an A.C./ii now. Well I am not an A.C., but I used to write A.C. because it does not really matter very much, and one feels the lowest of the low when continually being an A.C.ii. So it was really a matter of self–pride or respect rather than any progress on my part! Actually however we are not A.C.iis or A.C.s now, but 'Cadets' as we are on a Pilot's course. On official papers however we are still often referred to as A.C/ii though we are addressed as Cadet Hermolle or etc. We are cadets because as I have told you before we are potential officers, and the course may be also called an O.T.[2] course; but if you continue to call me A.C.ii: it will be all right. Apart from offending my pride it will do no harm!

By the way, I have paid my second visit to the M.O. this morning and am congratulating myself on getting out of a full kit inspection which is always a nuisance, besides getting off two days further drills etc. I have to see him on Monday and he will then see how my glands are going on before doing anything further.

Well I shall now conclude, and will look forward to writing my next letter which brings my leave a week nearer so for the present sending you all my best love and wishes I will say goodbye

From Your Most Affectionate Son
Philip

P.S. Would you mind forwarding those letters when you next write to Lorna and Monica and Kitty

---

1. Medical Officer
2. Officer Training

R.A.F. Grand Hotel
Scarborough
9th February 1941

My Dear Mother and Father,

Thank you very much for your two very interesting letters which I have received this Friday morning. At the moment the rest of our flight are on drill but as I am still on light duties I am having a rest; actually this last two days my knee has improved considerably, but the M.O. this morning gave me another three days light duties. This would suit me down to the ground but for the fact that one has to be within the camp by 6 o'clock every evening, which I like to have free at the weekends.

However I went out last Sunday night, and am quite disposed to do the same tomorrow because it does become rather boring not to go out at all. There is not much to do actually even when you do go out unless you go to the R.A.F. or Army dances which I do not; but I generally go to the pictures on Saturday nights for want of something better. Do not think I am therefore miserable here because I am not and in fact taking it all as a whole and the rough with the smooth I think I am having a jolly good time, and I get on quite well with most of the chaps here – which reminds me that yesterday in armaments class they organised a little 'sweep', every member contributing a penny and then guessing the weight of a revolver which was handed round and which is one of the guns we have to know something about. Well to cut a long story short, I guessed nearest and took the kitty within half an ounce!

Talking about yesterday also reminds me that it was eventful for other less fortunate events! We all had to scrub our floors out in the afternoon and I discovered what terrible hard work it is! Then at night I was on guard duty, but was fortunate in that my turn was from 7 o' clock until 10.45p.m. and although it was three and three quarter hours it did not interfere much with the rest of my night's sleep.

I notice that you, Mother, seem very anxious about me still, and I am afraid that I can appreciate how you must feel all round, if not to the full depth, at least to know how hard it must be for you. As regards myself however, I can assure you that I would be the last to cause you any worry by deliberately undertaking unnecessary risks, yet the more I think of it, the more I feel that I should not shirk flying duties. I would only feel that I was not pulling my weight if I did not offer my services, and it seems to me that I have no right to try and escape all the hazards of war – even the bombing – while so many others are having to bear it; I even feel rotten at not having had to share all you have had to go through so far. There are a number of fine young men here who have a wife and perhaps one or two young children, and I think that in many respects it must be harder for them than for me.

Then again, the fact that I have undertaken to train as a pilot improves the situation from your point of view as it will be a long time before I am through with this training; and even when one has one's 'Wings' one still has to do 100 or so flying hours before doing anything of operational importance.

There is also the fact that there is a variety of duties even as Pilot, as for example Coastal Command which must be very interesting, and whose casualty lists must be very low. But even if you take R.A.F. casualties all round they are not alarming, and even when brought down there is often the parachute, which would only mean that you would be a prisoner of war until we win the war. Of course this looks as though I am ignoring other possibilities but I am not; on the other hand it is no good simply looking at the dark side is it? Besides I am getting fed up of Hitler talking away in the boastful way he does! It is amusing to hear some of the chaps here; to hear their schemes and plans for when the war is over, you would think there was no possibility of their falling by the wayside at all!

Well as I say, I can understand how you must feel, but it is also hard for me and it is a sense of duty that urges me on, which my spiritual convictions only tend to stiffen, for it was only after many prayers that I decided to undertake flying duties in the very first place. Until the war is over, I am afraid that suffering will have to be the common heritage of us all and in the long run I dare say that all will turn out for the best, and I think we can at least say that Hitler has already made the world look to itself and examine its conscience, as it were, with the result that in England at least, better social conditions and schemes are being formulated.

Do not worry about my not having anybody at home during the daytime when eventually I shall get home, because I shall soon be able to occupy that time all right, and it will be enough simply to be at home for the week – at least, I mean I shall be so pleased at that, that the other part will seem a detail.

Yes I have heard from Bernard lately. He has just left Bristol and is apparently 'fed up to the teeth' as he is still on ground defence which consists, so I believe, of perpetual guard duties which is no pleasure in the weather we have been having lately. He envies me very much. I just forget for the moment where he is, but I think it is somewhere in Berkshire.

Last Thursday morning as we were getting up about 6.15a.m. two H.E.[1] bombs fell just in the gardens of the Grand Hotel, and two by the Catholic Church almost the same time, so you see we are not entirely safe here because actually the bombs were less than fifty yards from our room. Of course we had a bit of a shaking up, especially as we are so very high up (sixth floor on the Grand, which itself is on the top of a cliff), but the Grand Hotel is an extremely tough structure and I think we are pretty safe within its precincts. There were no casualties.

I hear that Benghazi (or however you spell it) has fallen to us today; it's good to hear news like this isn't it?

Well for the moment I will bring this letter to a close and I will be able to give you more definite information about the forthcoming leave in my next letter I hope. So for the present here is wishing you every happiness and my best love

From your Most Affectionate Son
Philip

P.S. This is an official photo we had taken about a fortnight ago. They are not really worth the money but still you will probably be interested. I did shave that morning! it is the photograph's fault!

---

1. High Explosive

R.A.F. Grand Hotel
Scarborough
16th February 1941

My Dear Mother and Father,

Thanks very much for your letter of this morning and the news therein.

Actually I see I have been set a very ticklish question with regards to the children and I am afraid that I do not know what to think. Of course I should very much like to see you all together again and can appreciate how pleased you would be as well, yet on the other hand I would never like to say that there will be no raids because one never knows when it will all flare up again, in fact as far as the R.A.F. are concerned it does seem to have started again. Then again you mentioned the weekend as such a time didn't you? I do not know the exact times of my leave yet, but it seems that I will be travelling some part of each weekend. I should be coming home sometime next Saturday (February 22nd) and travelling back on the Sunday week; this is only an assumption but I do not think it will be far out, for we finish our exams next Friday and so should be free if not Friday night, at least from first thing on Saturday. I do not know whether it would be practical to fetch them on my way home because my hours of travelling may be awkward, and indefinite, and I do not know whether I could use my warrant to go such a long way round. Well after all I cannot say really what I think but I would love to see them all again, and can guess you would.

Since writing the first part of this letter yesterday I really had a fright, for the week's programme went up last night, and it actually schedules our activities till Saturday night next when, as I have just told you, I had hoped to be home; however this morning the Squadron C.O. came round and informed us in a very hush–hush manner that official leave would commence on Monday am. but that he would endeavour to give us all a weekend pass from Friday night until Monday morning 07.59 when our official leave commences and surmount the difficulty that way. But there is no promise in this, and it largely depends on circumstances. If it works okay I hope to get a train from here about 7.25p.m. on Friday evening when we should catch a good train straight through to Birmingham on its way to Bristol from York. It is down to reach Birmingham about 2.30a.m. I think, but I will ask you not to put yourselves out in any way on Friday night because, as I say it is very indefinite at the moment, and then one can never tell what will happen to trains these times, and it might be more in the region of 6a.m. that it will come in. So if you will go to bed in the ordinary way (Jerry permitting) I'm sure you will not mind being knocked up in the middle of the night. If I am not home up to a late hour on Saturday you will know that something has gone wrong with the works and that I shall not be able to set out before Monday.

You will be interested to know that all our Squadron here have been asked to state whether they would like to continue their training overseas. Nearly all have answered in the affirmative but I have put down to go to an E.F.T.S. in England. If I could have been certain that they would go to Canada I think I would seriously have considered it, but it is far more likely that they will off to Rhodesia where there are some big schools. As a matter of fact I should love to go to Rhodesia but it struck me that once out there, you would be very handy to send on to Egypt or the Near East without further leave. I would not mind going out East if it was a matter of having to, but I would not like to find myself out there as a result for which I could only blame myself. I know that you would also prefer to have me relatively near at hand. I dare say that they will endeavour to train fairly large numbers out of the country and so ease the food situation but as far as possible they say they will try and get the men where they want to go i.e. at home or abroad.

I heard from Les this week and if Mary would just convey my thanks to him and explain to him that I have a very busy week ahead with various exams, and so unfortunately cannot reply for a while I would be very pleased. Perhaps with a bit of luck I may see him while at home.

You should have heard the din from aircraft on Wednesday night – you can tell, it woke all in our room up, I should think there must have been hundreds of them. But as it was about 5 a.m. and there was not an alert all the night we can only presume that they were the British aircraft returning from the heavy attack we afterwards heard they made on Hanover in Germany. In fact I had a suspicion at the time that they were British because there was undoubtedly a different note about their engines – I could almost express it as a cheerful note as compared with the long monotonous buzz of Jerry. I do not think actually that there is much doubt that they were British, because I know that all our planes, both when they go out and on return, have to fly across only one portion of the coast which is changed from night to night, and Scarborough was apparently the point where they flew out on their way to Hanover that night.

Well for the present I will bring this letter to a close and if there is any news or items that I have not given you now I shall be able to give you them next week in greater detail.

Very best of love and wishes

From Your Most Affectionate Son
Philip

P.S. Last night a soldier from Birmingham told me that he had been home by the train of which I have told you, and said that he did not get into New Street until after 4a.m. and there was no blitz or anything so you will see how unreliable the services might be especially if there is any trouble in the air.

R.A.F. Grand Hotel
Scarborough
5th March 1941

My Dear Mother and Father,

Here I am again back at Scarborough quite safely. I must say that I enjoyed my leave very much indeed but it is a pity that they go so quickly.

As you may well imagine, I was not too pleased at having to return, especially when I had to travel during the whole of such a nice day. The trains were all pretty good and we arrived in Scarborough at about 7.15 p.m. There was a two and a half hour wait at York and as the weather was so inviting I took the opportunity of walking around. I was making my way to York Cathedral when I saw a St. Wilfred's Catholic Church and going in I found that the Holy Hour had just started, and so I remained for that. I then went into the Cathedral just as the service had ended, and so I heard the organ for about a quarter of an hour which was most impressive. In fact the whole cathedral is most beautiful and magnificent, and I could not help feeling what a pity it is that such majestic cathedrals are not Catholic, and are therefore so meaningless. Among the names of the Bishops of York were those of several pre–Reformation Catholic Bishops, including Cardinal Wolsey.

By the way I have not heard officially, but I think it is safe to say now that I have passed the Navigation Exam. Four from our flight have not. Anyway I do not know what will happen after next week, whether we will remain here for weeks or whether we will be packed straight off. I am hoping that I will be sent to somewhere like Coventry, Shrewsbury, Nottingham or Gloucester in which case I HOPE to be able to get home far more frequently.

Well for the present I will close hoping the recent bombings of Cologne will bring no bad nights on Birmingham. Here's wishing you all my love and best wishes from

Your Most Affectionate Son
Philip

P.S. Would you please forward this other letter to Gerald whose address I have temporarily mislaid.

Philip was twenty one years old on 6th March:

R.A.F. Grand Hotel
Scarborough
7th March 1941

My Dear Mother and Father,

Well now that I have reached man's estate and am a full citizen with all its rights, I can therefore spit in the fire, kill the cat and all those other peculiar rights to which I have so long looked forward! To tell you the truth, however I feel very little difference from a few days ago when I was still a mere twenty years of age. But before I go any further I must thank you all very much for your very best wishes, for the £1 note which by the way seems to me sufficient in itself.

You asked me to tell you what I would like as a present, so I have looked round through many shops in Scarborough but I don't seem to see anything of particular note that I would like under the present circumstances, except as I told you at home would always prove acceptable, namely a camera. I have dared to mention this again because I have made small enquiries, which seem to point to the fact that they are not as damning as they might seem; however I will ascertain more about that later on. But really, especially since you find things none too easy at the moment I would prefer to wait until things are more settled, and if the price is not too outrageous perhaps that suite of records of Beethoven's Symphony in C minor, or Myra Hess's Pianoforte Concerto (Schumann) could be enjoyed by you as well as myself.

Well under the circumstances I really enjoyed my birthday very much. I had a rude awakening when my whole bed (me asleep inside) was tipped onto the floor by one of the chaps in the room who apparently thought it a fine way of wishing me many happy returns! The others were all desirous of kicking me twenty one times, but I managed to persuade them not to. I made a bad start when I got late for parade and with the others in our room was ordered to report to the flight sergeant, fortunately he was not in at the time and we have not bothered him since and I believe it has all passed over. Anyway we had a good feast in the room that night after 'lights out'! I bought a bottle of sherry and a large cake while the others smuggled some bottles of beer through the guard room, and got hold of one pound of margarine from somewhere, as well as bread, sardines and more cake on which we all feasted on our bed sides in our pyjama jackets. So you see, it did not go by without any jubilation at all, and you will be pleased to know that today I am feeling no worse for it; I was not sick nor drunk!

In spite of all, as you will imagine I should very much have liked to be at home for it all, and to have had just an ordinary supper with you all. I was very pleased with Kitty's, Lorna's and Monica's little letters which I will enclose for you to read.

I must have played rugger extra well that day as well for I am down to play for the I.T.W.[1] on Sunday against an East Yorkshire XV. Of course there is one of the squadrons away on leave at the moment and that may be partly accountable for it.

Well I think I can say that I am quite settled down now and we have had some beautiful weather this week, so that I feel I should like to see Scarborough in the spring or summer when it must be a very nice place indeed.

I hope that it will keep quiet at Birmingham for very much longer, that circumstances will be so changed that Hitler will not be able to bomb our cities to such an extent when the weather is once again more clement to him.

So for the moment I will wish you goodbye sending you all my very best love and wishes

From Your Most Loving Son
Philip

P.S. I not know what will happen next week. I suppose that anything may but I shall try and let you know quickly.

P.P.S. By the way it is a good thing you washed my shirt and collars, because the other was bombed and burned at Filey Laundry while I was away – we have others issued but nowhere to send our present washing as yet.

---

1. Initial Training Wing

My Dear Mother and Father,

Thanks very much for your letter which I received this morning. Yes I had heard that Birmingham had not been entirely forgotten by the German air force but I am glad it did not develop on too severe a scale, and I certainly hope that you will not be visited too strongly. One thing about it all, we do seem to be making some genuine progress in combating the night bombers which is a very excellent thing indeed; and it is heartening too, to know that in future perhaps the Germans will not view the raids from the same comfortable position as they have hitherto. I am pretty certain that we are dropping some far heavier bombs on German factories and important points than the Germans are using, with the exception perhaps of landmines of which they cannot drop so many. At last one feels now that we are not simply sitting down on the defensive awaiting German bombs to fall wherever they will.

The night before last I was one of the duty spotters for the night, and there was a six and a half hour alert on, in fact he actually dropped incendiaries about half a mile away, but nothing more exciting than that. However I was up spotting for nearly three hours in the middle of the night waiting to catch any bombs he might drop and throw them into the sea. It was a beautiful moonlight night and from the roof of the Grand, you could get an excellent view of Scarborough in the light of the moon, and that part of the sea that reflected it was almost dazzling to look on. That was a scene that you never saw at Blackpool, for both the sun rise and moon rise was on the other side of the sea, though of course there were some nice sunsets there, which you never have here.

The weather for most of this last fortnight has been gorgeous and I will not mind a few more weeks here if it remains like it is now, in fact I am only just beginning to appreciate what a nice place Scarborough is, and if it were not to become much more crowded than it is now I should think it an ideal place for a summer holiday, for there is something very quaint about the harbour, while the walks and gardens along the front are very nice even at this time of the year, when the trees are still stripped of their leaves, and most of the plots still lacking in the gay colours which should bedeck them soon. (The sirens are just off, and there is a large convoy just in front – in fact I can count 32 ships – we will wait and see!)

Anyway there is a chance that we will be here for some weeks more for the C.O. told us last Tuesday that this is a bad time of the year for hold–ups, and he thinks that we will be here for AT LEAST another month. He will give a limited number of weekend passes on compassionate grounds, so next week I will try and make up some excuse regarding my twenty first birthday, and will endeavour to come home but I ask you not to set store by it, because any number of things may happen to prevent it (eg. I may be on duty). The pass would start from After Duties, Friday, so if I am not home before tea–time Saturday, you had better not expect me. Otherwise I cannot tell you how or when I shall arrive, but I will have a good try at hitch–hiking, because I do not think that the night train will be worth taking, especially as you will most likely be at work during the morning. If I get to York or perhaps even further by nightfall and then find I can make no further headway, I shall be able to put up cheaply at some Y.M.C.A. or something like that and then set off first thing in the morning. Well whatever happens if you will be just prepared for me, but not disappointed if I do not turn up, everything will be O.K.

We have been issued with flying kit now which must be worth some few pounds. It fills a special kit bag.

I dare say that you have been wondering about me, whether I am due for L.A.C.[1] or not. Well, I think that we draw pay as L.A.C. from last Sunday, but apparently we are not officially classed as an L.A.C. until we are posted to an E.F.T.S. We are having a fairly easy life at the moment, in fact it is just nice as there is work to do, but we are getting more time to ourselves and things are not so bustling as they were before. We still do navigation, for the most part practical work, other time is taken up with drill, P.T., occasional signals and armaments, lectures and films on flying, map–reading, reconnaissance and etc. We are also putting in more time to Gas drill, using full decontamination equipment and fire– fighting.

I was very successful in the last rugger match we had. I was playing full–back and came very near to scoring what would have been the only points of the game with a drop kick from thirty five yards that missed the mark by inches. That sort of thing looks very spectacular, especially for a full back who has usually as much as he can do to keep his own line safe, and it is astonishing what an impression one makes by a thing like that. Up to that time I might have been doing fine work and remained unnoticed, yet a flash in the pan of such a nature as that makes them all tell you how well you played, even if you did not. However I held the lines intact and so discharged my major duty with equal success.

The All–clear is now going again, and the convoy is still lazily sailing but I can now only see the latter half of it.

I am very pleased for your sakes that you have the wireless functioning once more, as it should make the house a little more cheerful and homely for you. When, or if you hear some poor crooner sobbing his or her heart away, remember that that is what for the most part I have to be satisfied with nowadays, though I did hear a good lunch–time concert this dinnertime (B.B.C. orchestra with some lady pianist).

By the way that reminds me that last night I attended the Scarborough School of Arts class on arts (music night) and heard a very good appreciation of Elgar's

Enigma Variations and Beethoven's *Emperor Concerto*, which was demonstrated by records. The whole thing lasted just over two hours and was very interesting indeed and I am sorry that I did not know about it before. I was told about it by a chap here who also has a great interest in music and he told me he would take me down. Apparently it is on every Friday evening and open to H.M. Forces free, so I am on quite a good thing in future while in Scarborough.

It is now Saturday morning, not yet 8 o'clock, and at present we are waiting in our rooms for inspection to take place. Last night there was another very long alert, and more bombs were dropped in Scarborough again, this time H.E.s and I believe Hull has come in for a little packet as well, that is not far from here.

It is now a bit later and in the meantime we have just had a parade with full flying kit on – and it is certainly warm when on the ground if you need it when up in the air. The weather is once more brilliant and I believe we could almost sunbathe it is so warm. There is a slight haze above the water so there is not quite such a good view as usual, but there is a great calm, and quite a number of rowing boats afloat.

Well I do not think there is very much more I can say now, except that I am feeling very well and contented, and have lost that Monday morning feeling which lasted long after Monday morning when I returned from home. So for the present I will bid you adieu, sending you my very best love and wishes from

Your Most Affectionate Son
Philip

P.S. The 40 hours adoration is on at St. Peters up here, and I have bought a cheap candle which will burn for your intentions together with those of the whole family, in the hopes that we will all soon be re–united again in better times.

Yesterday afternoon (Saturday) we played against Leeds Training College (for teachers) whom we beat 29–5.

President Roosevelt's speech sounds pretty good doesn't it?

---

1. Leading Aircraftman

Philip had leave, weekend 22nd March

R.A.F. Grand Hotel
Scarborough
Saturday, 29th March 1941

My Dear Mother and Father,

At the moment I have not heard from you this week, but this morning's mail has not come through yet. I returned here in good time on Monday morning 6.30a.m., and though once or twice during the day I found myself almost dropping asleep I was otherwise quite O.K. The first thing we had to do was to scrub our rooms out, and now to make up for the other things that we are not doing they are giving us plenty such duties, all the banisters on the stairways, all the linoleum that they are just laying down will have to be polished every day. The windows, outside and in, have also to be kept clean, so I look like becoming quite domesticated by the time I finish this course.

I thoroughly enjoyed the weekend at home, and am hoping that in future will be able to make many such excursions; I am in fact trying to think what excuse I will be able to make on the next such occasion.

Michael[1] wrote and told me that he is now only sixteen miles from Scarborough and will come here tomorrow Sunday afternoon; if he does, he will be rather unfortunate however as I am playing rugger for the Squadron in the afternoon, and will not be able to see him until late in the afternoon. I have written to warn him, but I do not know whether he will hear in time.

We had very good news on Thursday don't you think? From the first I had not expected much of Yugoslavia, so the sudden reversal was all the more joyous and I should think represents a serious diplomatic set–back for Hitler and slap in the face for Ribbentrop if nothing else.

Last night I again went to that gramophone recital and heard a very nice symphony of Haydn, also a violin concerto of Mendelssohn in which the soloist was none other than Kreisler and with one or two other records splashed in, it represented a most enjoyable evening.

I have just read the account of the Battle of Britain just published under the auspices of the Air Ministry, and it certainly seems to have been most interesting and exciting while it was on, and makes one feel proud to be a member of the R.A.F. even if only still under training. I should think that that must have been one of the biggest shocks Germany and her air force ever had.

By the way, talking of the German air force I have just heard from two distinct chaps who come from Wallasey, that it is that place and Birkenhead that have taken all the brunt of Liverpool's bombing. Both places have apparently received a terrific thrashing, because they're both on the side of the Mersey, and all the roads leading down appear from the air just like docks. They say that the Czech fighter squadron made the same mistake when they first went there. Anyway, they say that the damage is simply appalling in these two places, that nearly all the residents have moved out, but that it is all kept very quiet, because these big raids of late are pure and simple waste from the German point of view; while the main docks themselves are unaffected.

You have probably noticed that I AM now L.A.C. and not a mere ACii (at least for the moment!) We get paid on Friday, and I will commence letting you have an allowance to help you manage things more smoothly.

I have just learned that there is no letter for me this morning, and so I will finish hoping that you will have a good time at Whitchurch tomorrow,[2] and that the children will all be very happy when you find them. I pray that the coming weeks for you will also be quiet and as peaceful as the times allow. Here then, is wishing you all my very best love and wishes

From Your Most Loving Son
Philip

---

1. Cousin
2. Philip's three younger sisters were now evacuated at Whitchurch, Shropshire

---

R.A.F. Grand Hotel
Scarborough
5th April 1941

My Dear Mother and Father

Thanks very much for the letter that arrived this morning, and am glad to see that you are all quite well with the exception of Kitty, whom I trust will soon recover.

I am going to have another try to get home for the coming Easter weekend, but I will just remind you again not to look forward to it as an accomplished fact. For one thing as the weeks go forward, the chances of being posted increase and you will possibly be interested to know that nearly all those that put down for overseas training have been on embarkation leave since last Thursday. It is almost certain that they are going to Rhodesia from certain facts we know.

The weather has also been rough round here. The sea has been very rough and high, and a north east wind has been icy cold. Today it still persists in raining very hard but otherwise the storm has almost abated.

After the spate of good news we have been having lately, the loss of Benghazi again comes as a nasty jolt doesn't it? However I hope it is only a temporary setback, and that it is not so bad as it sounds.

Last night I again went to that gramophone recital and again heard a good selection which included the whole of Schubert's 'Unfinished' Symphony, a record of Cortot playing one of those Chopin's 'Waltzes' that I used to struggle along with, and another record of Myra Hess, Mendelssohn's 'Fingal's Cave' and a fugue played on the organ by Cunningham at the Birmingham town hall!

During the week Auntie Annie sent me this writing set which I am using at the moment. It is very nice and compact, and therefore suitable for this roving R.A.F. life. I sent the letter to your address not remembering theirs.

By the way we received our back L.A.C. pay yesterday in addition to the last fortnight's ordinary L.A.C. pay, and we received £5.10 shillings so you will not think the £1 note I will include in this letter any too much. For my part I will be only too pleased to think that I shall be able to lighten your heavy burden in some way or other. Then after this I will try and send you regular sums every fortnight as we get paid.

Well for the present I do not think there is very much else I can say, so will ring down, wishing you all the very best and sending my best love and wishes

From Your Most Loving Son
Philip

P.S. If I am not home to partake it with you, I wish you a very happy and joyful Easter.

CHAPTER FOUR

YEADON

'I think this has been the most adventurous twenty six hours I have ever had. Within that short space, I suddenly find myself wrenched from Scarborough, and what is more, having had my first experience of flying.' (Monday, 7th April 1941)

Yeadon, nr. Leeds
Monday, 7th April 1941

Dear Mother and Father,

That bottles my weekend this Easter! Last night (Sunday) after coming in from a walk I was told immediately to report to the C.O. who told me to get packing, that I had got to be on the train in two hours! So I am one of thirty who has found myself at this aerodrome. I think this has been the most adventurous twenty six hours I have ever had. Within that short space, I suddenly find myself wrenched from Scarborough, and what is more, having had my first experience of flying! Yes I have been up for a full thirty minutes this afternoon and none the worse for it! But what a surprise I had when my flying instructor told me to move the stick forward; not realising how sensitive the aeroplane was I pressed it forward what must have been much too far – it was only about two inches – and the aeroplane fairly went from under me as she turned into a steep dive! I was so surprised (and I could almost feel my dinner coming up!) that of course I quickly released it again and we came back to normal. It was all only a matter of seconds however, and I suppose such hair breadth escapes (!) will soon leave me cold. Well it was wonderful and I am looking very much forward to tomorrow morning when we take to the air again!

Well I am sorry I will not be home for the weekend, because I was looking forward to it a great deal and had already put my application through so that I would be one of the first for such a festive season. However I always seem to be cheated in some way or another; but I am glad that I shall perhaps be able to do my whack, and yet not be thousands of miles away as I might have been. By the way do not worry about me and imagine me crashing and doing all sorts of silly things, because as soon as I get the general hang of everything I shall try and be as steady as possible. Meantime, the instructors will keep a sharp watch out if only to protect their own skins!

I see Germany is still going out of her way to protect even more countries against British intrigues! Really we must be a set of rascals mustn't we, to go causing all this trouble in Europe. Yes, and Turkey still cannot apparently make up her mind, and cannot even do herself what she seems to have demanded of others, though the trouble is right at her doorstep.

Well I suppose I shall have lots more exciting stories to tell you by next Sunday, or perhaps they will not strike me as exciting by that time – by the way isn't Leslie up this way somewhere? I must be quite near him I imagine.

Here's all my very best love and wishes,

From Your Most Affectionate Son
Philip

Yeadon, nr. Leeds
12th April 1941

Dear Mother and Father,

Thanks very much for your letter which arrived today Saturday morning. I see you say that you were well on Thursday morning, but there was another heavy raid on Thursday night, and I hope that things are still quite O.K. It is rather distressing to have to go to the wireless to see what has happened during the night and then to hear news of that nature, but I hope that you have suffered no more than a bad night. There has been a scarcity of good news of late, and I suppose that the two things combined tend to depress one a little; I feel at such times that I have no right to have a good time or enjoy myself, but I suppose that that is not a right attitude. I am already playing rugger for this R.A.F. camp of Yeadon this afternoon, but am not looking forward to it as much as I would normally.

It is a pity that I could not have come to Coventry E.F.T.S. in which case I would have been able to have at least one day per week at home, but as it is I am just out of reach for such a short time. I have been wondering how I am placed for paying a visit to Whitchurch but as far as I can make out I would have to go through Manchester which would make things rather awkward; the trouble is that it is rather across country and difficult to arrive at. Yeadon, by the way, is North West of Leeds and North East of Bradford and about equal distance from both, (four or five or six miles).

Tomorrow is our day off, and I think that I will take a run into Harrogate which is supposed be a notable beauty spot, though at the moment I think it is largely in the hands of the military.

I have made various enquiries about Leslie, whether he is here, but I have had no definite news. There are a number of WOPs but none know of him so he couldn't be just around here.

This is quite a good camp, and there is nothing to grumble at in the food considering the times. When I was up in the air the other day and had been trying out various things some miles away, the instructor told me to set course for the 'drome'. I searched vainly about in all directions and I am afraid could not have stated where it was at all as I could only see so many fields and a few villages about; however after telling him I had no idea he turned it round about 60 degrees and told me to fly straight and level, and sure enough after about five minutes the hangars came into view slightly on the right. It seems marvellous to me how they can do that because when I am up I lose all sense of direction all together. Between Monday and Thursday I have been up on five flights and had just over three hours instruction, but since that the weather has been too poor and we have had to be content with ground work of which there is plenty.

No, they believe in getting you into the air from the first as they say that half an hour in the air is better than a week on the link trainer (a kind of mechanical aeroplane on the ground which is just as hard to control and which registers in black and white all your errors). In this link trainer we are supposed to do one hour per week, but for the moment it has broken down and I have not yet been in it. To turn an aircraft is much harder than one would imagine, and whenever I turn to the right I have a tendency to bank her too much which turns the nose down to the ground and soon develops into a dive. That is what happened the first time I tried, and I couldn't correct it and bring her to normal again; however the instructor had everything under control in a matter of seconds, and he explained to me that I had made a steep turn which we do not come on to for some time yet, and which needs a different use of the controls. I made the same mistake the next day, but improved enough to gain full control by myself.

At the moment I cannot tell you very much about the course here; it sounds as though it will be a very stiff one, but extremely interesting.

Last night (Saturday, for it is now Sunday morning) I walked I do not know how many miles in the darkness, through silent narrow lanes, and across fields trying to find the church which is actually only about one and a half miles away, but which nobody around here seems to know anything about. At last in desperation I called in at an isolated house which seemed miles away from anywhere to ask about it. When the door opened I found it to be the presbytery, and I had quite a little chat with the Priest who told me the best way to get there. He said that the reason for the church's position was that it had been put up privately by a wealthy gentleman within his own grounds some thirty years ago. This morning I was able to go to Holy Communion, but have had no breakfast, which is not the ideal way of coming out of Lent is it?

By the way, our pay is now 7/6d. per day at an E.F.T.S once we have commenced the flying training, so if I make you that small allowance home you will not have to think that I am doing anything much at all. It leaves me extremely well off and I am afraid I would feel terribly selfish if I did not make some effort to alleviate your troubles, especially as you have done so very much for me – it is not as though it is even causing me to go without anything at all because it isn't.

I wonder whether there has been any outstanding damage done in Birmingham lately? Well for the moment I will conclude this letter hoping that it finds you well and in good spirits. I always pray that you will be safe before I go to sleep at nights, and remember that though things may be very quiet here, yet you may be having quite a bad night. Well here is all my very best love and wishes,

From Your Most Loving Son
Philip

Philip had obtained another weekend pass.

Yeadon nr. Leeds
Monday Dinner Time
21st April 1941

Dear Mother and Father,

Well here I am back again and I am feeling surprisingly awake considering the sleep I haven't had these last nights. I slept soundly all the way to Sheffield and almost failed to get off in time; I was again asleep in no time in the Sheffield–Leeds train and cannot remember it even starting off; somehow I again managed to wake up as we drew into Leeds station at a quarter to three in the morning. I then had tea, chips and eggs at a nearby Y.M.C.A. where I remained half asleep and half awake until the first bus went to Yeadon at ten to five a.m.

This afternoon we are going to fly again, and then after that I think I will retire to bed as quickly as possible.

By the way I forgot to let you have the £1 note when I was home so will include it in this letter, and remember that after this is deducted from what I get, I still have slightly over six shillings per day to myself and so am not curtailing myself at all, and am still doing better than the average total wage I used to get from Hercules!

So here's wishing you all the best and hoping you will find some speedy arrangements for Lorna and Monica[1].

From Your Most Affectionate Son
Philip

---

1. Lorna and Monica had left Whitchurch because of unsatisfactory conditions

My Dear Mother and Father,

Thanks very much for the letter received this morning. I have just completed the second and last of the most important of our mid–term exams, and so feel as though a load has been taken off my shoulders. How I have done is another matter and to tell you the truth, I do not think I have done very brilliantly and in fact, I do not think that the week as a whole has been exactly a sweeping success as far as I am concerned. I have not as yet mastered the art of landing, but that is partly offset by the fact that the weather is very bad for training and I have had less than an hour's flying for the purpose of landing. This afternoon in desperation it was decided that we should go up, but do further exercises which normally take place when you have done your first solo flight and as a result I have been doing climbing turns and steep turns and can manage these with ease – if only I could land as smoothly as I can do everything else I would be made, for already I feel quite at home at the controls of an aircraft. However nothing is achieved without effort and continual practice, and I am jolly certain that if Amy Johnson could fly a second rate aeroplane all the way to Australia, (or was it New Zealand?) that I am going to manage a circuit round the aerodrome!

By the way another lot have arrived here from Scarborough, and have succeeded in turning everything upside down with the result that we had to have our day off yesterday (Friday). It has upset many chaps' plans for going home this weekend, so I will just advise you that there is perhaps the same fate awaiting me next weekend. Anyway if you will just keep in mind that things are in a bit of a turmoil here and that I may not be able to come home after all, it will be helpful.

And now, how are Lorna and Monica getting on? And what does Auntie Eileen think of them?[1] Yes I can quite imagine their delight at being home once more and what a cheerful weekend this should be for you.

I hear that a Midland town did receive a little attention last night but no damage or casualties so that is a good thing. We too heard many aeroplanes and had an alert, but that was as far as it went. I have not as yet heard the Leeds guns in action, there are three within half a mile of the camp, so I should hear them quite well when they do start. I am writing this part of the letter in the crew room and have just been up on 'circuits and bumps'[2] and I was told that I am now getting into these quite well – so this is a little stride forward.

Tonight I think I will go to Leeds Cathedral for the Evening Service. I have been before (on Easter Sunday Night) and it is a very nice church, but not what you would expect for a Cathedral.

As you say the news is not so good as it might be, and there seems to be no stopping these Jerries in Europe. However we are quite used to bad news by now, and so long as we can get the armies away in fact should not be unduly depressed. I thought that Lord Halifax's[3] speech was very significant where he pointed out that even with all these victories, the German people were at heart profoundly anxious that Britain was still being left intact and unbeaten. So long as we can hold Egypt, that is the main thing, and we seem to be regaining our balance there don't we? We have certainly a big job, but I think Hitler has a bigger one when you look all round.

Well for the present I will finish by sending you all my very best love and wishes.

From Your Most Loving Son
Philip

---

1. They were temporarily at Auntie Eileen's
2. Bumps = landings
3. Foreign Secretary

Yeadon nr. Leeds
9th May 1941

My Dear Mother and Father,

I fear that you will find this letter the harbinger of some rather unwelcome news. For tomorrow Saturday we are being posted to a place called Wilmslow which is about thirteen miles south of Manchester and I am afraid that this from all accounts, is a stepping off mark to going abroad. Nevertheless I will now try to give you some consolation from the advantages that will accrue to it.

First of all, it seems that Wilmslow is a place where they wait to go to Canada and I do not think you will mind that so much, as I ought not to be away for too long. Secondly you might find some consolation in the fact that it should delay the completion of my training by many weeks. Thirdly I certainly hope that I will get an embarkation leave before we go.

Whatever happens, I shall do all in my power and never cease to pray that I shall finally be back in England and that you will all be very safe and happy in the meantime.

You may be interested to know that twice this week I have flown solo to Brough aerodrome near Hull and returned safely. Though on the second time I got lost and pin–pointed myself some ten miles to the North of Hull by my map; however I turned right knowing I was bound to come to the river Humber (I couldn't see it, there was such a heavy haze above it, that it was obscure from that distance). Finally I came to it and then soon found the aerodrome when I was glad to find myself on Mother Earth again after sixty five minutes in the air, which represented about seventy miles journey because there was a strong wind against me. Well I have now finished flying for perhaps several weeks.

Hope I will soon be able to give you more news – and perhaps be seeing you. Anyway don't worry, and remember the war will not be lasting for ever – the end might be nearer than we can imagine.

Very Best Love
Philip

CHAPTER FIVE

WILMSLOW

'All pretty well fed up . . . hanging about here doing nothing much'
(Sunday, 18th May 1941)

My Dear Mother and Father,

I am writing this letter in complete ignorance of what the immediate future holds in store. Even a short leave seems most improbable though we have each put in a special application and leave form in hopes of it. I am afraid that we are all pretty well fed up with the hanging about here doing nothing much, yet incapable of going home. The whole affair seems most unfortunate, but it will not be too bad if we are returning fairly soon. I think that our destination is somewhere in Canada; of course we are not supposed to say anything about this but if it will save you any worry I shall think it quite justified, and it need not get past you.

In the event of my being pushed off suddenly, I will of course do my utmost to let you know, and I ask you not to forget to weigh up the advantages of it against its disadvantages; especially in so far as it should delay my period of training for many weeks.

We have just had a bit more hanging about on parade, again giving in names and numbers and ranks etc.! That's all we seem to be here for! I have just decided that I will try and let you have the news more quickly by trying to catch Fr. Boland on the phone this afternoon and he will then be able to tell you this evening, while I shall ascertain that all's well after the latest blitz – was there one last night? I have heard no news yet, but there was a long alert on here but no gun fire. I do not know as yet know Fr. Boland's phone number but will have to do something about it.

When we will go from here of course, I have not the remotest idea, but if you wish to write to catch me I would advise you not to delay.

I cannot really find much more to say as things are, so will end by sending you my very best love and wishes

From Your Most Affectionate Son
Philip

P.S. Many Happy Returns for Lorna on 29th of this month!

Hut 28 'A' Squadron, No.1.
P. D.Wing, R.A.F. Wilmslow
Cheshire
20th May 1941

My Dear Mother and Father,

Things have been moving very quickly of late and I hardly know where I am. We have been kitted out and it is NOT tropical kit, neither is it plain clothes for U.S.A. so this seems to make it more certain that we will ultimately arrive in Canada – just for a course which is not more than twelve weeks at the very most! Anyway it will probably be more than that through being abroad, and by the time we get settled down. Hope you will all be well and safe, and will try and let you have word as quickly as possible when we get to the other side. Hope we will all be together again soon. Aren't we unlucky! Our group is the only one that has not had at least seven days embarkation leave and quite a number of them have had even fourteen days and some even twenty one days. Yet we cannot get an hour.

Well will have to hurry and let you have this, so here's saying goodbye until I contact you again from somewhere in the Atlantic or in Canada. I'll see whether I can see anything of this great 'battle of the Atlantic' and give you some firsthand information on it!

Well good–bye and all my love and best wishes

From Your Most Loving Son
Philip

P.S. No more trotting home for week–ends I'm afraid! Not for a few months anyway!

Philip must have got home leave after all:

Hut 28 'A' Squadron, No.1.
P. D.Wing, R.A.F. Wilmslow
Cheshire
Friday, 23rd May 1941

My Dear Mother and Father,

This letter is just to let you know when I will be finally going, and I am trying to post it at the last minute. I arrived back here quite early with three hours to spare which was quite a pity really. At the moment I know nothing more than before, so may be off at any time.

Well I cannot really do much more than send you my best love and wishes, and the promise of my prayers for your continued safety and good fortune.

From Your Most Affectionate Son
Philip

Hut 28 'A' Squadron, No.1.
P. D.Wing, R.A.F. Wilmslow
Cheshire
31st May 1941

My Dear Mother and Father,

Somehow I have a feeling that they mean business in the near future and that I will not be making many more excursions home for some time to come. Somehow someone has found out where 34 S.F.T.S.[1] is in Canada, and if it all turns out correct, we will have as long a train journey as we have in the boat, as it seems to be near to the Pacific side and only about 100–150 miles from the U.S.A. border. This afternoon we have an idea that they are going to break another tradition of this camp by paying us – we are due for it of course – and if this proves correct I shall be letting you have something more before we go.

There is not much in life here, and we are not even allowed out at nights now, with the result that there is a spate of frayed tempers and general dissatisfaction.

I suppose that at the moment you are thinking that the news from Crete is not too good, and are wondering when we will have to conduct another exodus. Well do not give up heart, for up to the moment at least, we still have not lost Crete and I for my part have an idea that we may yet win the day there.

Today, Saturday, we have just been paid for the fortnight in advance as well so I have rather a lot on my plate and am trying to send this in registered mail which I want you to take in its entirety as I will not be able to allow you to the same extent when away. This still leaves me a very full margin for the voyage across including a fortnight afterwards, so don't think that I am doing without at all.

There was quite a bit of air activity around here last night and the night before, but it did not disturb my repose very much.

Well for the present I will now draw to a close, wishing you all the very best of love and wishes

From Your Most Loving Son
Philip

---

1. Service Flying Training School

A cartoon 'Western Desert Roundabout' is enclosed:

Hut 28 'A' Squadron, No.1.
P. D.Wing, R.A.F. Wilmslow
Cheshire
Sunday tea time, 1st June 1941

My Dear Mother and Father,

Well I imagine that this will be the last letter I write you from this part of the world, and it is not at all outside the bounds of possibility that I will be already plying my way over the broad expanse of the ocean when you read this. Our 'deep sea kit', as it is called, has already gone, and there are persistent rumours that zero hour is at something like four or six o'clock tomorrow morning, i.e. Whit Monday. The weather is wonderful and the countryside particularly delightful at the moment and it grieves me to think that we may have to leave this and return to arctic conditions around Iceland or some such place on our way across.

At this moment an N.C.O. has just informed us that Reveille is at 2a.m! So as I just inferred things are beginning to move!

I am awaiting tonight's news of Crete at the moment but am still hopeful of the outcome here, and at worst I think we have done very well. At any rate Hitler is having to fight harder and harder for each fresh victory, and I do not think it will now be long before the scales will be turned, and in spite of all he does he will have to taste the bitterness of defeat.

By the way, I hear that the crossing is sometimes fourteen to sixteen days so don't worry if you are a long time in hearing and remember that no news is good news. I hope that you will have received by this time the registered letter in which you should find £5. I have still £5 with me so am quite alright financially. Did I tell you there is a chapel on this camp and I have been able to go to Mass and Communion every day?

Well, here's saying goodbye to you all and sending you my very best love and wishes from

Your Most Affectionate Son
Philip

CHAPTER SIX

AT SEA

Thirteen days

From H.M. Ship
Tuesday, 3rd June 1941

My Dear Mother and Father,

I could of course fill in all these interrogation marks (four of which accompanied this skeletal address) but for various reasons as you know I must not. However we are aboard and have been now for some few hours, and it looks as though we are going to have a rare time and good grub. The Navy assures us that they will look after us, so what more could one ask?

By the way, I was in the Manchester blitz of Sunday night, I don't know whether you heard of it because I haven't heard the news for some time now. There seemed to be numerous planes, but I don't think it was unduly heavy like the proper blitzes and for all I know it might have been worse at Merseyside where there did appear to be gunfire.

There are many illuminating things that I have seen lately and I should love to be able to write of them not only to satisfy your curiosity but because they are so reassuring – to me at any rate.

Well I will now conclude hoping that you will remain safe and well, and sending you my very best love and wishes,

From Your Most Affectionate Son
Philip

Atlantic Ocean,
8th June 1941

My Dear Mother and Father,

It is Sunday June 8th. as I take up pen and paper to write this letter. I have been keeping a diary of events since we left Wilmslow but I doubt whether the censor would approve of my passing them on. Of course at the moment we are still somewhere in the Atlantic and miles and miles from anywhere; I am hoping that we will dock in by about Wednesday for there is not very much one can do here except sleep, read, eat, and lean over the side watching the water swish by. I have of course been wondering much about you all at home, and wondering what sort of nights you have been having and what is happening over in Europe and Africa, for I have heard no news since last Monday when the ship's wireless 'conked' out.

I suppose that you have been wondering about me and how the battle of the Atlantic is affecting me. I fear that it has affected me in a manner far from what I anticipated. In fact from the minute we started the full might of the Atlantic has been in play against my stomach. The latter was holding its ground in relatively calm waters during the first three days, but was gradually giving way under the relentless pressure of the surging waves until a climax was reached during the night of Friday – Saturday when we came into real rough waters, but perhaps if I quote from my memoirs of Saturday June 7th it will give you a better idea.

'The sea was not *kind during the night, which proved very rough for me; full of continual nightmares, being tossed about, with my stomach being turned inside–out I could not even face a breakfast of sausage and bacon. I was just about to brave a cup of tea when I decided it would be more prudent to race to 'B' deck to the nearest open side of the boat. I heaved and gulped, gaped and gurgled, whilst I hung over the side and the rain beat down – but all to no effect as my stomach was presumably empty, or its organs so badly mangled that they could not even perform that simple operation. However I was just about spared the degradation of being sea–sick, though this was small consolation at the time, as I felt for all the world like a dying fish that is out of water and does not know what to do with itself.'*

However there were other phases in this 'battle of the Atlantic' and I hope that it is quite alright for me to tell you that during the first two days we had no less than six or seven air raid alerts. But I think they must have been German reconnaissance planes for, apart from slight anti–aircraft fire from one of the destroyers, nothing extra happened. There were one or two other minor incidents but they were of no great consequence and as yet we are quite safe and sound.

Wednesday 11th June

You may remember that I said I hoped we would dock by Wednesday, yet still we sail apparently as far away from land as ever. However we have been told that we will dock on Friday morning which will be a relief. My writing may betray the rocking of the boat at the moment, which I can assure you is very considerable. The sea on Monday as well as today is far rougher than on any other day, but apart from finding that you cannot help running upstairs, while at other times you cannot make any headway down, and such other odd inconveniences, I feel very little effect and I certainly enjoy watching from the side of the boat.

Well, to tell you the truth I do not think there is very much more I can say (or dare say!) and as the mail bag closes tomorrow at 4.30p.m. (11.30p.m. where you are) I shall conclude and add anything extra that might interest you.

So wishing you all the very best and hoping this letter will find its way to England as safely as I have reached this present spot, I am

Your Most Affectionate Son
Philip

P.S. Thursday dinner time (tea time for you) and still we sail – not a sign of land though we must be pretty near, as they say we get in port during tonight. Well will have to finish to get it in the mail bag. By the way, you will be able to write to me at this address for the present

Royal Canadian Air Force Headquarters
Ottawa,
CANADA

CHAPTER SEVEN

CANADA

'There is a war on, though you would hardly believe it over here'
(June 29th 1941)

TELEGRAM: *16th June 1941*

'ARRIVED SAFELY CANADA. BEST LOVE. HERMOLLE'

TELEGRAM: *21st June 1941*

'ALL WELL WRITE HUT 14A 34 SFTS RAF MEDICINE HAT ALBERTA LOVE PHILIP.'

Alberta, Canada
Tuesday, 17th June 1941

My Dear Mother and Father,

As I am making a start to this letter, after an exceedingly long and tiring day, I reflect that at home it is no longer Tuesday but Wednesday, furthermore I can well imagine that the alarm clock will perhaps be going off any minute now, bidding you rise to yet another day. Yet as you get up I will just be commencing to go to bed, i.e. in about half an hour when it will be 10.15p.m. here, and 7.15a.m. for you at home.

At last! After fifteen days of continuous travelling here we are at our final destination right in the heart of Canada. We arrived at a Canadian Port Friday last at about 10a.m. and, while much preparation for the train journey was going on, we had dinner aboard and entrained almost immediately afterwards.

Twenty seven hours later saw us arrive in Montreal, Canada's largest city, on Saturday evening. There we went to another station and were soon on a Canadian Pacific Railway Express, and off again – we came off that train about 6a.m. so you can tell what a journey it has been. However it was a journey brimful of interest and one which I found never in the least boring. My only regrets were that I had to miss much of it during the hours of darkness, and that I could not look out of both sides of the window. Well for the moment I will have to close down once more for it is now almost lights out and I have not as yet made my bed.

I have now about thirty five minutes, so will see what else of interest I can say. I did keep a day to day account of things on the boat which did not amount to much; I had also intended to on the train but I found it was almost impossible to write on the train, much less to try and concentrate while there was so much to see outside. I suppose that what has struck me more than anything else about Canada is its vastness, for everything here seems to be about ten times as large as it would be at home. For instance, when the train was winding its way through woodlands, it seemed almost interminable. Then when after many hours we could see the river St. Lawrence on our right, we could not see the other side of it at all; and the train must have run for well over an hour very near to it. When finally we actually crossed this same river about nine hours later it took us about five minutes when we were doing quite a good speed.

Twenty hours after this we touched on Lake Superior about 6p.m. on Sunday night, and it was well on into the night before we left sight of it through darkness, and yet we had only travelled along a fraction of its coast line. Indeed, Lake Superior, when one can get a complete view of it, appears exactly as a seaside coast, especially when one sees the sun setting over its waters as we did.

Of the country around this vicinity, well it simply baffles all description. For hours and hours the train puffed on and on, in and out of rocky crags and ravines, now plunging deep down through shady thick forests, now suddenly sailing merrily aloft over an ocean of tree tops, and then plunging forth into wide open sparkling lakes – or what we English would term lakes – and all this time the sun scorched down out of a cloudless sky. The country on the East of Lake Superior and a little to the west of it seems to be literally full of pools and lakes, of small hills and valleys and woodland. As one nears Winnipeg the land becomes more flat, and from then onwards one sees large fields of corn and other cereals, and at times where there are no apparent boundaries to the fields and very few trees, it gives the impression for all the world of being on the sea, especially at eventide and when looking at the horizon.

On the way we stopped at one or two small places for thirty or forty minutes, and in the Quebec province especially (around the St. Lawrence river) I was struck by how patently Catholic the place was. There were many churches which were obviously Catholic and on one or two hills large illuminated crucifixes stood overlooking a small town or village at its foot. In the three shops into which I went there were pictures of the Sacred Heart, with a prayer in French seeking for protection in this time of war. This prayer in French also reminds me how surprised I was at the vast areas in Canada where French is the spoken language, where all the advertisements and newspapers were written in this language, and where the similarity in style of the houses and churches with those of France was extremely noticeable.

This place, Medicine Hat, seems to be a very nice little town, something of the size of Melton Mowbray, but I hope I will be able to tell you more of this a little later. We have apparently a very stiff course ahead of us which will take ten weeks. What will happen after that I do not know, but I do not think I will be sorry to leave all the bright lights and excellent food of Canada for good old England – even the siren will be music in my ears! I won't talk about the food here because it might only make your mouths water. Suffice it to say that there is more than even I can manage!

The people from what I have already seen are exceptionally generous, and even coming up on the train we had baskets of apples and oranges given us. Montreal, all lit up at night was also a very strange sight nowadays – I am not yet quite accustomed to these new conditions, and more than once I have frowned at seeing a bare unshaded light![1]

I fear that so far I have spoken only of myself and have rather left all you out of it, but I can assure you that even now (Thursday afternoon) I realise that Birmingham is in darkness and that many things might be happening. It is not so easy to get the news here, but from what I gather there does not seem to be much doing in the way of German air attacks, for which I am very glad.

There also seem to be rumours of Russia floating around but I do not know what to think of it all, or even know how true much of it is. I hope you will have received my former letter which was actually posted aboard the boat and should by this time be well on its way across the Atlantic again. I hope by this time you have also received the two cablegrams I have dispatched and that they have not caused you too much disturbance. Anyhow weighing it up, I thought you would like to know of my safe landing, even if it did mean almost heart failure before you opened it! I wonder now whether I gave you the correct address on the second cable; this is Hut 14A 34 S.F.T.S. The rates are very cheap for H.M forces and each has only cost me the equivalent of $^2/_3$ pence in English money.

As I'm trying to have this sent by air this evening I will now finish, so here's my very best love and wishes to you one and all, and promise of my prayers.

From your most loving son
Philip

---

1. Britain had been in blackout since the beginning of the war

Canada,
Saturday, 21st June 1941

This evening heard Germany has just invaded Russia

My Dear Mother and Father,

Your letter was posted last night at the Post Office to go by air mail. This is the first attempt since I have been on the camp to try and keep a diary of events.

Today the weather has been simply scorching. In the afternoon I was flying for the first time here. They are twin engine Oxfords, very similar to Oxfords[1] and extremely complicated to manipulate. I certainly have not as yet mastered 'rules of vital actions' (necessary actions for ensuring that aircraft will fly as it should i.e. putting undercarriage down to land, as well as flaps; putting on rich mixture etc.) There is a tremendous difference between these and the old Tigers. I was up for two hours fifty minutes and made two fairly successful landings and one not so good – in fact I all but swept the undercarriage off!

In the evening I went shopping, buying a new tie and a camera. I then proceeded to go to the Church for the first time for nearly three weeks, and Confession. This is the one night in the week when we are allowed out after 9.30p.m. but we went back again at about 11 o'clock.

Sunday 22 nd

My squad was altered and I found myself flying again today, in the afternoon. I was able to get to Mass in the morning. Back again in the canteen, trying to cool ourselves with ice cream, we heard wireless announcement that Churchill would be speaking in one and a half hours (noon). Just before dinner, we all gathered to his words of wisdom which came through exceptionally clearly. At the end, for the first time for many weeks, we heard a B.B.C. announcer 'You have been. . .' when it was cut off.

The heat is terribly severe, and the wind blows as though it has come out of an oven. In the evening I managed to get to Benediction, while sweat literally poured down my face and back.

Monday

We have been on ground work all today. The heat is even worse – temperature 102 degrees in the shade! This evening I simply dare not stir from camp.

We had quite a good concert and sing– song in the evening, sponsored by the local Y.M.C.A.

The weather proved somewhat cooler but still very hot. By the way I hope you do not mind this small and rather cramped writing, because I cannot use more than three sheets at the very most if I wish to send it by air mail on account of the weight. Today I had my second trip up in the air, and was encouraged by my instructor saying that there was a big improvement, and that my instrument flying was good. This evening there is a terrific thunderstorm – the worst I've encountered – but there is no rain.

Wed. 29th June, Thurs., Fri., Sat. and Sunday

I fear that I have not kept up to date as I should have done. But there is not very much to say. Thursday and Saturday I had a little flying, and was not doing too badly. Saturday there was a big stampede (display by Red Indians etc. and quite a big event) but we could not manage to get there. Heavy rain set in last night and continues with unabating violence this morning, my one day off in a fortnight! By the way I am very pleased with the news lately because you do appear to be escaping some of the more intense raids owing to this Russo– German conflict. I can never tell what to make of what little news I can glean, but though I do not doubt Germany is having big successes, I should imagine that they have had one or two hitches in their programme.

There seems to be a poor news service out here as compared with home, and I am afraid that neither the Canadian Broadcasting System, nor the National of U.S.A. is half so reliable or clear as the B.B.C. Talking about radio also reminds me that the standard of programmes out here certainly does not compare with those of the B.B.C., though one can plainly see that in many ways the Canadian is endeavouring to follow the same style as the B.B.C.. There never seems to be any decent music on the Canadian at all, and from what I can see Canadians seems to be even less musical than the British.

However, in other respects, they seem a very good set of people and they are certainly heart and soul in the war. I was astonished by the large number of houses that have a large Union Jack (sometimes the Canadian flag as well) flying from their house or one of their windows. You would come across this too in the heart of the prairies where you would see one little wooden house miles and miles from anywhere. In some cases in French–Canadian parts you might also see the French Tricolour side by side with our own Union Jack. There are plenty of notices up: 'Bury Hitler', 'Buy Savings certificates' and 'Finish the Job'.

Most of the people refer to England as the 'Old Country'. They have much to say about the visit of the King and Queen (who by the way, passed through Medicine Hat and remained for an hour or two here). The other night one gentleman showed us a film (movie) that he had taken on this occasion, of which he was justly proud!

I am gradually becoming accustomed to the 'peaceful' conditions here and when I hear an aeroplane at night as we often do, I do not immediately think 'Ah Jerry's at it again', though I admit that the other day when I first saw the lightening in the distance my first instinctive thought was 'who could be having the blitz?' As a matter of fact some chaps said later on, when the storm was fully upon us, that they would rather have a London Blitz than such a storm. It was pretty bad too, but of course it is easy to say that when many thousands of miles from London!

Well it is now five weeks nearly since I heard from you, but I trust all is still well with you as it is with me. I, as you see, am up to the moment all in one piece and will endeavour to remain so, until such time as we will be on our way home again! By that time let's hope that you will have no cause for worry, for somehow I have still that feeling that the end of the war is much nearer than it is possible for us to see with clarity. At any rate I am praying hard for that end particularly for your sakes and those of other people who feel its effects so much more than I do or ever have done.

I wonder whether by this time you have received one of my letters; it is just about possible that you have done though I doubt it. I bet you would see a great difference in me just now if you could see me, for one thing I am in khaki uniform (tropical) and in the daytime we only go about in light khaki slacks and a khaki shirt with an open collar, which is quite pleasant after the other uniform. I also imagine that I am far browner and tanned in complexion than when I left England, and for all I know the better food may be having its effect, but if it is then I do not notice it very much.

By the way, Mother, I am hoping that this letter will reach you by the 25th July, and I would like to take this opportunity of wishing you a very happy birthday and many happy returns of the day when it arrives. I can assure you that I will not forget the day, nor Monica's birthday on the 16th (or is it 15th?) I think you will not mind not having a separate letter all to yourself, because as I say I am limited with paper from reasons of weight in the post. I hear that air mail services from here and to here are very haphazard and though a letter may occasionally arrive within ten days or so, at other times it is more likely to take in the region of three weeks, and longer by sea.

However, mail is not so liable to submarine intervention from the air and I will endeavour to let you have a fairly constant flow as far as possible. I think I told you in the last letter that this is another course that seems almost beyond my scope – however at both I.T.W. and E.F.T.S. I seemed to get through what appeared an impossibility to me and I'm hoping that the third and most vital occasion will not prove unlucky for me. If it were to I am afraid that it would be some time before I saw England again for they simply send failures to another station in Canada for some other type of work, and that would have very little appeal for me. I do not suppose you have heard any more about Bernard have you? And has Leslie got on to his gunnery course yet? I suppose he might easily be a Sergeant by this time.

By the way, this reminds me that at the beginning of this course, in one of the forms we had to fill in there was a question 'Do you wish to obtain a commission if possible?' Well I have never consulted you on it, but I put 'Yes' mainly because I thought it would give a better impression, and also because I do not think there is much chance of my being offered one. Otherwise I am not terribly keen, and do not know too much about it.

Well time is running along reasonably quickly this side of the world, life is reasonably happy too, so I should not find the time I have to spend here too irksome before we are on our way back again. I do hope that I will be able to have a better view of Canada than I have had so far however, and that at the end of the course we might have the opportunity to look round one of Canada's large cities such as Ottawa, Montreal or Quebec. It seems so silly to travel one half the globe nearly, to be so near places of interest that one may see but once in a lifetime, and yet have to pass them all by. I suppose the obvious retort to that is that there is a war on, though you would hardly believe it over here.

And now I think it is about time I draw to a close because there seems little more to say and no room to say it in. Enclosing, therefore all my usual love and best wishes to you all, I am

Your Most Affectionate Son,
Philip

---

1. De Haviland was the only other plane he had flown

Canada,
7th July 1941

My Dear Mother and Father,

It seems a very long time since I heard anything from you, and I am eagerly awaiting some news. I see that Birmingham has just had two raids but I trust all is perfectly well and normal.

As for things here, they seem to be going fairly well, but I will be greatly pleased when the course is over and finished with, for one reason it is a very strenuous and hard course which I would like to see the back of, and for another reason that Canada with all its present advantages and generosity, is a very poor substitute for England – at least as far as I am concerned. Although we are all having a pretty good time and enjoying the life, I think that this is the view of most of us. The weather still continues very warm, and I imagine that we must all be as brown as niggers. When possible we try to counteract this by swimming in an open air bath that is quite handy for the camp. I am also making the most of the facilities for tennis that we have on the camp, and have had some very enjoyable games.

How do you find things at home? It is amazing what a different picture one gets out here of things at home. One reads of things in American papers and journals that would never appear in print in England, this especially regarding the purpose or significance of different moves of a military character. It is especially interesting to read American commentaries written last summer on the momentous happenings at France and Dunkirk and the 'Battle of England'. They evidently took a very poor view of our chances of long surviving.

We occasionally get B.B.C. programmes that are broadcast on Canadian stations, as for instance last Sunday morning when I was having a cup of coffee in one of the cafes after Mass, there was a programme direct from London on which a number of schoolchildren were singing, and Canadian soldiers were speaking to their people over here. They were saying what a warm afternoon it was, but I would like to bet it was no warmer than it was here though it was only 9.30a.m. Do you know that the other morning at such an early hour as 7.30a.m., it was already 87 degrees in the shade! Yes it is wonderful to hear so directly from home as one can over the radio, and some of the programmes are very well done and very clear indeed. But should Lorna be interested, I have never heard Sandy McPherson yet, but of course that may be because I am there at the wrong time.

And what do you think of the war situation now? Do you think that Russia being involved will lengthen or shorten it? Personally I am still optimistic enough to think Hitler's days will not be long now, although I am apparently in direct contrast with such considered and authoritative views as those of General Wavell and Mr. Churchill. Do you ever play those records now? I dare say that you have had that one of Gigli on once or twice, but I am afraid that I shall remain starved of music for most of my life in the R.A.F., for there does not seem to be much over here.

Saturday, 12th July 1941

I am snatching a few moments before I have to go on the Link Trainer for one hour (10p.m. – 11p.m. on a Saturday night!) Yesterday we had a much appreciated day off to allow those who wished to visit the 'Rodeo' or stampede at Calgary, which is for Canada what the Derby or the Grand National is for England. I went with four other chaps starting by a hired taxi at 3.30a.m. and arriving there at 9.30a.m. The town was in a very festive and gay mood; flags and bunting bedecked the streets, cowboys in their colourful costumes and large hats strolled lazily about in the mid–day sun, military bands played and paraded, quaint rustic carts drawn by lazy oxen formed a strange contrast to many of the luxury stream–lined limousines of visitors from the States and other places, and even the notorious police motor cycle, common in America with its terrible siren, nor the colourful and dignified Canadian Mounted Police, were absent.

Furthermore we breakfasted at a cafe in wonderful style: with four rashers of bacon and two fried eggs, fried bread, toast, bread, butter and marmalade and really delicious coffee (and of course you can help yourself to sugar)[1].

After an hour or two of sightseeing, a cool ice–soda proved sufficient for dinner, after which we went into the stampede – which is a kind of fair, exhibition and horse and cattle show all combined. However it proved exceptionally interesting and has given me a much better idea of life and sports and the spirit of Canada. The cowboys (who do exist!) are very smart indeed with a rope, and several had chased, lassooed and completely bound bullocks or a calf in an average of 21 or 22 seconds (some in about 18). Then again, others proved very stubborn in sticking to bucking horses which had not been broken in, and if some of them fell pretty hard they certainly had a good clap from a large audience of some 50,000 who were very appreciative of their efforts; others showed how practical they were by arresting fleeing wild cows and then milking them – which appeared to be no easy job! I shall never forget the peculiar wit of the commentator who had such a mournful expression on, when somebody had failed to succeed in his particular effort.

Still this was only the commencement of the real fun and adventure which oddly enough took place on our way home. I do not know whether I have mentioned it, but the roads in Canada do not compare with our English ones, and are for the most part beaten down tracks which have been hardened by small stones and gravel. In the dry hot weather a car leaves a thick smoke screen of dust and dirt in its trail, in rainy wet weather a car will stumble along through ruts and holes. Anyway we had to make a detour of six miles on an even worse road because of repairs that were going on. At this point I should also explain that there had apparently been a heavy thunder storm in the afternoon, and the soil is so soft that when moistened it will not bear the least weight. Such was the nature of the surface that we had to traverse to get back on the main road! We made the first hill after some very anxious moments, but when we arrived at the top we saw three or four other cars waiting, and another three or four on the other side striving might and main to get past the others! You never saw such a hopeless traffic tangle right in the middle of the prairie, miles and miles from anywhere. Then an old fat vicious looking bull slowly walked up and stood staring at our frantic and vain efforts as though registering utter and complete disgust and contempt at our inability to overcome a few inches of mud.

This attitude of the bull seemed to pull us all together, and we set about to prove to him that if our machines (wonderful as they were) showed themselves ineffective in such circumstances, that at least we were not quite so bad. We therefore took socks and shoes off, rolled up our trousers, and by dint of much slithering about and pushing and pulling, extricated the vehicle from the mess. Our troubles were not over by any means, and the sight of other cars which had fallen by the wayside down into ditches gave us continual cause for caution. It took us about an hour and a half to do this detour of six miles. The people in front of us were holiday– making in Canada from U.S .A. so I do not know what they think of Canada, though they said that some of the roads in the States too were pretty rough. We finally arrived back in the camp in the early hours of the morning, sometime after we were due but nothing has happened and at least we had a good excuse.

In the morning I also received your letter which appears to have made very good time. I am glad to hear that all was well up to the 24th June anyway. This evening (it is now Monday I fear) I have just heard a recording of a speech made by Mr. Churchill this morning all about bombed London and beleaguered Britain to quote an oft–used expression in this country. But apparently England is not the only country now being bombed! Although bombing is so ridiculous really and so insane, one finds it hard to remain unpleased that Germany is now receiving her due, especially as I believe it will hasten the downfall of Germany more quickly than anything else.

By the time this letter reaches you, Russia may be one other occupied territory, but for the moment they seem to be causing a little trouble. This German– Russian war appears to have had a rather bad effect on many Americans who seem to prefer Nazism to Communism. I read an article by a Jesuit this last week, in which he blames both U.S.A. and Britain for helping Russia. He brings out his argument by recounting all Russia's past and her crimes up to the present. However this seems a very illogical line of thought to me, to expect Britain to cease fighting simply because Hitler has added to his crimes. It seems fairly obvious to me that we are not fighting to uphold Russia, but to defeat Germany. And of course it is simply pure hypocrisy to make out that Hitler is now fighting a crusade, for he fights for military reasons primarily. I know that I have certainly no qualms of conscience about our position.

You will probably be interested to know how I enjoy the flying here and how I am getting on with it. They have nearly all gone 'solo' now but I am one that has not. I was awaiting my test all Saturday afternoon and then did not have time for it. However it should not cause me much trouble as our instructor (not my usual one, whom I do not like too much) told me that I should 'walk it' and that my circuit and approach was perfect. So I think tomorrow should see me through without much bother. These machines of course are very large as compared with the 'tiger moth' and far more complicated and delicate to different altitude and attitudes of flight, but they are very nice to fly once you get into the hang of it.

Flying in Canada is also a far different prospect to flying in England, for once you leave Medicine Hat you will not see another town or villa for miles and miles; roads and railways are not very apparent either. There is just one vast yellow prairie spread beneath you, with an occasional ploughed land or plot of green rye. This is not altogether a disadvantage however as there is no mistaking a landmark once you find it, as there may be in England. Also the visibility in Canada is much more clear than at home.

Well I want you to have this letter as soon as possible, and to let you hear fairly regularly, so wishing both you Mother, and Monica, very happy birthdays – they are still in the future as I write – I will conclude sending you my very best love and wishes

From Your Most Affectionate Son
Philip

P.S. I <u>have</u> now gone 'solo' and have done an hour and a half on my own in these Oxfords, and found myself quite at home.

---

1. Sugar was rationed in Britain

Canada,
Friday, 18th July 1941

My Dear Mother and Father,

It is now evening but I have a couple of hours to wait around before going on the link trainer, and so cannot go out for the evening or do anything special. Since the sun still persists in pouring down mercilessly on all who care to brave its fearful barrage, I am indoors trying to keep cool. I have been here now getting on for five weeks and I can say the truth of all the time I have been in Canada there have only been three days when we have had no sun at all, and on those days it simply poured with rain the whole time. However at the moment I imagine the heat is reaching a climax for yesterday was the hottest day of the year, and it seems even hotter today to me.

This week we are not flying in the afternoon, but in the morning from 4a.m. until 1p.m. which is a jolly good job, because the cockpit is just like an oven as the day grows warm, unless of course you rise to 12,000 feet or so and contemplate a trip over to the Rockies where you can see the blessed spectacle of white snow!

I have not been over there as yet, but those who have tell that the scenery, even from the air, is really wonderful. When we went to Calgary (of which I told you in my last letter) we actually saw the long chain of Rockies very clearly with the snow topped peaks, but I suppose that even so they were about forty or sixty miles away. I should like to be able to get over there before I return home. By the way do you know that here we are 2,500 feet above sea level, almost as high as England's highest mountain I believe! (or Wales it is, isn't it?)

You will see that I enclose one or two snaps, though not many because of extra weight and the fact that they are very disappointing. I have a little number taken, most of them unsuccessful, when we were at Calgary, because another chap who shared the cost in films etc. seemed pretty keen on taking a number of long distance ones, which I knew would be no good. I fear that I have been very extravagant, because I have now bought another and better camera that will take better and bigger snaps. The former was quite a good one but it is the size of the snaps I do not like.

Thinking it over I thought I may as well get what I want as I have the money and will not be able to take much of it out of Canada, and I thought I could possibly give this other camera to Gerald, because I can imagine he might grow quite interested in photography, and it might open out a new line of thought for him. Anyway, you can say what you think of that idea, because I dare say you will have visions of Gerald asking for all sorts of things for it! I dare say you will tell me that I should have thought more before I purchased the former one! But that of course is quite obvious to me as well!

By the way, I have heard that all the letters we wrote on the boat have failed to return to England, so it looks to me as though hours of patient writing with an extremely vivid description of how I was feeling when I was almost seasick, and had to rush to the side of the boat early one morning, has all been in vain! I will probably find out from your next letter whether you did get that letter. In case you did not get it, I will just say that the crossing over was not entirely uneventful but was not very exciting. We had several air raid alerts in the first three days but apart from slight anti–aircraft fire from one of the neighbouring destroyers, nothing more materialised from the air. It was however a great relief to reach land on this side.

You will be interested to know that somehow I have become quite pally with the curate of this church at Medicine Hat. He has lived in U.S.A. until very recently and has told me some very interesting things about them and their attitude, and of course he's very interested to know all he can about 'the Old Country'. I say he has lived in U.S.A., but I think he is actually of Canadian nationality. At the moment he has to help in taking a census and last night I met him on his round and he was very amusing the way he told me of some of the embarrassing moments he gave some of his people to be censored, as in this hot weather they apparently leave things in a very haphazard manner and are very economical with the wearing of their clothes, at least while at home! The sight of a Roman collar at the door appears to throw the whole house into a turmoil of confusion!

Saturday 18th July

This morning I was up with the crack of dawn and before most people had thought of getting up had been on a two hour cross country flight! (with instructor of course). I have since been up for nearly five hours, three of which were solo. The weather is not quite so bad (or good I should say!) today as there is a slight breeze and a few clouds in the sky. Well if you do not mind I will make this rather a shorter letter and let you hear a little more regularly than I have hitherto.

Well with this I will finish, sending you all my very best love and wishes

From Your Most Affectionate Son,
Philip

Canada,
22nd July 1941

My Dear Mother and Father,

Though it was only the day before yesterday that I dispatched the last letter, I think it will be a good idea to make a start on this, or else if I leave it a little, it seems to get left behind. I do not know whether there is much more to say, but I shall have to try and say it anyway. By this time you will be growing tired of my talking about the hot weather which still keeps up its reputation, so I will say no more of that.

I wonder how you are all getting on nowadays and whether conditions are much changed since I left England. I expect there must be some changes, but I soon hope to be back again with you all to share your hardships and see what I can do to help you get out of it. If I make this course okay, I am trying to get on to coastal command aircraft; however they tell me that for that, one's Navigation has to be pretty good, and you also have a long period at O.T.U.[1] for you have to learn quite a lot about Naval Procedure, and to be able to identify all types of naval craft, and know what things to take note of etc., in addition to all the other things that one normally does at O.T.U. But on the other hand it is quite interesting and not quite so bloodthirsty as normal bombing, which has no great appeal for me. Anyway this is all very much up in the air at the moment.

Meantime, what do you think of the war now? I am beginning to wonder whether 'Adolf Hitler' (as they call him over here) has bitten off more than he can comfortably digest. Anyway this campaign should help to destroy the Stalin regime and provide a better Russia in its place, and if at the same time they can hold Germany for a little longer I think it should prove to our great advantage in the end. I see that the Midlands are visited occasionally these nights; I do not know how intensive these attacks are but I never fail to pray for you all at home, and that it will soon end. By the way, it is almost embarrassing sometimes to hear what the Canadians have to say about the English people. There is no doubt about it that Canadians and Americans think the English are far more wonderful for the way they stuck to it last summer and held through during the winter, than the Germans for all their striking victories. From what I hear of Americans, they think there is nobody so wonderful as the English; they are apparently wholeheartedly behind giving all help in a material way, but are a little afraid to take the final step of entering the war.

Thursday

I have a little more time on hand, but I do not know what I can write about. It is only about 10.15 in the morning here and we await flying this afternoon, but I realise that it is about 7.15p.m. and that you will all be home after a hard day's work, and after having a little of something to eat, and listening to the news (which I have just heard direct from London, and is mainly about this Jap business in Indo–China) you will be retiring for what I hope will prove a quiet night's rest. At 3 o'clock this afternoon I shall also try to recall that your birthday is just beginning for you; so that actually when I eventually waken here on the 25th. your birthday will almost be over! Anyway, I hope it will be a very pleasant and enjoyable day, and of course I am at this moment wishing you all those things I have expressed in my previous letter which should have reached you by this time.

Sometime this week I have to have a Navigation test in the air, and immediately after that have to fly to a small town about 120 miles away, and having found it and taken a photo (for evidence) am to return back to base. This will be solo! I hope to have done it by the time you have this letter. After this there are four cross–countries, but only one of them will be solo. In the other cases I will either go as navigator or have a navigator to navigate me. (I mean I will have to practise both.)

Today Saturday 26th

I am writing this in the crew room while I await the other chap under my instructor to come down, when I will go up for an hour or so. I was very pleased this morning to receive your letter posted on the 10th. July and to hear that things are not too bad at home. From the news, one really does not know what to think, because it cannot be said to be bad, yet on the other hand one is afraid to say whether it is good. However

I should imagine that in a month or two the position should be clarified a little, and we will better understand how things are going. I am grateful for your prayers because there are times when one feels that one needs a bit of extra help and power of endurance to carry right on regardless of all dangers and hazards. I am afraid that I worry more because I know that you are worrying, and I pray for my own safety mainly for your sakes because I know you have already more than your fair share of burdens, and I am not anxious to add to them at all. However don't worry because if we are all trying to do our duty, we cannot do more and I feel that if we pray hard enough everything will come right and the war will soon be over.

Well for the present I will conclude and try and get this letter off tonight with a few more snaps. I expect the one where I am standing outside one of the hangars, and where I look more like an American Ball Player, will make you smile. It was not my helmet but another chap's who stands about 6 foot 2 inches tall! I have one or two more interesting ones, but I would prefer to show you those when I come home.

For the present then, until next week I will bid you adieu, sending my best love and wishes to you all

From Your Most Loving Son
Philip

---

1. Operations Training Unit

Canada,
Tuesday, 29th July 1941

My Dear Mother and Father,

Well here I am once more at the start of another letter. As I write at the moment there is a programme coming over the radio from America which is very similar to some of our English Sunday Evening broadcasts with the B.B.C. chorus and orchestra, consequently it reminds me very much of home and makes me ache to get on the way again. Talking of the radio also reminds me of a very long programme broadcast to Canada and U.S.A. from the B.B.C. last evening about different things of the war. It was very interesting and well put over. England seems very tough and efficient when you view and hear it from the outside!

This morning I must have gone about 300 miles in one single trip on a triangular course for an Air Navigation Test which I have come through O.K. I think. I was in the air for about two hours ten minutes and must have been within quite a few miles of the Canadian–U.S.A. border. What a long frontier these two countries must have and yet as far as I can make out there is not a single fortification or soldier to man them the whole way along.

Talking about the flying, we have just had a little more 'gen' (as we call it, which is anything from a rumour to real genuine news) namely that there is a chance that some of us will be able to go on night fighters at the end of this course which is really what I have been wishing for, but thought I would not be able to get. Anyway it shows there may be a chance, and Beaufighter aircraft should present no difficulty after these Oxfords, which we are told are some of the most difficult aircraft to handle especially in this warm weather.

Saturday morning

This finds me in the crew room once more awaiting my solo trip to Shaunavon and back which will be a total distance of 210 miles. By the way, I went on my first solo at night flying the other night. It was a peculiar sensation when I found myself in the air just off the ground with just a few lights here and there, the only things I could see – and all by myself with the knowledge that I had got to come down on terra firma, somehow, if I hoped to see the light of the next day! However it is not really so hard and I can manage it all quite well. When you actually land, you hit (or I do!) the 'deck' with more of a bump than you would in day time, but then you do not take much notice of that, as you feel quite a hero for getting down at all! Anyway there is no need to worry, since I will have finished my night flying hours by the time you receive this letter. We have only to do ten, and I have already done five and three quarters and it is quite good fun on the whole.

Well what of the war lately? Russia is still fighting and every extra day she fights, the better it will be for us. I cannot help thinking Hitler's intelligence officials have badly let him down on certain facts. Anyway it is about time he made a serious blunder, and if he manages to get out of this even fairly soon, it will not pay him to make many more.

I am sincerely hoping that with this course ended in about a month from now (somewhere about September 1st) that we will be able soon to set off home once more. However there is the possibility that we may have to do our O.T.U. training over here as well, in which case we will have to wait a little longer; but I am hoping for O.T.U. in England, and there should be a leave coming!

Have you a parcel of foodstuff yet? I think you should have it by the time you receive this letter, and I will get another one off tonight. The trouble with this of course is that it has to go by boat, which makes its eventual arrival a trifle more doubtful.

By the way, while I remember, I should not reply to any letter after this one, since there is the chance that I may not be here to receive it. Your letters take from thirteen to fifteen days by air. They are held up by the censor sometimes, a delay which you do not get by boat as they do not seem to get censored by sea, but they generally take three or four weeks by sea.

There does not seem to be very much in this letter, but for the sake of letting you hear regularly I will now finish and get it off tonight.

Here's wishing you all I can and hoping things are looking a little brighter and sending you my very best love and wishes

From Your Most Affectionate Son
Philip

Canada,
Tuesday, 5th August 1941

My Dear Mother and Father,

I will just endeavour to snatch these few moments to get in a few lines while I can. I notice that yesterday was August Bank Holiday, but I did not notice any difference here; did you have your day off at home? At the moment I have only just got up from bed although it is 11 o'clock! No this is not the normal routine in the R.A.F., but as a result of being up from 12.30p.m. until 5.15 a.m. during the night, during which time I finished off my flying time for night time.

This afternoon I will be flying again and I expect to have to make another cross–country, this time of 122 miles, but with the difference that this time I have to go with another pupil pilot, and either I have to navigate him there and back, or he will have to navigate me. Anyway I shall have to make the trip twice in both capacities. Last Saturday I made the trip to Shaunavon quite well. Of course the Wind Speed they gave me was quite a bit out, but I altered course about twenty miles out when I saw I was about three miles north of a small village I should have flown straight over, and eventually I came dead over Shaunavon and then turned back again and found base without undue difficulty. The weather seems to be a little cooler of late which is a very real blessing.

I hope you will not mind if I continue in pencil, but at the moment it is more convenient. Today is Friday 8th. August and tomorrow looks as though it will be a busy day for me as I start flying at 6.30 a.m. and am not due off until between 7– 8 in the evening. Of course I will not be flying during all that time but I shall probably do enough to make letter writing a difficult project, so want to get it in while I can. I imagine next week will be a very full one because the 'wings' exam comes on the last three days, although the present course will not end for another fortnight after that. What will happen after that I do not know but I will be more than ready for the long journey back home.

I often wonder, since all of us out here are so anxious to get home, yet our standard of living is so good, how the poor Tommies in the trenches for such long periods in the last war, must have longed to get home and rest from the perpetual strain and risk of war. Then of course there are those others in the Middle East at the present moment, who no doubt are very impatient for the war to end.

To tell you the truth I find there seems little I can find to say, however I shall just mention about two of these snaps I shall insert. I put that one of the train in because it is one of the famed C.P.[1] Railway Engines; I am afraid I really spoilt the picture by using the wrong focus lens, but will learn better next time. How do you like that one which I will call 'Sunset on the River'? As for the other snaps there is little to be said for them. I hope that I will be able to show you one or two more when I get home, but for the moment these will give you a slight idea of what I am looking like and what I see over here. I am sorry that this letter is a little short and not very interesting, but I am sure you will be pleased to know that I am still jogging along which is the main thing.

I hope that you too are still quite well and happy and that jerry is not causing you too much trouble, so until next week, here is sending you all my very best love and wishes,

From Your Most Loving Son
Philip

---

1. Canadian Pacific

Canada,
Saturday, 16th August 1941

My Dear Mother and Father,

I hope you will excuse pencil, and the hurry of the letter but for the moment my main preoccupation is to get it off and let you know that to date everything is quite well. I received your letter this morning, and was sorry to hear that up to the time of writing you were still awaiting news of me. I remember that I did leave a letter until three days after the week before it finally got posted, but I have tried to keep them on an average of once every week, and I hope that there have been no further delays. By the way, I have waited three weeks for the one I have received this morning so it looks as though we are both having to wait.

Yes, the 'Wings' exam is finished off now, but whether I will have to sit for any of them again, I do not know. I have two more cross–countries to do, both as Navigator and Pilot and a few more hours of solo, some practice in formation flying and then should be pretty well finished. This morning I also had the Chief Flying Instructors Test but in that I do not know exactly how I have done.

Last week I went on a trip to Calgary by air with two Wing Commanders which is a journey of about 190 miles. On the way there I went as passenger, but on the way back I was Pilot and came back the whole way under the hood (i.e. you have a hood over the cockpit and have to fly only by instruments, as you would at night). He instructed me to alter course on two occasions and there I was after an hour and twenty minutes back at base.

You ask about Edmonton. All I know about it is that it is the capital of this province of Alberta in which we are now. But I think it is some hundreds of miles away.

The Duke of Kent was here on Thursday last, but I was flying most of the time he was here. I saw his plane take off as he departed.

Well, for the present, here is sending you my very best love and wishes,

From Your Most Loving Son
Philip

PS Will try and write very soon but main point is to let you know I am still O.K.

Canada,
18th August 1941

My Dear Mother and Father,

Well I was surprised this morning to receive the second letter in three days, yet I see it was eleven days later when you posted it. I am glad that you had those three letters, and hope that you will not worry too much at any further delay you might have to experience. Thanks too for Auntie Kathleen's letter which you also posted and arrived here at the same time.

This morning I was up in the air at five past five, off on my fourth cross country as pilot. It was almost three hours later that we circled round the aerodrome to land. During that time I had flown through the worst storms I have encountered during my short experience, when visibility was absolutely nil. However they were of rather short duration and were more of a nuisance than anything else. I am now feeling quite at home in the air and, given a map and normal conditions, I think I could quite easily find my way to anywhere and be able to return again. The longest and final cross–country is still to come, but I rather look forward to it. I might add that besides keeping a log of the cross–country we have to take photographs of certain cross roads or rail bridges etc., and have to find the direction and speed of the wind by aid of the bomb–sight, and to get in touch with base by radio–telephony. Of course you do these things when you go as Navigator, but it also entails close cooperation of the pilot and all is very interesting.

We hear that a fortnight from today we will all be presented with our Wings and promoted to the rank of Sergeant (i.e. September 1st.) if all goes well. I have passed all the exams rather well for a change and have passed the Chief Flying Instructors Test I think.

Yes and after that it will be home I hope and a leave of some duration at least, before we start O.T.U. Yes I can imagine that you are praying hard for the war to end and I dare say that many people are. You know I have often told you that the war will not be continuing by next Christmas, and it is mainly on that that I base my hopes and I might add that I am still as hopeful though I cannot see any positive reason for it. On the other hand Russia's resistance, whatever it is just now, has proved very tenacious, and Hitler will not be able to afford many more victories at such a price. It is also heartening to see that apparently the war is having a good effect on religious life in Russia and it is not too much to hope that, terrible as it is, it will act as a purgative for the whole of Europe. I find it harder and harder to follow Marshall Petain's foreign policy; it seems to differ fundamentally from his home policy which is very good on the whole I should think.

Anyway I don't suppose that talking about it all will do very much good, and I have noticed that things in this war invariably take the most unorthodox methods of solving themselves. I am very glad that you are having the month off to be with the children and that Gerald will be home and I hope that it will be a very happy one.

I am afraid that it was the 18th. August not the 10th. when I received your letter, so of course the concert you were getting up has been over a week and a day now. Still I will pray in retrospect that it was a great success. The weather just now is very fine and though the sun shines most of the day and rain is very rare, it is not near so sweltering as it was when we first came.

I was very surprised to hear you talk of Victor[1] 'being back again at the Gas department' and more so to hear he could even be contemplating joining the Navy and the Fleet Air Arm at that! He is certainly very ambitious, because you have to be top notch to be successful in the Fleet Air Arm. I did not hear much more than what was a rumour about him before I left, so I can only have a hazy idea of what happened.

Yesterday I was talking to a chap who is on this course, and to whom I have spoken several times. In the conversation it came out that he was from Birmingham. On asking further I discovered he hailed from Albert Road!

Last week I had a long letter and about two C.T.S.[2] pamphlets from Fr. Murphy of St. Francis, that he had posted to Yeadon two days after I had left. It was all very interesting and not lacking in humour. He told us that 'there were three weddings scheduled for the same time at St. Francis on Whit Saturday, but somehow things became a little mixed up – and at one period we had the bridegroom of one party, and the bride of another, both without their respective life partners but neither of them keen to adopt the obvious suggestion'.

I have just heard on the news on the B.B.C. overseas service that Mr. Churchill will broadcast once again on Sunday. I wonder whether I will be free to hear him then? I hope so for it should be interesting to hear what he has to say of the war at the present stage and after his talk with President Roosevelt.

The other day another chap and I got into conversation with a man and his wife from St. Louis in U.S.A. who were passing through Medicine Hat on a holiday. They seem to think no end of the R.A.F. and told us to go down to their place any time we could and said what a big fuss everyone would make of us. They seemed very disappointed when we explained that it was out of the question, that it is just as much as we can do to get free one day in a fortnight to have a look round Medicine Hat.

That seems to me to be the trouble with Americans, they are furiously pro–British for the most part and think us proper heroes, yet they still seem to think we should not allow the war to prevent us having a good time; and I rather think that it is this rather selfish attitude that has prevented them from coming into the war before now. If they are not careful they might meet the same fate as France, for you cannot have your cake and eat it. There is one redeeming feature however, that their leaders do not seem to be of the same opinion and it would seem to me that they are continuously waiting for public opinion to swing round before they take big decisions.

Well I will now conclude and try and let you have this with no more delay, so sending you and the whole family my very best love and wishes. I remain,

Your Most Affectionate Son,
Philip

---

1. Victor Hermolle, cousin
2. Catholic Truth Society

Canada,
23rd August 1941

My Dear Mother and Father,

Well here is another weekend arrived, and I see that you are due for another letter so I had better try and make as good an attempt as possible. I have not heard from you since I last wrote but that was only five days ago so am not really expecting one for the moment. The last few days there has been a fresh burst of really fine and hot weather, but it will not now be long (I hope) before I am enjoying the good old English fogs and rains and able to see you once more and hear some of those records. It will be quite a change to walk about in the black–out, without the bright and colourful neon lights that bedeck the shops and cinemas in Medicine Hat and other Canadian cities; also quite a change to see shops without full shelves, and cafes that can only give you very limited variety of meals. Nevertheless I will not regret leaving all this behind me one bit.

I suppose that at the moment the children will be preparing to return to school and your usual routine will be recommencing. By the way I should not worry too much about Gerald not doing too well at school because at his age it would be really unnatural if he took things too seriously, and I have noticed that those of his age who do, are very often not particularly desirable characters and either think far too much of themselves or are of very one–track types of mind.

I dare say that you are now wondering what Mr. Churchill will say tomorrow evening (or midday for us over here). I am pretty certain I shall hear him as well, since it will be broadcast on the Canadian Broadcasting Corporation as well. I hope that he can tell (or intimate) something pretty good, and that President Roosevelt can as well on Monday. I am sure that you are all longing for the war to end, and I can well imagine that you do not relish thoughts of next winter, but I am hoping that it will not be so bad as we imagine.

I am often wondering what England will look like when I return again. The thing that causes most concern to most of the chaps over here is that it is reported there is a shortage of beer at home, and already out here they are almost dying for want of it as there is none in Canada.

I do not suppose that you have heard anything more about Bernard have you? I have no idea where he is at all. And what of Leslie lately? He's been fortunate enough to have another leave so I see, but is it because he has completed his gunnery course or is he a sergeant yet?

By the way I have been doing a few hours of formation flying lately, and yesterday three of us had to go up for an hour and a half so we decided on a little cross–country. One chap was leader from here to a town called Maple Creek (45 miles away) then the other chap took lead from there to a place called Cypress

Lake, (about another 30 miles) and then I took lead on the third leg back home. It proves very good fun though it is a bit of a strain at first. And it is about the most difficult exercise in flying that I have as yet come across – and sometimes the most frightening! However when solo we all take good care not to have the formation too tight as some of the instructors do, and at such times I always think discretion the better part of valour.

Next Saturday we are going to have a Squad dinner which should be pretty satisfying if they maintain the usual standard of Canadian meals, which are certainly not lacking in quantity and are pretty good in quality.

Well I fear that for the present I seem to have exhausted all I can find to say, so will let you have this so as not to keep you waiting too long. Here then is wishing you all my love and best wishes,

From Your Most Affectionate Son
Philip

I would just like to take this opportunity to wish Mary many happy returns of the day on the 7th September if this letter arrives about that time.

The next letter from Canada is dated 7th. September. Either a letter is missing or the men were given a sightseeing leave before they left Canada – a theory substantiated by the fact that there are no flights logged after August 24th. and the next address is not Medicine Hat as in the previous letters but is Halifax Nova Scotia.

Halifax

Nova Scotia

7th Sept. 1941

My Dear Mother and Father,

Today is Mary's birthday and I hope that she is having a very good time. I remember that it was this time last year that I had my first trip home in uniform and that night London, it was announced, had its first big night raid which I think scared us all a little.

This last week has certainly not been monotonous and during last Thursday I spent the whole day in Montreal and it is a wonderful city, and I am hoping that my snaps will come out O.K. and then I will be able to show you a little of it. There are also some very good views around Lake Superior, but how those snaps will come out I do not know because there were about three or four of us trying to take them through an open train window at a speed of between 60 and 70 miles per hour. But I think that Eastern Canada is much better than where we were, though people say the Western Coast, Vancouver etc. are very good.

Well this letter is mainly to allay any fears you may have for my well–being, so don't worry. Today it is a day of National Prayer as it is in England, and in the Cathedral (St. Mary's) there will be exposition all day, with special services throughout the week September 10th. to 17th. (It was September 10th. when Canada declared war on Germany). I hear from B.B.C. news from England that Cardinal Hinsley has once more broadcast, and has uttered one or two warnings. This same news comes to us now at 1p.m., whereas it used to be 9a.m. at Medicine Hat.

Well I will now conclude hoping that if this letter does not entirely satisfy your curiosity that it will at least leave you reassured. Once more then I send you all my very best love and wishes.

From Your Most Affectionate Son,

Philip

CHAPTER EIGHT

BACK HOME: BOURNEMOUTH

'You see that here I am back in "the old country again"
and how pleased I am too' (*30 September 1941*)

My Dear Mother and Father,

You see that here I am back in 'the old country again' and how pleased I am too. It looks grander than ever, especially after a fortnight on the high seas and pretty poor conditions and fairly rough weather at times. There are of course lots of things I want to tell you about, but I am hoping that soon I will be home and able to get it all out then and of course I am just itching to see you all and hope you will be well and happy. I should turn up within about a week, I think, as this is only a depot (and a very nice one too!) but if I do not turn up that soon, never mind because I think leave is pretty certain, and it may be only a matter of a day or two or three. Perhaps just in case will you leave the key in the usual place if I happen to arrive at an awkward time of day or night.

I must tell you however that by some stroke of luck Denis Crisp[1] was on the same boat coming across, except that he started coming home from the Mediterranean on the same boat last July! What a coincidence wasn't it? And he has certainly seen action out there too.

Well until I see you, all my love and best wishes to you all,

From Your Most Affectionate Son
Philip

---

1. Member of family in the same parish of St. Augustine's, Handsworth

CHAPTER NINE

JURBY, ISLE OF MAN

'I have been enjoying myself lately, especially when I have been on bombing details' 30th March 1942

The short gap between letters suggests that Philip had home leave (see letter to sister Kathleen in appendix, when he writes to her from family home for her birthday, Oct 9th)

Sergeants' Mess
Jurby, I.O.M.
30th October 1941

My Dear Mother and Father,

This will be nothing more than a short note to let you know that I am quite all right and have been here a day and a bit, but still find this camp highly mystifying. I am fortunate enough to have with me a chap who was next to me in the hut at Medicine Hat. There were only four pilots sent here and we are all to start flying Blenheims, but we have not been up yet and things seem very happy go lucky at the moment. From what I can see we were the only ones who had anything like three weeks leave, so for once I seem to have been lucky.

Well I shall now have to go into one of these Blenheims and get used to a totally new set of controls and remember one or two additional things like the variable pitch air screw.

We are getting treated well for a change and the food is good. By the way could you send me my post office bank book? I think it is on top of the cupboard in the kitchen but if you cannot find it do not bother.

Well for the present I will conclude and send you all my very best love

From Your Most Loving Son
Philip

P.S. Will write again soon.

Dear Mother and Father,

Sunday unfortunately here is a normal working day while Saturday is the day off. However as I still wait in the crew room here I think I may as well try and get this letter written and give you such news as there is.

As I have said before this seems to be a very happy go lucky camp and I have up to the moment not left Mother Earth, though I expect that before the week is out I will have done. There is a small examination on various points about the Blenheim coming off some day, but I hardly feel that I am being overworked. I can see that the Blenheim will take a little getting used to as the controls of vital actions are all in different places from those in the Oxford and there are one or more things to do. I cannot yet quite make out whether it is more difficult to land a Blenheim than an Oxford but I rather think I will find it a little harder as they all seem to be making three–pointers whereas we made wheel landings on the Oxfords. The Blenheims land at not less than 90 mph. but that should not be noticeably different from the Oxfords.

The ultimate object of all this appears to be to fly these Under Training Observers on their navigational flights or if I am more unlucky merely taking these and Wireless Operators round for gunnery practice and practice bomb–dropping. I do not know how long we will be left here though, but I suppose you will not mind how long. I would rather prefer to be in the navigational flight of the two, since I was always more fond of the cross–countries when in Canada and I hear that in some cases we take trips quite well into the Midlands and sometimes well up into Scotland so there should be plenty of variety. There are four Polish, two U.S.A., six Canadian, one N. Zealand and one Australian pilot in this crew room so we are not too badly represented are we? (There are only six English chaps).

I am afraid that I do not know what it will be like for leaves here, and from what I can see there are no weekend passes going, but anyway I shall find out more about that later on.

The food in the Sergeants Mess is the best I have ever had in the R.A.F. and there seems to be plenty going in Ramsey itself. We are seven miles from Ramsey up at the camp, but I am billeted in a bungalow just outside Ramsey for sleeping and we have a lorry to take us to and from it. It calls for us at 7a.m. and if we are not ready in time then 'We've had it' as they say in the R.A.F.

Well it is certainly a nice feeling being so near to home after being out in Canada where you realised that there was a whole ocean and thousands of miles of land separating you. The countryside here is wonderful too and the autumn seems hardly to have made a difference at all. Yesterday I paid a brief visit to Glen Auldyn (of ancient and happy memories) and it looks as magnificent as ever.

Well for the moment I will once more conclude by sending you all my love and very best wishes,

From Your Most Affectionate Son
Philip

Sergeants' Mess
Jurby, I.O.M.
Friday, 7th November 1941

My Dear Mother and Father,

Up to the time of writing I still have not heard from you, but the post does not get here till evening and if it is anything like the daily papers, it is very irregular as well. I don't know what you will think when I tell you that even now I have not so much as taxied an aircraft and see no signs of doing so before this week is out.[1] In fact I am beginning to wonder whether I will ever get up at all. However while they are paying me thirteen shillings per day I do not suppose they will be content to leave me long in this blissful state. By the way I have to pay seventeen shillings per week in income tax and if I were a civilian with the same weekly wage or money, in spite of having to keep myself as well, I would have to pay 21/6d. per week. Perhaps that will help you decide whether it would be better if I made an allotment or not. If you just tell me what you think I will see to the same, but I do not want to cause you to have to pay a higher rate of tax than I already have to pay and as you know I am quite ready to, and would like to, make an allowance in a private way if it would help.

Last Sunday I was U.T. Duty Pilot, more or less helping the official Duty Pilot of the day and gaining experience for my turn which will come shortly. I happened to be on my own for about three hours towards the end of the day. It was a dreadful experience dashing from one telephone to another (or so it seemed to me) and forgetting all about the weather reports which I should send out every hour. Telephone calls came through from Pershore and Squires Gate (nr. Blackpool) aerodromes and one from Air Ministry, so I was getting in some long distance experience as well.

In all, Duty Pilot is quite a hectic business, for you are more or less responsible for preserving correct discipline as regards flying around the aerodrome; it is the

Duty Pilot with whom responsibility rests for laying out the runway, flare paths etc. and to decide as to when to make such changes as circumstances may dictate; and he is responsible for initiating all calls for the M.O., fire tenders etc. if and when crash occurs, while in addition he has to book in all visiting aircraft and their crews when they come and when they go. He has to send the signal (or have it sent) through to the aircraft's home station to state its safe arrival, or to expect it at such a time. Then, most important, he has to phone up operations to warn Fighter Command of the intended route, height, speed, and E.T.A[2] and the point where it should cross the coast, of each aircraft leaving this drome for a long trip, and to ask their permission. So you see when you get a number of aircraft in there is plenty to do.

I do hope I have not given away any special secrets, but I do not see that I really have, for it must be quite well known to him[3] and he could not do much about it even if he did not know.

You know I don't know how you feel about it, but I could just about do with another leave! After all I have almost been here a fortnight now and reckon that another three weeks would just put me right to come back for a week or two! Still the awkward part of the scheme is that I have grave doubts as to whether I could persuade the authorities to adopt that view for they are awfully old fashioned and narrow minded on these subjects.

By the way, we have now been issued with R.A.F. battle dress and consequently I have had more sewing to do and I think that I am becoming quite expert at this sort of thing.

Well the weather is not all it might be here, but I suppose that is one of the least of our present trials, and for the present I think I will conclude sending you all my very best love and wishes,

From Your Most Affectionate Son
Philip

---

1. The next entry in the Pilot's Log Book is dated December 8th and is an isolated flight until these begin again regularly from January 6th
2. Estimated Time of Arrival
3. Colloquial term for the Germans

My Dear Mother and Father,

This is just a hurried note in case you don't get my other letter. I wrote quite a long one, stamped and addressed it, and then lost it somewhere! 'Just what you would do', I suppose you'll think! I'm hoping that someone will just pick it up and send it on to you. I said in it that I still hadn't heard from you; however that too was a mistake and my own fault for not reading D.R.O.s[1] every day as I ought and where it states the persons for whom the adjutant has registered mail; but even then I never look down that column! By some chance I did today and discovered that it has been waiting there three or four days.

Thanks very much! I still haven't taken to the air and am still quite O.K. but am badly in need of another long leave as I feel that it would ease matters considerably and raise my morale to new and even undreamt of heights! I imagine that one day perhaps I will get another leave, but at the moment as the wind howls and the rain pours without and it is none too warm within, my spirit rather echoes Cardinal Newman's sentiments in Lead Kindly Light: 'The night is dark and I am far from home'.

Well, I'll have to turn to the more practical side of getting this letter finished and despatched or else you will be wondering whatever is the matter with me particularly when you read the above, so without more ado I will now conclude sending you all my very best love and wishes

From You Most Affectionate Son
Philip

P.S. Will probably write again during the week in case the other letter doesn't reach you.

---

1. Daily Routine Orders

My Dear Mother and Father,

Thanks for your letter which I received this morning though I think it arrived here last night only that I wasn't there – we are billeted just outside Ramsey, and sometimes are gone before the post comes in.

You know you shouldn't do so much sympathising for me or one of these days I shall really begin to think how hard my lot is! After all I think we chaps in the services are having the best time, for at least we cannot complain of boredom, or that we are not getting about, while we seem to do much better than civilians for food, and are out of blitzes etc. And after all if we have to do the fighting I think it is a question as to which is the worst, i.e. having to fight yourself or remaining at home in the same old routine while you know someone else whom you love is in danger of being killed or wounded. Personally I feel far more sorry for mothers and wives than the actual men in the forces, for they must feel so powerless to help and must scarce know what to think but must bear all with patience. I pray very hard that I may be safe but it is mainly for your sakes.

Anyway, thank you very much for the gloves which I can assure you are very warm indeed. I hope however that you have not had to forfeit a coupon on my behalf. Did you knit them? I hardly like to assume you did since I made that mistake about the parcel last Christmas!

I had a very busy 24 hours from last Wednesday morning till Thursday a.m. when I was Duty Pilot all on my own. I explained all those duties in a letter which is apparently lost for good. The Duty Pilot is for his period of duty responsible for seeing to the correct flying discipline, on and round the drome, that everything is in readiness in case of an accident etc. He has to lay out the landing T and flare path and get weather forecasts. In fact he is the one in authority to route aircraft if they are going some distance, tell them what weather they will meet, any special signals or orders of the day and to get permission for the flight from Operations (Fighter Command). The latter have to be informed of all details such as course, height, speed, time of arrival etc. etc. On top of all that you have to send out a signal to the station of destination to warn them.

You will see from this that it is quite a hectic job at times and I have used the telephone more in those two days than ever before in my life. Once I was directly in touch with the Air Ministry concerning a special signal for that night.

No, I have still not spread my wings – for one thing there has been practically no flying this week as the hills round here have been totally obscured most of the time. However I have been putting in some good practice on the link trainer and trying to get hold of the ZZ landing and approach, as I hear that they are going to start using it here, which may be a very good thing if the weather closes in sometimes while we are up in the air. I have become far more appreciative of the link trainer since I have been here; for one thing I don't think of it in terms of some necessary evil which I have got to do, and I can also take it with some leisure. I have also heard now that for a civilian flying in peace time, one hour's instruction on the link trainer would cost six pounds six shillings! So now I like to hop in when the occasion presents itself and when I feel like it, and then I just think of the six pounds six shillings that are being expended on me just at my whim and pleasure! Mind you of course the time is far from wasted and is all excellent practice.

I am glad that your concert at St. Francis[1] went down so well. Are you going to get up a carol concert for Fr. Boland?[2] So Fr. Boland blames me for going to St. Francis every morning does he! I rather think he is treading very dangerous ground when he makes a point like that, which surely is in fact the very contrary! But I don't suppose he meant it as a genuine grouse, and certainly if he knew how hard the bed pulled in the mornings he wouldn't have me get up two hours earlier to go to St. Augustine's!

You express the hope that I will be home for Christmas, but I fear that there is pretty well no chance of that. You see that in the first place I am one of the newest pilots here, and I can claim only after the last of the others, and out of all the others there will be two lucky ones! I seem to have come to a relatively bad station for leaves for they only allow two off at a time, When a leave eventually does come round there will be the consolation that it will be a fourteen days one, I think. As you see, as well, it is not very practical here for weekend passes, and I think the best thing for me to do will be to lose myself somewhere about dusk and make a forced landing – quite by chance of course – at Castle Bromwich or Elmdon; perhaps the authorities there might see fit to prohibit my returning for a day or two owing to inclement weather!

Well I will now bid you adieu, sending you my very best love and wishes

From Your Most Affectionate Son,
Philip

P.S. If you could see me now I wonder what you would think of my new uniform? R.A.F. battledress has been issued and is what we knock about in while on the station.

---

1. St. Francis RC Church, Handsworth
2. Parish Priest of St. Augustine's RC Church, Handsworth

Sergeants' Mess
Jurby, I.O.M.
21st November 1941

My Dear Mother and Father,

The weeks seem to come round very quickly don't they, and here I see it is time to get off another letter already. Thanks for your last letter received last Monday or Tuesday. Fancy your receiving that lost letter at the end of the week! No I had not found any trace of it at all so I suppose someone else has had the good sense to drop it in the letter box for me.

No, the camp is not an O.T.U. nor in place of one. I thought I had made this clear, but of course I have not tried to raise your hopes too much because one never knows how long I will be left at a place like this. Before going on to Operations however, I should still have to go to an O.T.U. and should be all the better for it by the experience I gain here. This is now a school for training observers and from what I can make out I will have to fly these observers on cross country runs for them to practise their navigation, so that if they lose their way it's up to the poor old pilot to extricate them out of the mess and somehow or other return here. It now looks too that I will be mainly flying Ansons and not Blenheims, as they are lately bringing large numbers of the former here.

I am not certain yet whether we will have to do night cross–country flights but I think we will. We have had a few lectures recently on the automatic bombsight and I now have a pretty good idea how to use it; also on these hedge–hopping flying tactics, and of course we have been given full instructions for use of sighting enemy aircraft, and what to do in the event of sighting enemy submarines etc. but up to the moment I still have not done any flying mainly owing to the terrible weather over here. From all that I am learning recently I am becoming rather thankful that I will be able to get much more flying experience before I do go on to operations if I ever do, because the more one learns about all these things the more one realises what high pitch of skill and alertness is demanded of a modern pilot and I should imagine that quite a large percentage of our losses in the air occur with the pilots of lesser experience.

I can quite see how on the whole we have such an effective air force, for there is an Australian Fighter Squadron stationed at Andreas taking a rest from Operational duties and it is wonderful to see them practising dog–fights and flying in perfect formations of all types, the way they can break off and fall in again then deliver their attacks in line astern diving at their targets at terrific speeds. I think that many of our chaps have several times been 'shot down' by them! I have discovered that some of the chaps on my last course are at an O.T.U just south of Stratford and are on Wellingtons and they only had eleven days leave.

By the way talking about leave, I will have a try at Christmas, if by that time I still have not been posted to navigation flight; but I cannot say that I am at all optimistic about it, except that there is nothing to lose in my asking and everything to gain.

Did you hear Beethoven's *Fifth Symphony* last week? It was broadcast in the evening by the London Philharmonic Orchestra, but I couldn't hear it as there is no radio in our billets.

I was talking to the Catholic Padre of this station last Tuesday and on learning that I came from Birmingham, he remarked that the M.O. here was also a Catholic and from Birmingham. I asked his name, just as a matter of course, and found it was O'Dowd and he is about 25 years of age. I suppose that he must be a brother of the O'Dowd I knew at Cotton and a son of Dr. O'Dowd. Anyway he is going to tell me more a little later. Perhaps Gerald could ask D. O'Dowd at St. Philip's if he is still there?

I have just received your letter tonight, Friday and thanks very much for it. No, of course I will not mind what paper you write on. I am very sorry to hear that the children are not as well as they might be, but I hope that all will soon be well. One thing, as you remarked in a former letter, times are not as bad as they were this time last year from the point of view of raids or anything, while we are one whole year nearer to victory than we were – and a year I would not like to go through again.

I see we have also commenced a new offensive into Libya and we can only hope and pray that success will attend their efforts and that casualties will be extremely light. Let's hope too that we can clear every German out of the place so that he cannot come back and cause any more trouble. It was a great pity to hear of the Ark Royal meeting her doom at last wasn't it? But there is much cause for consolation and gratitude in the knowledge that her huge crew are safe and sound.

No, I did not hear that orchestral concert and in fact hear very little of the radio and even then it is nearly all on the Forces programmes. I have heard on two or three occasions some of those songs of Gigli and Maria Caglia.

Yes I dare say it would cause you all a little amusement at my being called HERMOLE! but that is almost what I am called. I now purposely give the pronunciation in the old way as when we were at Kings Heath, because it saves no end of trouble: but then some people <u>WILL</u> give the "O" the long sound as in hole!

Yes I remember Hartley quite well[1] and I hitch–hiked home from Wilmslow with him most of the way as he lives in Coventry – he also had his Elementary training there, lucky chap! You should find his photograph at home on that picture of the course with his name underneath.

Well I will now conclude sending you all my love and very best wishes,

From Your Most Affectionate Son
Philip

---

1. F. Hartley who left Cotton College in 1937 and who was in the RAF during the war

My Dear Mother and Father,

Today, Thursday, I am Duty Pilot once more, and I am trying to catch a quiet minute to make a start on this week's letter. Of course the phone may and will cause me many interruptions, not to mention other sundry things such as visiting aircraft, and different chaps coming along with all manner of enquiries, however I will do my best. You will note that I can give you six of the films, the other two were not printed which is a pity. Though Leslie happened to take those two, I take full blame for their defect since I have looked in the little booklet and I find that I used the wrong stop which has distorted the focus somewhat. The same has happened with the two I took. However I shall know in future and perhaps this summer will give us chance to take many more.

Well this war still seems to be raging and many people seem to have extremely diverse opinions especially regarding the Japs. I had a long letter from Thornton[1] only yesterday and from the way he went through the long list of places we and the Americans . . ., I had reached this point yesterday when something interrupted my writing and after that I never had time to put pen to paper again. But to continue, I imagine I was going to say that though you can pull out a long stream of places we have lost or where we are retreating, it seems to me that even in the war with the Japs there are three vital places that the Japs have to take, and we to hold, according to who will eventually be victorious. These points seem to me to be Rangoon, Burma Road and Singapore. And the most significant part about all three places is that they seem to be the only places where we have good air defence and command of the air. Singapore seems to be better fortified than any Japanese counterpart judging from results of air fights, and I notice, it is the only place in the Far East from where night fighters are operating. I have noticed too that Japanese anti–aircraft defences would appear extraordinarily weak considering what small forces they have to repel, and even their warships seem very vulnerable from the air. How then will they show against larger air forces? In any case Germany seems to me to me the core of trouble, which when we have dealt with it, will leave to die all its other offshoots (I hope!)

I see now I have wasted much time and paper in talking quite a lot of trash which I cannot even understand, but at the same time I think it is always a good idea to count your blessings rather than your misfortunes, to dwell on your assets rather than waste tears over spilt milk which does not make things any better and can make one very dissatisfied. However with me my main source of optimism has always been that such a criminal cause as that for which our enemies fight can never win the day no matter how gloomy the situation looks. That belief or its strength suffered what you might call a slight tremor in those hectic days of Dunkirk, but even then was never really shaken. That we actually survive still cannot but make me feel this way all the more, for it seems nothing less than miraculous by worldly standards.

There! Now I see I have turned philosopher from military commentator, yet I do not see whence I derive my authority in either capacity, do you?

Well to get now to some facts. Thornton once again mentioned how he enjoyed that evening so it rather looks to me that he spent quite a happy evening in our midst!

Last night the night was made a little more exciting for me by the message over the phone from operations that a spitfire was coming to our drome, that we would have to make preparations hurriedly to bring him in, since he would be over within four minutes. Then from that point messages flash this way and that, and the personnel in charge of the flare path skurry hither and thither getting everything ready. Sure enough, just within about four minutes, the high pitched note of a spitfire roars in the darkness above, accompanied by the high whistling note caused by the wireless aerial being sped through the air at such a high speed. The challenge signal is then flashed up from the Duty Signaller by red aldis lamp – this must be done, though how this could be an enemy I don't know! The spitfire then signals back the appropriate letter and after a few more odds and ends a small red light can be discerned gently floating down to the runway, and so our spitfire pilot once again reaches the security of 'terra firma', and the hospitality of an aerodrome from the wilderness of the black night! It was an Aussie Pilot Officer, but he wouldn't delay long in the watch office as he said he felt like a drink or two in the mess.

However that was not the only bit of 'panic' (as we call this kind of thing and that is just about the word for it!) because later on in the night one of our own Ansons just back from a cross–country radioed that he could only get one of his wheels down and then the one he had got down would not go back. For this the station Duty Officer came down and later the O.C. flying when there was real 'panic'! Messages were made to be radioed up – new ones received, previous ones cancelled and so on. Meanwhile the Anson was circling and roaring round and round the aerodrome for almost an hour. Finally he couldn't wait any longer and radioed that he was going to land in spite of it as his fuel was running low (he had been up four hours). Then as we saw the navigation light take its downward path to earth, the fire tender and ambulance raced across the aerodrome to a point where they judged it would land.

All's well that ends well however, and though the aircraft did a complete revolution when it touched down, the pilot did very well and kept it balanced on one wheel until the speed had slackened somewhat and was little the worse for his experience.

Perhaps you can now see why I did not get much time to finish this letter when I was Duty Pilot.

Well for the present I will conclude wishing you every happiness for the coming week and conveying to you my very best love

From Your Most Affectionate Son
Philip

---

1. A Cotton friend

Sergeants' Mess
Jurby, I.O.M.
Early December 1941

My Dear Father,

As your birthday comes round next Monday (8th December) I want to get this letter written in good time so that I may at least wish you very many happy returns of your birthday, with the hope that it will go by as happily and pleasantly as our present circumstances allow. I do not know really what I could buy as a present that you would really like just now, so for the moment at least I can do no better than send you my very best wishes. Of course there are little odd luxuries that one can get better over here, but just lately the I.O.M. customs are looking into all parcels going outside the island.

There is slight talk here of pilots being able to volunteer for flying with the Chinese Air Force, and one or two have already entered their names, but this famed Burma road seems rather a long way away to me and in any case probably nothing will materialise from it.

Well for the moment I can find little else to say and so will now conclude again wishing you a very happy birthday (and free from fire–watching!) and sending you my best love, I remain

Your Most Affectionate Son
Philip

P.S. I have just received this letter which you sent after I had left the boat.
(*The envelope contains a re– directed envelope*)

My Dear Mother and Father,

What wretched weather we are having nowadays aren't we? As the sea roars just beneath, and the wind whistles just outside, my thoughts inevitably fly back to mid–Atlantic on the Empress of Asia and remind me of those pitch black nights when with much stumbling, and after many uncertain steps, I successfully combatted the rocking of the boat and finally found the particular stairway or door that I wanted, and was able once more to take a fair amount of shelter from the beating rain and biting winds. However in my present circumstances I cannot complain that the floor or ground is unsteady, which is a great blessing, for nothing gets on one's nerves more than continually being thrown off one's balance especially when in the act of walking!

It was funny that the other day I met a chap who was in my billets at Blackpool; he is here just finishing off his gunnery course. I couldn't help being tickled when he said what a pity it was that I had not been here a little sooner for then I would have been able to take him up for his practice, for it struck me that were I in his place I would thank my lucky stars for my escape! However that is a curious thing, that we pilots are far more scared of allowing ourselves with any other pilot, than ordinary air crew chaps are in risking everything with us, which shows how much truth there is in the old saying 'When ignorance is bliss, 'tis folly to be wise'.

I wonder how the children are now? I hope that they are all enjoying very good health and are quite happy, and that they are not causing you undue worry, trouble or expense. I trust too that you will not allow the carol concert effort to get you down unduly either! It amuses me in a way, the number of times you promise yourself you will not do such and such a thing, and then almost before you can say the traditional 'Jack Robinson', lo and behold.. you are at it again!

I have just now finished reading your letter which has just arrived, (Wednesday) and I can see that, not satisfied with a carol concert, the aim now is a Nativity Play! Well, Well! I cannot help smiling, and I hope you will excuse me. Anyway I see that the children seem to be better which is a very good thing isn't it?

By the way, I noticed that in my old writing pad, I still have those notes I wrote up in diary form when on my way to Canada, and I shall let you have them to read if you will find them interesting enough. I have also had several prints off some of the negatives the chap here took while in Canada. As I was with him when they were all taken, it gives added interest to them, and in fact we both took our photographs with the idea of sharing the best prints when we got to some place – somehow it hasn't materialised until now, but those I have are very good and I think you will find them worth looking at. When I look back now on all that was crammed into those few weeks in Canada, I cannot help feeling little regrets that I didn't see more, and I don't think I shall ever forget it all. It is peculiar also how one always seems to appreciate these things when they are over. Looking back I can see that I had a wonderful time out there, and yet all the time I was there my thoughts were in England.

I notice too that two or three of our modern songs that have just made their appearance here, were all the rage in Canada all the time I was there; and now every time I hear them, I can picture myself outstretched on the bed, sheltering from the terrific heat and dazzling rays of the sun, or having a really first class meal in one of the cafes, while the brightly coloured penny–slot gramophones played those same tunes! But alas! now when I look outside I no longer see the brilliant sunshine or cool clear twilight, but only our leaden clouds being hurtled across the sky! However I am more than satisfied to be where I am and am not anxious to pay another visit under our present circumstances at all.

While I am talking about Canada, I cannot help thinking what a wonderful idea it was to have it as the main training ground for all our pilots and observers, especially when I look at this school here which is apparently one of the most successful in the British Isles. Lately at this school some of these U.T.[1] observers haven't been up for a fortnight or more, and many of those who have, have not had much practice because they have had to turn back on account of the terrible weather, while night flying has been practically negligible. Yet in Canada nearly every day, every aircraft is flying maximum hours, and even in the winter the clouds are fairly high and visibility very good with the result that they have only to fix skis on the aircraft and they operate almost as much as in the summer. The observers trained in Canada also get 40 hours night flying exclusively by means of astro–navigation, which is hopeless to attempt here as things are now.

Talking about astro–navigation, I see that I had almost forgotten to tell you that we pilots here are now going through a course in this subject whenever there is no flying, and I must say that it is proving extremely interesting.

Today, at my own request I have had a little flip in an Anson with a Squadron leader, mainly because three months on the ground has made me a little anxious as to how well my powers of judgment still work as they ought. In a general sort of way I don't think that I have lost much, but I noticed that when he came in to land at only 75 miles an hour, the speed seemed similar to what it appeared on my first few trips in Oxfords. More important however, it will take one or two trips now for me to judge my height accurately when landing, i.e.in those last but crucial 40 – 50 feet above the ground.

I think that I had better finish now or else you will not have it even by Tuesday, but before doing so I just wish to ask for Auntie Kathleen's new address, and also I have forgotten her new name. Now I fancy it is time for me to wish you goodbye and all those other good things which you need or desire, not last of which are my prayers and love,

Your Most Affectionate Son
Philip

Sergeants' Mess
Jurby I.O.M.
Wednesday, 10th December 1941

My Dear Mother and Father,

Today I am Duty Pilot once more and I write now from the Duty Pilot's Watch Office while there is some lull in the day's activities. As a matter of fact it is now about 7.30 and all normal flying has finished, but I shall have to remain on duty till 8.30 tomorrow morning, ready for any weather reports, and others that might come in, or for any aircraft in distress that might want to land here etc.

I fear that I have lost much of my good spirits today by the terrible news I have been told – namely about two of our battle ships being sunk by those wretched Japs. I can hardly believe it; to think that within two or three days they have done far more than Italy under more favourable conditions has done in eighteen months! Still it is to be hoped that our Navy can take it in good spirit and perhaps when the time comes give it back good and proper. I bet old Hitler has already sent a telegram congratulating his new ally! Isn't it galling? At any rate when you see how the Japs have acted and what the Germans are doing it makes you want to knock it out of them and risk anything to do it.

When on Monday morning I was at breakfast and the eight o'clock news came on with startling news of Japs attacking Malaya I shall never forget one of the Polish chaps opposite me when he said 'I think I go home to Poland in tree months but now. . .' he plainly showed what he meant the way he waved his hands in despair.

Thanks for your last letter that I received on Tuesday. It would seem that my letter arrived before I intended it to, but I sent it much earlier realising that you had not received my other letters until Tuesday. I'm glad that your birthday, or the day before, passed pleasantly. I hope that you get the wireless mended by Christmas, because undoubtedly there should be some good programmes at that time, with the King speaking on that Empire programme on Christmas day.

You ask me about how much free time I get here. Well we generally get all the evenings to ourselves, except for nights like this, but the trouble is to know what to do with it. Our rooms are not really too warm and it is rather hard to stay in and read or do anything like that, but if you go into Ramsey there is nothing to do there except go into a Y.M.C.A. about which there is nothing very attractive. You can go to the cinema, which I do more than I would do normally, but I do not really enjoy most of the pictures. As a matter of fact last night was an exception, when I saw one called '*Kipps*' and strange to say it was by H.G.Wells, 'a Story of a Simple Soul' and lacking in all the forced drama and artificial mannerisms of most pictures.

Apart from the evenings however we have been working seven day weeks because of the rotten weather we have been having. It seems terrible weather this year and even when it is fairly reasonable here, the priests say that it is terrible on the mainland. Yes I heard from the same sources too about all the snow you have been having, but we have none here except on the tops of Snaefell.

I have been doing a little flying in an Anson lately, but have not got really far from the island and, even when I have, it has been more up in the direction of Scotland. The sea sometimes looks magnificent from the air, especially when you can peep at it through little tanks of cloud. That is one thing about flying in England, there are some really beautiful sights way up in the Heavens!

Last Saturday being a day off, I went to Douglas for the first time since I have been here. It is a typical seaside resort and I would have had a very good time were it not for the fact that about 7.30p.m. a slight headache made its appearance. It would not have been bad were it not for the fact that it was one of those when it is imperative for me to go to bed rather hurriedly to prevent consequences. However I was in the pictures, and when I came out we had to go into one of the cafes for a supper of egg and chips – Yes, egg and chips![1] – but when on the bus coming back to Ramsey I knew the end was come and I warned the conductress that I wanted the door open, and to be in a good strategic position for any eventuality – and a good job too! And that is the sad end of those egg and chips. By the time I had walked the two miles from Ramsey to our billets I was more than ready to go to bed. The effects I am glad to say are no worse, and Sunday saw me as full of beans – not egg and chips I must confess – as ever.

Some U.S.A. ferry pilots of the R.A.F. delivered some Blenheims here this morning and I asked one or two if they were anxious to get home now, (they came into Duty Pilot's office) but they seemed quite content to continue with their present job, and do not think that America will really need their services. They are very nice chaps though, and they all seem to be more generous than the average Englishman.

Well Christmas is well on the way once more, and I think that we have much to be thankful for in that the worst part of the winter has passed so calmly as far as air raids are concerned. Let's hope that the latter half will prove just as good and then perhaps we can finish with all this wretched business.

Thursday

This afternoon I heard our excellent friend Hitler saying a few words. I don't suppose there was much new in them, or that they portended much good for us, and from what I could make out he did not (nor his audience) think too well of President Roosevelt. I heard from Garvey[2] at Oscott the other day; apparently Victor was up there recently and he has made known that he is to become engaged next Christmas. Did you know anything about it?

By the way, if you will be writing to Auntie Kathleen in the future, or whenever you do, perhaps you would send her one of those photos I sent last week, if you think it's worth it. If you don't, well there's a paper shortage and you know what to do! The photo that I enclose is from a November issue of '*Flight*' and is a picture of an Anson which I am flying for the time being.

It looks now as though I have come to the end of my letter, and that being so, there is little left for me to do, save convey to you one and all my very best love and wishes,

From Your Most Affectionate Son,
Philip

---

1. Eggs were hard to come by
2. Fr. John Garvey – a friend from schooldays at Cotton College – later became Fr. Garvey (see book jacket and letter in Appendix 3)

My Dear Mother and Father,

Thank you very much for your last letter that I received yesterday. You appear to be going through one of those awkward periods when everything adds to make things hard for you, but I hope that you will not let these things upset you too much and that by this time Monica is as bright and cheeky as ever! Yes I would like you to buy those records for Christmas if you consider that they would like them; it certainly seems a good idea to me.

Flying is going on at a better pace this week. I spoke of November being a peak month as far as NIGHT air raids were concerned and I thought I said December was a very good second; but that is because the nights are longest and generally speaking better weather conditions prevail in November with the clear and starry nights. This year has been below average, but in any case when aircraft haven't always efficient wireless and when the observers are striving to train, they want fairly good conditions when they can see where they are to check up on their course and etc.

Apart from all that, there is the additional danger at this aerodrome that hills of over 2000 feet are quite near and if you get cloud below 1000 feet you cannot see all the hills, and if a general mist comes up your position is very much worse. So obviously they have to be very careful of the weather at a place like this; then there are no runways in this aerodrome which is at least a disadvantage at such times. One of our chaps back from a cross–country the other day said that he saw a Birmingham Balloon barrage on his way down to Oxford, quite near on his left, so you see one of these days perhaps I will be passing quite near; however I don 't think that I will risk a tussle with the balloon cables.

Things are always much the same here and there does not seem very much to do at nights after we have finished up at the camp so I have taken to doing a little reading when I can bestir myself, otherwise I walk down to Ramsey with one of the chaps and we invariably argue about some question or other all night long, on such things as 'How shall we prevent further wars after this one?' 'Whether there should be a United States of Europe', and other social questions.

These debates nearly always turn on to religious questions, or rather ethical questions and I can generally manage to dominate thanks to a pretty good grounding at Cotton. Actually conversation of this nature is very common amongst air crew personnel, and if you listen in you can hear much talk of Christianity, but unfortunately, though many seem to recognise that it will be essential, they are very vague about most of it and are a little slow to translate words into action. At least though, it is something to have started thinking on those lines.

I am going to enclose a few photographs. I don't know how you will like them.

Lately we are having a proper 'spit and polish' parade every Tuesday, i.e. the whole station. We have the bag–pipe band playing and they look very smart in the R.A.F. blue version of the Scotch kilts etc. Then of course the C.O. (a Group Captain) gets up and they hoist the R.A.F. flag and then a parson reads prayers for us all. It makes me think what a wonderful sight will be furnished by all our victory marches when the time comes.

For the present then I think I will conclude as time is getting short and I cannot find much more to say.

Here's then wishing you my very best love and wishes

From Your Most Affectionate Son
Philip

Sergeants' Mess
Jurby, I.O.M.
16th December 1941

My Dear Mother and Father,

I received your letter today, and thanks very much. You see that I am getting it started early this week (Tuesday) just in case the Christmas mail will make any difference.

You spoke about my 'snaps and photos' and you go on to say 'I like them and am sending some of them away. . ..', which do you mean, the former or the latter and which do you want more of? Thinking about it I do not suppose that you will send any snaps away, so I will see what I can do about the photos. I am not certain because they are limited with their supplies owing to paper shortage. I will try and persuade them if that will be any good. Of course I don't mind you sending them away if you want to, since I bought them mainly for you; I have still another one here if you want it. About those films in my camera: I had intended to ask you weeks ago whether you had taken them, because I instructed Daddy to tell you to have them taken and get them printed, as I knew you wanted more of the children. I put everything in order on the camera (i.e. focus etc.) and said that they could be taken right away. There are four more films. Number 5, which is now showing in that red (or is it green?) little aperture, has not been taken, so you can fire straight off.

No, I have not met Sergeant or Flight Sergeant Carpenter yet, though I think I recollect the name. I will look out, but especially as you say he is instructing, I imagine he must be an Observer or Wireless Operator.

Yes, as you say, it was terrible news about 'the Repulse' and 'the Prince of Wales'. We are not too much affected by all Hitler's or anybody's victories on land, but once we lose powerful warships like that, there is real danger in the air. It is a good thing that there is such a good spirit in our Navy for I am sure that that will make up for a great deal, and I do not suspect that the Japs will get it all their own way by any means. Still the Navy has done a marvellous work during this war, and I think has been Hitler's main stumbling block, as well as our protection.

It simply beats me how the Japs have done all they did, for it must all have been done by the work of aircraft carriers, whose aircraft are never so effective as those of land based aeroplanes, and even Japan's land based aircraft wouldn't compare with ours or Germany's. Of course that is partly offset as our aircraft out there are not our best at all. Then again if they registered those direct hits on to moving and dodging targets from 17,000 feet as Mr. Churchill said (excluding the other low flying attackers) then the Japs in one raid have accomplished something which neither England, Germany or Italy have managed throughout the whole war. Yet with everything considered, the Bismarck appeared to take much more punishment than our Prince of Wales, and even then took many hours to sink.

However all will come right in the end. I read that Hitler did not care what Mr. Roosevelt said because he (Mr. R.) was insane. Do you remember Hitler saying the same about Mr. Chamberlain and Mr. Churchill? One cannot help thinking things about Herr Hitler himself, when he says that about all his foes, can one? Mr. Roosevelt's speech last night sounded exceptionally good from what I have heard about it, and it is a good thing we have a man like him on our side.

Did I tell you that this Christmas day we Senior N.C.O.s, as well as the officers have to take over most of the duties on that day so that the airmen can have the day to themselves and be served by the officers? If I did not tell you, well that is true; however I wouldn't grumble at that, and in many ways I am exceptionally well off here and the food is very good and exceedingly well cooked. There is no doubt that Waafs[1] are far better at cooking than their male counterparts. The trouble is that the chaps who really deserve better cooking are the very ones that are worst off, such as those in the desert or any of those overseas.

By the way, I forgot to tell you before, when on the subject of the Navy, that I saw H.M.S. Repulse in Halifax harbour when we arrived there last June. Then I remember looking at her huge grey guns and the massive armour plating around them, while fifty or so sailors were being drilled on the upper deck under the brilliant sunshine; all then was so quiet and peaceful and I never thought that the same ship would soon be rusting away many fathoms under the sea.

You also ask in your letter why I am here at an A.O.S[2] Well I don't really know except that they must have some more pilots than they can at present cope with for operations; they were a little short–handed on this station before. One thing,

I'm jolly glad that they did not keep me in Canada for this job. No, I don't think that you can say that the pilots here are more experienced or better than the others; the very fact of me being here disproves that! It is true that there are some very experienced and good pilots, but there are also a number of raw and inexperienced ones like myself straight from S.F.T.S. In fact in Canada they retained the below average pilots for work at A.O.N.S[3] and bombing and gunnery, but I think they generally flew single seater Henleys or Fairy Battles, used for towing around drogues, which the gunners use for targets in their practices in the air.

However in my case I don't think for one moment that it is a reflection one way or the other, and in navigation flight, to which I will be posted, there is quite a bit of responsibility and concentration demanded, not only for oneself but for a crew of two or three or four others, who in their early stages at least are liable to land you anywhere from mid–Atlantic to Norway or France, not to mention Eire, if one does not keep a check on them! Notwithstanding, on the whole I hear they are pretty good, and in many cases not a little helpful.

There seems to be much talk lately of heavy air raids again, but somehow I do not think you will have them, this winter at any rate; they are now currently needed in so many places that I should hardly think they could afford to launch large scale operations against us, especially since our night fighting defences have improved so much and their losses in Russia must have been very large.

I think I have dwelt too much on the war in this letter, a subject which I generally try to avoid, though it is rather hard to in times like these. Nevertheless it all comes out from me almost before I realise it and I am afraid all my letters are alike, in that the subject matter is very far from the point and jumbled together in a very rough and ready fashion. I only hope you do not mind too much, and so with this apology I will now conclude by wishing you a very happy and merry Christmas – this year you will at least have all the members of the family around you, so make the most of it!

Meantime I send you all my love.

From Your Most Affectionate Son,
Philip

P.S. It was an alert that made me make that last crossing out. I was so surprised – the first I have heard since last May! There is night flying on our drome as well!

---

1. Women's Auxiliary Air Force
2. Air Observation School
3. Air Observers Navigation School

My Dear Mother and Father,

Sad but true! Here I am back again at camp with some sixty miles of deep and restless salt water separating me from the mainland – as we refer to England from this little island. Yet I have only to think that it might have been an ocean or oceans, with some 6000 miles distance between us and I soon see how much worse things could be – then I would not even have a leave to come back from would I?

On the way back here I lost my leave pass just to make things a little more awkward. When the train arrived at Fleetwood an hour late, the boat had already gone and some 400 troops had to be billeted at various points of vantage. I just missed being put Sergeant–in–charge of a crowd of about eighty airmen who had to put up for the night at Squires Gate Aerodrome; for which I was more than thankful that evening, when I saw the other sergeant having to march a tired, hungry and angry mob of airmen (many with heavy kit–bags) from place to place at Squires Gate, where nobody seemed to know what to do with them or where they could accommodate them. On the other hand, I rather quickly got settled up with a meal and bed which is one of the advantages of being a sergeant. We caught quite a large troop ship early the next morning which generally runs between England and Ireland, and I could not help thinking it was something like a troop ship after the two I had been on. The sea crossing was a little rough and affected me enough to make me go and lie down when I fell asleep for the rest of the journey and only woke up to find that the boat was almost deserted and alongside the quay at Douglas.

Judging from what I heard of the Christmas here I am glad I was at home. Several of the chaps say that I was better out of it and that they wish they had been. Apparently beer played a predominant role in the festivities, and what with the officers coming up to the sergeants' mess and vice versa, drinks were being thrust down people's throats. Anyhow I suppose that people who like a normal amount of drink will in such circumstances try to make up for not being at home by really throwing restraint to the winds at a time like Christmas, but I am afraid it would not have helped my Christmas to have been a very pleasant one.

The weather appears just as bad over here and I see they are now trying to get in some flying in spite of it. There has been quite a big change here since I went home; the course for observers has been extended by many more weeks and the other day the C.O. Group Captain gave all the pilots a lecture about it, and the new organisation to meet it. In future, he says, we will be guaranteed one day off a week, Saturday the one, and Monday the other. This is so that there will be continuous flying throughout 24 hours and seven days of every week. The observers have now to do a large part of what would be their O.T.U. here which includes 25 hours night flying. However I am not really sorry to see that the standard of their training is going up, because I have long ago discovered that you can never learn too much about this flying business, while I am pleased to think that I should be able to gain useful night flying experience on Ansons.

Night flying is really very much more exciting than day flying, and so long as I remember a lesson I learned in Canada I should be quite O.K. That lesson was that you still have to be just as careful during day flying. I found that out when I had been doing one or two hours one day after I had been doing some night flying and I had almost made the mistake of thinking that day flying was too easy for words after night flying, with the result that I noticed my circuits were getting careless and my approaches and landings bad. However I fortunately pulled myself together at that point and I shall see that I don't fall into the same attitude again.

Please excuse poor writing as I am writing this on my knees. At this point I think I will conclude and bid you farewell, so here's wishing you my very best love and wishes from

Your Most Affectionate Son
Philip

P.S. Parcel and letters etc. received for which thanks.

Sergeants' Mess
Jurby, I.O.M.
Friday, 2nd January, 1942?

My Dear Mother and Father,

'Blow blow, thou winter wind, Thou art not so unkind as man's ingratitude' – says Bill Shakespeare, but I doubt whether he could have been at Jurby or experienced the icy east wind which now courses across the Irish Channel cutting through everything that comes in its way! Yes, it certainly is cold just now, but we have no snow here as I hear you have on the mainland, so you are probably worse off than we are; one certainly feels thankful at these times for our warm uniforms, and our great coats seem capable of withstanding anything.

Thank you very much for your letter which I received last Tuesday. You did not mention how Auntie Eileen was so I am hoping that she still continues to make great improvement.

Through going home on leave at Christmas I have missed my turn for the flying instruction prior to being posted to Navigation flight. The new chap has however taken me up, but this time in a Blenheim. I have been up three times now but my total time only amounts to 1 hour 40 minutes. But on the last occasion I was very pleased, because I made the whole circuit and landing on my own (not solo, he was just there in case!) and I think I have done remarkably well considering that I have done practically no flying since last August, and that even then I never had to make three pointer landings. Just after that effort my starboard engine cut and as I couldn't get it started without the help of the fitters; we had to pack up for the day, for it was then late afternoon. Since then the weather has intervened, and here I am tied to the ground.

I will of course have more dual instruction, for one engine flying, and one or two other things, but I hope soon to be off solo on it. It is a very nice aircraft and much better than the Oxford or Anson, but Hampden pilots tell me that as much as the Blenheim is superior to the Oxford, so much is the Hampden better than the Blenheim. I must admit that the first time we landed in a Blenheim we appeared to be going so fast as we touched down that I did not see how we would possibly stop before the end of the aerodrome, but you have to wham the brake on almost straight away and then you don't do so badly, and I'm getting more used to it now. Later on I may possibly be flying Hampdens, but you can never tell what you may be doing next in the R.A.F. You just simply await what the fates will next decree.

Fancy Mary and Leslie thinking of becoming engaged! At least when in future years Leslie comes moaning to me 'accursed be that day'! he will not be able to say that I did not give him full warning! I am afraid that he has eyes but sees not, and ears, but hears not! Anyway does that mean that everybody is expected to buy presents for them, or does that have to wait till later? To be a little confidential, I secretly hope it is the latter because I already owe Mary one Christmas present and it would look bad if I was two in arrears.

My particular pal at this station the other day flew between the Coventry and Birmingham balloon barrages and he was telling me what a fine peaceful sight it was with the tranquility only disturbed by the factory smoke rising vertically from the chimney tops, with the brilliant sunshine, clear visibility and shining silver blimps high in the sky. I am hoping that one day I'll witness all this for myself – only I shall make a point of pin–pointing Castle Bromwich and Elmdon aerodromes in relation to my position and Birmingham just in case! After all if I ever do get lost or have any particular trouble, there is no sense in coming down far from home is there?

I had a letter from Bernard – he is apparently (or was until December 17th) at Trentham which is a sort of Wilmslow or pooling camp. He does not know what he is going to do but up till then he was not doing anything special. At the time he had managed to get 14 days leave which he is spending in Toronto, Ontario with some people he had met on his course. They are Catholics I believe and are being very generous and hospitable to him. He mentions, as being almost beside the point, the fact that he is getting on very well with one of their daughters! Otherwise as usual he seems very fed up and apparently does not think much of Canada; he even says that had he been able to peer into the future he would never have packed in his Observers Course. It's a pity that Bernard does not seem to have learned yet that you cannot have your cake and eat it. However I must admit that it is rather tough having to remain so far from one's own country and it is very easy to make mistakes when you are too keen on trying to arrange for the best, particularly in such an organisation as the R.A.F.

By the way, will you get those records with the coupons or vouchers, whatever you call them, as I did not have time; they were closed after Christmas. I see there are some new records just out of the Boston Promenade Orchestra playing Ballet Music from Faust which should be very good indeed (H.M.V.) That is the Orchestra I have playing 'the Sleeping Beauty Waltz' and the 'Poet and Peasant Overture'; one which you remarked as being very good. I forget the number or numbers of the records, but they were in the paper recently advertising new H.M.V. records. I hope that you will not allow the three months time limit to expire, no matter what you get – even if it is a Paul Robeson record for Gerald. (But you won't, will you?)

Well, for the present I will once more bid you farewell, sending you one and all my very best love and wishes.

From Your Most Loving Son
Philip

P.S. I fear I write these letters very quickly and when I do read some parts through again, I have to wince at the poor grammar that appears from time to time, not to mention the laborious repetition of words and adjectives – I don't notice the bad spelling so easily! Nevertheless I don't suppose that you will pay undue attention to that, as to the fact that with me all is well and 'according to plan' which I hope is the same with you.

My Dear Mother and Father,

With the continued advance of the Russians, even their winter seems to be retreating before their oncoming, seeking to establish itself in our islands. At least I cannot think of any other explanation of the terrific snow drifts around our billets this morning, when even the transport could not get up the road from Ramsey. All night long they have had work parties on the Ramsey–Jurby road striving to maintain communications and the R.A.F. seem to have taken over Ramsey itself as far as keeping the roads clear. The snow itself would not be so bad were it not for this east wind which whips up the fine snow with almost blinding fury. For these reasons the long drag down to Ramsey this morning was anything but pleasant, especially without the reinforcement of a breakfast.

They have just formed a musical circle for this camp, and the first meeting was held last Tuesday evening, when the 'Emperor' piano concerto was played on gramophone records and I must say it is something to which I will be able to look forward as it was a wonderful success, with everybody most surprised with the number who turned up – and they all seem very keen and as though they mean business; many chaps who might be interested would quite possibly not know, because the announcement only took the form of a short insignificant note in D.R.O.s and it was a wonder I noticed it. I also heard a record of Caruso and I was wondering whether, in spite of the worse recording, I didn't like him better than Gigli. There was a record of 'Jesu Joy of Man's Desiring' too but it was sung by a Bach Choral Society with Leon Goossens as solo oboist.

I have also just discovered that we have one or two celebrities on this camp. When, last Sunday at tea–time I heard the B.B.C. announcer say that 'we present L.A.C. Clinton with the B.B.C. Theatre Orchestra and Chorus as the artist of the concert' (he is a baritone I think) even then I didn't realise that he had special leave from Jurby to go there and sing, that he only sleeps three or four rooms from me. It's funny how little you know about the chaps who actually live with you, isn't it? He is bringing back a good set of records for this music circle and will himself sing for us accompanied by his wife who, I am told, is quite an accomplished pianist – but I don't think she is an L.L.C.M.[1] yet!

I have had a little more flying in a Blenheim since I last wrote. We went up and the visibility was so bad that I couldn't see the aerodrome even on the circuit just around. I had to do my best on instruments (on which I was not quite as I should be, for lack of practice) and more or less guess when to turn in for the landing. I seem to have got hold of the technique of flying and landing now and even earned some measure of praise for one or two – something I am quite unused to after my instructor in Canada. The chap who takes me here, by the way, is a Flying Officer Primavesi (sounds Italian doesn't it?) and I am glad to say he is quite a good Catholic as well as being good to get on with.

I haven't heard this week from you, but I hope you are all very well and in good spirits and that Aunty Eileen is getting brighter and better. Tell her from me not to worry because everything is under control (I hope). If you don't get those photos of me in this letter, I will send them in my next. It is all a question as to whether I shall be able to get down into Ramsey in this raging blizzard or no.

Well for the present I will once again ask you to excuse my drawing to a rather early close to what must be a very careless and hurried letter. However I find it hard to concentrate on writing with cold hands and feet. Here's sending you my very best love and wishes

From Your Most Affectionate Son
Philip

(*NB Family had just moved back to 128 Farnham Road, the house from which they had been bombed out*)

---

1. His mother was already a Licentiate of the London College of Music

My Dear Mother and Father,

I received your short note yesterday, and I had gathered beforehand that you are now probably too busy to think much about writing letters, so I will understand quite well if you would like to attend to first things first. But I would like to warn Mother not to go making herself ill by trying to undertake herculean work in too short a time, and for want of a better word I will use a piece of R.A.F. slang by asking her not to 'panic'. After all if you look at it this way, it is all a vicious circle isn't it, for the more you do, the more there is to be undone again! The maxim therefore is to do nothing so that your efforts will not be wasted and hence there is nothing to put right again!

After the very severe snowfall of last week it quickly dispersed within two days and has turned relatively mild but I heard that snow is still widely spread over the mainland and that it is very cold there.

The other day I was talking to a Warrant Officer Pilot in our mess about things in general when he mentioned the fact that he had heard I was from Birmingham. It turned out that he comes from Thornhill Road! He got his wings in 1937, was in the V.Rs[1] and had all his training at Castle Bromwich; he was posted to Jurby at the outbreak of war and has been here ever since! He is a very decent sort of chap as well.

Last night I went to that music circle again and had a very enjoyable evening; the main item was Tchaikovsky's *Pathetique* symphony. There was an amusing sidelight in that there were a number of Waafs there as well, one of whom looked exactly like Dorothy[2] from the back. 'Well', I thought, 'What on earth could she be doing in the Waafs?' However the answer was not long in coming for when I got a broader view of the face, the lipstick and the powder was so overpowering and the eyebrows so scanty that I bid a hasty retreat, wondering whatever Dorothy would think if she could be present to witness the sad mistake.

Apart from that sad little episode, everything else was very successful and the number there this week was considerably more than last week.

Well the war seems still to be in full swing and poor old Australia is now getting the jitters and one cannot help feeling sorry for them under the circumstances, though I do think that all their accusations of us are not as reasonable as they should be. Still they are a small and growing nation and it is very understandable, far more understandable than De Valera's grouse against the American troops coming over.

What flying I have done has been quite successful; I have now done about three and a half hours on Blenheims and have got the hang of it quite O.K. I think, but have not gone solo yet, though I am quite confident that I could. The trouble is that at this place they mess around awfully until you finally get going, but then you don't have a minute to breathe hardly – but I think I would prefer that to the present hanging around. I hope that now you will like 128 Farnham Road, and that it will help to allay most of your troubles. One thing, I don't think you will again have much trouble from Jerry; I hope those days are now past and done with.

By the way though, I would like to help you buy an allotment (official or private) especially if you (i.e. Mother) want to give up work but want to keep the children at St. Paul's. To tell you the truth I have rather a guilty conscience with so much money on my hands when you have done so much for me, and when your difficulties are so manifold. I know that you will not feel like saying yes, but really I think that under the circumstances I ought to help you and that it is rather selfish of me to stand idly by when things go so hard for you, so I hope you will consider it and not say no.

For the moment then I think I will adjourn until sometime next week, sending you one and all my very best wishes and love from

From Your Most Affectionate Son
Philip

---

1. Volunteer Reserves
2. Dorothy Timmins who worked with his mother

Sergeants' Mess
Jurby, I.O.M.
Thursday, 24th January 1942

(NB encloses cutting from the Times 23 .1. 42, on Libyan Desert – with note about ships)

My Dear Mother and Father,

Thanks for your last letter which I received last Monday and for the other you forwarded on. That one by the way came from Transvaal in South Africa from that chap whom I met in Blackpool and who is incidentally about the best Catholic I've met in the R.A.F.

The weather here continues brilliant but very cold. That's how it is on this island, for when every other part of British Isles is enjoying good weather, you can depend that this place is in the centre of a depression or something like that; but when everywhere else the weather is pretty bad, we enjoy continuous sunshine.

It was only yesterday that as second pilot, I was on a NAV. trip down to Kidderminster, Brise Norton and base (Brise Norton is in Oxfordshire) and was very excited with the thought of flying over the Midlands and so near home. But as soon as we crossed the coast over Rhyl the weather became exceedingly dull and over the mountains of North Wales visibility was almost nil, so the first pilot simply turned round and came back again. The same is true again today, though I have only been doing a spot of local flying. We have to do three trips as second pilots before we go with pupils, mainly for experience, though I'm rather dubious as to how much good it does. Personally I nearly always know much better where I am when I am piloting the machine, though why I don't know.

A number of chaps have lately been posted from here to Canada. It would be rather funny if I were sent out there again wouldn't it? However I certainly hope not; it is nice to have been there, but it is better to be at home. Last week a Wellington came down here with engine trouble, and I was most surprised to see that the observer in it was one of my pals from Scarborough (I think I used to mention him to you, as he was very fond of music and invited me to that gramophone circle at Scarborough). He was one of the chaps who failed at Yeadon on the E.F.T.S. course. Since then he re–mustered to train to be an observer and got a commission (he is a pilot officer). He is now finishing off O.T.U. and in a few days time is flying to Malta to take up active duties there – the most bombed place in the world!

Well after all the excitement of the loss of Singapore last week people seem to have quietened down somewhat, though why I don't know; it all seemed pretty futile to me in the first place. I think that we are jolly lucky still to be able to retreat without being beaten, and that we have done jolly well to be still in the fight. The more I look through the eight months following September 1940, the more magnificent I think is our achievement, the more splendid I think was the work of the Navy, the greater the mistakes of our enemies and the more miraculous our present position.

Is it to be wondered that after such prolonged strain of fighting for our very existence, for every scrap of food we have eaten and even for every ounce of war material we have produced – is it to be wondered in such circumstances that we have had such a temporary blow and that our nerves are a little on edge, and that we tend to wait for other countries to take a little more of the strain. The sufferings of Russia and her people have been great and her position perilous but I often wonder whether her people could have faced such a dark and bleak winter as we did in 1940–41, when we fought alone and when such friends as we had could do little more than encourage us.

I wish that our press would not do so much of this belittling of our position and of our organisation and compare us so unfavourably with Russia. They blandly say

Russia does this and that while we do nothing, omitting of course that only from two very important reasons that Russia still <u>can</u> do this and that, namely that we filled the breach during 1940 when even Russia was hostile, and that the R.A.F. prevents Hitler wielding his Air Force to his full capacity as he did against us and France, not to mention the work of the Navy which is almost incalculable.

I am pleased that Dr. Temple is the new Archbishop of Canterbury; he has good social views; even the Daily Mirror spoke well of him yesterday, so he must be good! I should like to see him and Cardinal Hinsley get together to try and tackle some of the many problems that face Christians as a whole, such as Education, Youth and general social questions. It seems to me that they could do untold good if they formed some sort of Christian common front.

Friday

Today there does not seem much more to say, except that I see I am down to practise ZZ Blind approaches[1] tomorrow in a Blenheim. There are two of us, the one keeps watch that the other doesn't go colliding into other aircraft or obstacles while he 'has his head in the cockpit' – as we say.

By the way did you hear Cunningham with the City of Birmingham Orchestra last Sunday on the wireless? I was fortunate on that occasion and had the whole mess to myself and heard it all in comfort. I thought it was extremely good. We will have to encourage Kitty to make that her ambition! The organ combines very well with an Orchestra don't you think?

Well at this point I will conclude and wish you goodbye until next week rolls around, with all my love and best wishes

I remain Your Most Affectionate Son
Philip.

P.S. All my landings to date have been happy, if on occasion they have been a trifle bumpy!

---

1. A ZZ landing was a method to assist the pilot to land in bad visibility, using a series of radio bearings. This was before radar and other more sophisticated radio aids.

Dear Mother and Father,

A new system has been introduced this week whereby only two pilots do Duty Pilot for the whole week – and I am one of the unfortunate two for this week. It is not too good while it is on, but on the other hand it should be a long time before my turn comes again. Yesterday unfortunately was a day of continuous 'panic' for one thing or another and I sincerely hope that the days to come will not produce anything so bad. It would take too long for me to go into it all, but in the daytime two of our aircraft were overdue and the action to be taken by the Duty Pilot, though clearly laid down, is of a very worrying nature. Fortunately both aircraft are O.K.; one landed down by Swansea and the other at Ballyhalbert in Northern Ireland, both on account of very bad weather.

Then, just to keep me awake all night, I was informed that Jurby would have to prepare to bring in a number of aircraft since weather conditions on the mainland were so bad that it would be impossible for them to land anywhere over there. Not that the weather was good here, but apparently it was better and the need was urgent. I think they must have been out on raids; however in the end they took them to safer aerodromes in Northern Ireland from what I could make out.

All this rather puts an end to any prospects of flying this week that I might have had, and I was doing very well last Saturday on the Blenheim. One of my pals here had an extremely amusing story about the trials of a night flying across country which he went on the other night, when his observers soon became completely lost and when he himself later lost his bearings altogether. To make matters worse his wireless had gone unserviceable or his W/opp could not manage it. He was telling us the feeling of absolute helplessness that he was experiencing when all of a sudden great numbers of searchlights sprang up some distance in front of him, dexterously fingering the sky. He had a feeling he said, that they were on the lookout for him and he began to wonder where he was, and visions of balloon barrages and ac/ac[1] made an unwelcome picture in his mind! Anyway as he drew more near he thought it would allay suspicion if he switched on his Navigation lights when to his relief every searchlight went out! Half an hour later the searchlights proved themselves a real friend in need, for with their long thin beams they pointed him on to another one, which in turn pointed him on to another and so finally brought him to the most welcome sight such a pilot could wish to see – a lighted runway, and a few aircraft on the circuit!

I wonder whether you will believe me when I tell you that just lately we have been having so many eggs that I am almost beginning to tire of them! This morning for instance I had two fried eggs, while yesterday teatime I had fried egg and bacon – but I won't tell you any more or else you will be desirous of moving from '128' again to the I.O.M. I often think what a pity it is though, that I cannot forego some to give to you at home, where I know they would be appreciated much more highly than they are here.

Fancy us losing Bengazi again! It makes one wonder, doesn't it? I suppose that it is the fault primarily of the Japs, but still it is most disappointing. It seems that the army cannot win such decisive victories as the Navy and Air Force has done – there is always something to snatch victory from them, though I do think there is still a lesson or two that they can learn from the German army. It's very annoying because it is delaying the outcome and victory cannot come too quickly for me, but I suppose as you say, all these things come to try us.

How are things with all you now? Is the house getting straightened up? And I am hoping too that the bad weather is not taxing your health unduly. So far I still have no knowledge of Auntie Eileen, but I am hoping I may hear this week sometime. As far as I am concerned, I do not think I could ever be in better health than I am now – there is this much to be said for life in the R.A.F., the outdoor life is very invigorating and does much to keep one's spirits up. I am afraid that I have a great weakness for the countryside and the sea, and the quaint old fishing towns like Ramsey and Scarborough, and I imagine that nine months shut up in all the dust and fumes of Hercules did much to deepen that appreciation.

Sometimes as I have walked solitarily from Ramsey up to our billets during some of the more peaceful evenings and have heard sheep bleating on the one side and the sea murmuring on the other, I have often thought what a pleasant contrast this forms to the busy hum of machinery with all the odd noises one cannot escape within our cities. On the other hand to be walking along alone in the silence of the countryside on a pitch dark night and to be greeted suddenly by the mooing of a cow, it's head poked unconcernedly over the hedge, is something which can be infinitely more terrifying than the largest H.E. bomb falling in one's back garden, and I'm sure that it made me jump much further the other night than any blast has thrown any one of its victims! The cow in question, however, appeared to be very aloof and indifferent to all the sensation she had caused – at least it didn't move, or moo any approval of my antics!

Wednesday

I managed to get to that music circle last night and heard a Rachmaninov piano concerto with himself the artist, and accompanied by the Philadelphia Orchestra under Stokowski. There was also a recording of part of the *Dream of Gerontius* which was very enjoyable, and one or two other things.

This morning I am in the Duty Pilot's hut but the weather is absolutely hopeless, and aircraft render a mournful spectacle as they stand motionless, littered around the edge of the aerodrome and more often than not, parked in the centre of a sea of mud and water – still it makes it easier for me, and as I look out I can only see hundreds of seagulls 'taking off' and 'landing', and I notice that they keep much better flying discipline than many of our aircraft, for you will never see them try and land downwind as one of our chaps did yesterday with disastrous effects to the aircraft, nor has the pilot heard the last of it!

Friday

This is my last day on this D.P. (Duty Pilot duty) which is one consolation. I hear from the weather reports and from what pilots have seen that England and Scotland are once more under a thick blanket of snow, but here the weather is quite mild except that cloud and rain still constitute a deadly enemy when they get stuck around these hills. Yesterday, however, it was an exceptionally fine day with brilliant sunshine, so good for flying in fact that I asked to do a little more flying even though I was entitled to the day off. As a result I had a really enjoyable afternoon practising one engine approaches and landings which I was doing unusually well, for me. I have now done just over six hours on the Blenheim and am ready for solo tomorrow; after that I should do about five hours on my own, and then switch over to five more hours on the long nose Blenheim by which time I should be ready for flying in Navigation Flight, to which I am looking forward very much. I shall probably be flying Ansons as well, especially if I get details for night flying early on. By the way, I received your letter last night, for which I thank you very much. I am pleased to hear of Auntie Eileen's good progress and I hope that Mother's sore throat (or does saw throat seem more appropriate?) is also by this time better.

Well at this point I do not think there is much more I can find to say so I will not make you late for work or otherwise waste your time, or strain your eyes simply through endeavouring to decipher this scrawl, so without more ado I will end in the usual way, sending you all my very best love and wishes,

From Your Most Affectionate Son
Philip

P.S. I have just read this letter over, and it struck me that I have written a great deal which is possibly of little or no interest to you – if you do occasionally find my letters lengthened with much uninteresting accounts of things that happen here just tell me, and I will endeavour in future to keep more to the point, and perhaps take a bit more trouble over them. I can realise that much of what I write must make hard reading for you.

PPS. Just before I post this letter you might be interested to know that today I have done two and a half hours solo on the Blenheim.

Anyway, best love
Philip

My Dear Mother and Father,

Thanks for your letter which I received yesterday and the various items of news.

Yes I know how cold it has been over in England this last few weeks, but on the whole it has been very mild here by comparison. Things have been getting more lively for me here lately; during the weekend I did nearly six hours solo on the Blenheim and really enjoyed getting off on my own again. Of course I had a good look round the island and paid a visit to Douglas and, after taking a good look at it from all aspects, went off all round the island when I suddenly remembered that the last time I went round was nine years ago in a charabanc in Boy Scouts uniform! Then as I swept low across the sea towards Peel and obtained my first view of the old castle since that last occasion, it struck me that I wonder what I would have thought nine years ago had I been told that the next occasion when I would see this castle would be from the air! And that furthermore I would be in a twin engined bomber on my own! I simply wouldn't have believed it.

I did a little reconnoitering over by the Scottish coast, but as visibility was bad and I had no maps or signal cartridges in case I was challenged, I didn't delay long. Still it was all most enjoyable after my long rest and I found the colour scheme made by the sun on clouds and sea particularly beautiful, I wish I could show you all the hidden beauty of the heavens, which at present is known only to those who fly. There are some magnificent scenes on occasions. Yes the old Blenheim is a very nice aircraft and I feel much more confident with it than I used to with the Oxford; it is however very startling to land with one engine, as you make the final approach at 100 miles per hour or faster with the angle of glide very great i.e. you get almost over the aerodrome edge at perhaps 1000 to 800 feet and simply push the nose straight down, with the result that you find it hard to keep in your seat. At the moment I am awaiting a long nose version, the Mark 4, which is slightly difficult to land. We do not have dual on this though, and it shouldn't prove any worse, in fact most chaps say it is slightly easier.

At the music circle last Tuesday we had Beethoven's *Fifth Symphony*. You can guess that I enjoyed it. At this the fourth meeting, attendance has grown to such an extent that they now have to arrange larger accommodation. There must have been at least fifty present, and when you consider all those who cannot come for various duties etc., I think that figure is very good. Next week they are having Mozart's *Thirty Ninth*, which is another very famous one.

Lately I am beginning to wonder whether the news is worth listening to or the papers worth reading. Certainly Singapore is now in very great danger, and by the time you read this letter I can imagine our papers talking of the scorched earth our troops did before they retreated from there, if even a retreat is now possible! I am hoping and praying that this may not be the case, but I am afraid I expected that our troops would have made a stand somewhere on the mainland of Malaya. I am afraid that now England is unequal to the task of defending her entire Empire alone, and in future I shouldn't be surprised at America having a good share in it – but perhaps it will be for the best in the long run. The most disconcerting fact though is the boomerang effect of our offensive in the Middle East which is most disappointing. However in the last resort it is still Germany that has to be beaten, and if we make a better show at holding the Burma Road and Rangoon, the Japs will still be in a perilous position particularly as our strength grows.

I have been wondering lately what you would think if you had seen the number of times I have been in various pubs since I have been at Jurby! Not that the number of times is very big, but considering that before I never used to frequent such places you might find it somewhat surprising. However I seem particularly fortunate in the good type of friends I have here, and it has seemed to me that it is a little better to fall in step with them in certain respects like this, especially as I know they are very moderate. Otherwise in this sort of life you have only the choice of living a life of hermit or getting with a much worse set of chaps altogether; and besides, there is very little else to do other than go to the cinema, and at least it is nearly always warm with a good fire burning – which are mighty alluring temptations when the other alternative is the black–out and pouring rain or sleet.

You talk about my next leave in your last letter, but to tell you the truth I cannot see any signs of it up to now. A new order has come out which states that we have to get in 220 hours before we can get a fortnight. So far I have 14 hours but I am hoping for some relaxation in this as time goes. There are other ways and means as well – for instance one might get the M.O. to say one is in need of a short rest from flying and etc!

Thanks for your long letter which just this minute I have finished reading. Truly a startling request from Auntie Celestine though! What sort of girls are they? What sort of letters do they want writing? If, as Auntie Celestine suggests, they think the R.A.F. chaps wonderful and 'would love to have a line from one' then of course I could soon write and disillusion them! However at the moment I have quite enough on my hands, and if I am going to write letters it may as well be to girls I know. Anyway to satisfy Aunty Celestine I will probably make one or two feelers, but I don't promise success at all.

As you talk of my skill as a pilot with a little doubt, I would like to tell you that at this job you can never get too good or be too careful – for your own skin! I am convinced about that, and that is my main reason for taking this practice so seriously, for I can assure you that nothing would be easier than to neglect some of this training. For instance when you are flying solo with everything going smoothly it takes quite a bit of will power to voluntarily cut one engine and fly on the other alone to make a landing; but on the other hand if the emergency does come, you are far more ready to tackle it.

I see you also think of my use after the war, which now that you mention it, is also an aspect which I have given much thought to, and I can tell you too that one of the primary reasons of my deciding to undertake flying duties and especially those of pilot, was that I saw in what a wonderful position a pilot (N.C.O. or Officer) was to influence his colleagues and subordinates for good. Of course I had my other reasons as well, but that one weighed most heavily.

I am afraid I fall short of my ambition, but on the other hand my endeavours have not been entirely fruitless. And though I don't wish to raise false hopes in you as to my future in the R.A.F. there is a saying that "once in training command, always in training command". To me, personally whatever happens would be O.K., but for your sake I hope that I will come through everything. However it is just as well you continue praying for me for hazards exist even in training command; but you may be interested to know that never do I take off without first of all saying a prayer that all may be well, and when soon I take up other passengers and my responsibility will be greater, I shall extend the intention for them and their relatives as well.

Yes, I can well imagine that you are war weary, who isn't? And today's communique about the two German battleships and the cruiser, though it is thrilling, is hardly reassuring. Still as Mr. Churchill said 'Our faith will not flag or fail. . .' and that is the main thing, and perhaps the common adversities of the allies, and the agony of so many other millions of people will in the near future blossom into an age of much greater social justice, prosperity (though it be more frugal in character) and general tolerance and good will.

I am now at the billets and believe it or not there appears to be a full scale blitz on at the moment with flares all over the sky and the air vibrating with the purring note of heavy aircraft. Guns are going from somewhere and we are awaiting the results. I wonder whether there are some more Yanks arriving at Belfast.

Well at this point, I think I will conclude, wishing you all that I can, with all my love and best wishes from

Your Most Affectionate Son
Philip

PS. This full scale blitz turned out to be practice. Our own Wellington Bombers were the culprits. Yet everybody swore they could distinguish the German planes!

Sergeants' Mess
Jurby, I.O.M.
Wednesday, 20th February 1942

My Dear Mother and Father,

I hope that you are all still quite well and happy and that things are getting somewhat straighter than they have been heretofore. Somebody has just rushed in here to say that the news is much better tonight 'What is it?' we all asked, 'there's nothing' was the answer! That seems to be the general temper lately. However, there is a pilot up here just now from a coastal command station in England, who was in this Scharnhorst and Gneisenau do last week[1] and he tells us that for days and days all their personnel had been standing by awaiting the event – they even had to sleep in their clothes – so it hardly looks as though it were out and out negligence. Apparently the opposition they met was absolutely furious, and the visibility excessively bad. I cannot think that all this criticism can do much good in our present situation and things are bound to turn soon; they say that it is the darkest hour that comes before the dawn, so let us hope that the dawn is near at hand.

Today I have been flying again in a long nose Blenheim – I don't like them so much as the short nose version, and I find them at present a little more difficult to land. The conditions today are not ideal for flying, and visibility was very poor – however it is far better than doing nothing and merely hanging around.

Last weekend I went again to Douglas and had quite a good time – some good meals and a general look around and this time I wasn't sick! I haven't found anybody to write to Auntie Celestine's girls and I really do not know what to do. I don't even know whether she meant Catholic pen friends and I do not know exactly how Auntie

Celestine would feel about it; if it would save her from feeling rebuffed, of course I could write short and occasional letters to one of them; and somehow I can imagine that she would feel a little hurt if it was simply ignored. In fact it is a bit of a snorter and I can imagine that chap on the radio (I've forgotten his name) saying 'What would you do chum?'

The weather is still cold lately, but there do appear to be signs that spring is in the air, which is very welcome. Perhaps this coming spring will be one of the most vital in the history of the world; certainly big things will happen, but I don't think Hitler will be quite so confident as last year and certainly I don't envy him his position.

By the way was it from you that the second Universe[2] came this week? Last week I thought it was from Fr. Boland as usually he sends me a Catholic Herald, and didn't last week. However this week came two *Catholic Heralds* (this week's and last) and again last night came *The Universe* again. Thanks very much; but if you would intend to keep it up perhaps you might tell Fr. Boland, for it would save him doing it. I would be willing to pay all the post and everything. However, suit yourself, because Fr. Boland has more time for it, hasn't he? Still as I say thank you very much for it makes very interesting reading.

I have just received my ration money for my last leave so I will forward that to you in this letter. That is yours, it is no allowance from me, but I do however want to make that offer again, because I shall be growing very selfish if I have all this money on my hands. If it were only a small amount I would at least feel I were doing something.

Today (Friday) I have been to Scotland as second pilot just to get some idea of the work. We landed at Prestwick, just North of Ayr on the west coast which is a terrific station. There were a number of American Liberator bombers there and all sorts of other stuff. But I have yet to find a sergeant's mess which is as comfortable as ours at Jurby, or where the food even approaches what we get. Visiting crews to Jurby invariably marvel at our food and especially the abundance of eggs on the Isle. As I always think, a satisfied stomach makes up for a lot of things.

Tomorrow will be a very full day for me as I am scheduled to do six and a half hours flying on the Blenheim, and at the end of the day I am Aerodrome Control Pilot, and if night flying goes on as normally, I will be in the centre of the aerodrome best part of the night, directing the aircraft – it makes me shiver to think of it!

Time is now getting short so I will ask you at this point to receive all my very best love and wishes to you all, while I remain

Your Most Affectionate Son
Philip

---

1. On 11–13 February 1942 the two German battleships made a daring "dash" through the English Channel to reach Germany. Caught off guard, the British were unable to stop the ships with air and surface attacks.
2. Catholic newspaper

My Dear Mother and Father,

I am supposed to be on two details today, but this morning so far not one of our aircraft have left the ground, and unless things improve they will not do this afternoon.

Thanks for your last letter which I received on Saturday. I was very surprised that it wasn't you who sends that *Universe*. The address is printed very similarly and the postmark is Birmingham; I simply do not know who it could be. Talking about postmarks reminds me that one of the letters I received from you early in January was posted in some village I have never heard of in Lancashire – how came that about?

I have now my own Blenheim aircraft with my own W.Opp., air gunner, and my own pupil observers on this station which rather gives me a sense of responsibility and importance at last. At least this is so in theory – in practice things don't run so smoothly at all, and if your own aircraft is not available they give you anyone that is going.

At the moment I haven't heard a word of news for at least three days so for all I know the world could be upside down. There is something I have heard about our parachutists which is said to be pretty good but I don't know as yet.

There are some American troops now in Douglas I saw on Saturday when I was there, and rumour has it that very shortly they are going to replace all British troops garrisoned in the I.O.M. I cannot tell you much about them just now as they have hardly had time to become either popular or disagreeable whichever the case may be. I have heard that they cannot get on very well with the British troops in Belfast, but I think the reason is that the American troops have so much more money than poor Tommies who have to withdraw to play only second fiddles in the various social events and entertainments.

I am very glad that Mother has bought those two records. They seem to be very good choices and I look forward to the day when I shall be able to hear them. I already have my eye on one record at least, and that is the second movement of Tchaikovsky's *Pathetique Symphony*.

Well after long deliberation with myself concerning Auntie Celestine's request, I have either wisely or otherwisely decided on a sort of compromise. The trouble is that I hardly like point blank refusing Auntie Celestine and after all I realise that she is trying to be helpful, so I have written to tell her that I shall endeavour to write to one occasionally from time to time. I cannot see that there can be any harm in it and if it is going to help make others a little happier you might do much worse these days.

Last night at the music circle we had a very good programme with the *Nutcracker Suite* of Tchaikovsky, and Schubert's *Unfinished Symphony* and one or two overtures of Wagner. I look forward to these weekly events very much and they produce easily the best entertainment I get up here. Yes I think it is a good job that you are back on A.C.[1] and have the radio readily available. I hope that you don't ever forego any music you may desire for want of my records. Especially those of Gigli.

How is Gerald these days in his new billets? I suppose he is doing fairly well for himself.

Saturday

I shall have to finish this with speed now or else lose the post. Thanks very much for the letters and birthday greetings which arrived on Thursday night – a good job as no post came through yesterday owing to weather. Thank you very much indeed for having a Mass offered up for me; thank Dorothy very much for the Communion intentions.

I finished up the last three and a half hours of my birthday with a terrific religious argument with two chaps, one of whom was most dissatisfied that the Pope hadn't excommunicated Hitler, amongst other things, whilst the other was more concerned to convert me to Russian or Marxist philosophy of materialism. So it was rather a three cornered argument. However the former later became very meek and mild, and after he has read the pamphlet 'Pope and the War' which I have given him, he may learn to admire the work of our present Pope. The other chap I intend to tackle when he is on his own – he is unfortunately rather under the spell of what he has picked up from Manchester University.

Well now I shall have to conclude sending you all my love and very best wishes from

Your Most Affectionate Son
Philip

---

1. Electricity supply

My Dear Mother and Father,

Hardly have I finished writing you one week's letter when it seems I have to start on the next, so here I am again ready to put a few more of my thoughts or reminiscences, or my hopes or desires on paper, with the idea of making something of interest of my general routine duties of which I can tell you.

I suppose I should begin by thanking you for the letter which I received this evening. Also I am pleased that you are going to accept an allowance from me, which I think is very well warranted; while it is officially going through R.A.F. channels I will send some by letter as well.

That you should cast grave doubts as to the wisdom of writing to girl pen friends certainly should leave me with no occasion to take offence; any humiliation of being told I have made a mistake can surely do me no harm, while from other reasons I have nothing to regret as my intention was mainly to satisfy Auntie Celestine who appeared to me to be the initiator of the idea. It is one of my weaknesses that I find it always hard to refuse people favours, and this I am afraid was one. However with the use of a little diplomacy and with far too much on my hands already, the affair will soon be a thing of the past – in fact I wouldn't be at all surprised if it is already.

Yesterday was a very nice day here and it is particularly spiriting to hear so many birds whistling and chirruping as the first light of day breaks one's slumbers each morning. Then after hurriedly dressing (always a very desperate affair with me!) the drive along by the broad blue expanse of the sea sets off the day on a very optimistic and joyful note. If on the other hand I find myself having to do most of my dressing in the van as it bounds and bustles and swings and sways over the rough surface and round the sharp corners – a very uncomfortable and rather unnerving affair – then there is always a lot to be said for the good breakfast that awaits us at the end of our journey. In spite of this however the weather is very cold, and the last ten days has seen it snowing heavily, and heavy frosts alternated with cold sleet.

Last Saturday I was doing ZZ landing in a Blenheim, and on Sunday I was on two 'details', the first of which saw a quite extensive flight over Northern Ireland during which I saw quite a good view of Belfast from its South side. In the afternoon it was nearly all over the sea when we touched the South tip of Scotland, a light vessel in Morecambe Bay and a point three miles off the coast of Eire where I had quite a good view of Dublin.

An Air Vice Marshall is here at the present moment and I think he will begin a shake–up of this place. They certainly need it here as they have certainly been very careless in the past. The American troops are only army chaps; I don't suppose for a moment that they will interfere with R.A.F. training command – they will have enough on their own hands, and they can do all that much better in their own country where conditions are almost ideal for this type of work.

I am very sorry to hear of Mr. Sheehan and will certainly pray for him; but I am very pleased that Auntie Eileen is making improvement even if it is slow. What are these clubs that Kitty says she plays at? Does she mean with the Children of Mary?

Fancy you having seen the King and Queen at Lucas's[1] and from such a point of vantage! By the way, in addition to your letters on my birthday, I received a parcel from Auntie Mabel and Uncle Walter with a chocolate iced cake within, which I thought was very generous when things are so scarce.

The news does not appear to get much better lately, but I am hoping America may be able to produce one or two more pleasant surprises during the coming months. They are certainly becoming very severe on this rationing business lately and it looks as though Mr. Cripp's (or should I say Sir Stafford's?)[2] words are beings borne out that we shall have to live more austerely in the future.

Well for the present time I will draw this to a close until next week, and meanwhile send you all my very best love and wishes from

Your Most Affectionate Son
Philip

---

1. Philip's mother worked at Lucas's during the war
2. Government Minister of Aircraft Production

My Dear Mother and Father,

It is Wednesday once more – and I always feel as though I must make some start on your letters if I want to have them finished by the weekend – but the trouble is what to put down! That is a question that has to find some answer week by week, yet as each successive week comes around, becomes progressively harder for I feel that I have told you all that I can and all that you wish to know about aeroplanes and the fools that fly them (as they say in the R.A.F. . . ., 'only birds and fools fly'); while if I mention the weather that in itself is an obvious sign of weakness that must bore you to tears for the simple reason that I can find nothing better to say.

In any case this week has seen no flying, or hardly any, which throws some light on to the state of the weather, which baffles all description. There was one incident which I must not miss, when one of our navigation planes crash-landed in Eire, as was in the next day's papers. But rumour now has it that all the crew are now in Northern Ireland, whether by foul means or fair I could not say. The Pilot was a Pilot Officer and I have since heard, is a millionaire!

By the way, could you tell me at which Post Office you would like to draw the allotment from? If I remember rightly Newcombe Road Post Office has been take away hasn't it? This time I trust I have to make it out to Mrs. Hermolle, isn't that so?

It was a funny thing, but last night I dreamt that Gerald was in the A.T.C. and came up to this camp to have a look round (as they do) and that I took him up for a ride! The most astounding part was, however, that we landed in the Bull Ring (just as though it were the most natural thing) after which we went somewhere and purchased a terrific black dog whose bark was the most mournful sound that you could wish to hear – I afterwards woke up and heard the fog horn off Maughold Head blowing a sombre note every half minute! It is very funny isn't it what tricks dreams play on us! How I could land a Blenheim in the Bull Ring I don't know what with all the traffic, the crowds of busy people, the high buildings and church spires on all sides – and I had not even had my supper!

The other day when I was awaiting my turn to do a little link practice, I discovered that Winco was in (that is our pet name for Wing Commander Edwards who is in charge of all the Navigational flights here). It was a great source of consolation to me however when such a renowned 'high up', as he, went into three spins during his effort – and the rest of the exercise was not too good either. But to see a Wing Commander who has first of all been careless enough to get into a spin, and then trying to get out of it is a sight which I wouldn't have missed for worlds – it seems so undignified especially when it takes place on three occasions.

Tonight I have just received a letter from Mr. Duffy on behalf of St. Augustine's.

This morning a squash competition has been arranged for Pilots (to help them keep fit!) I was paired against the supposedly best player we have here, and the astounding thing is that I decisively beat him though I have never played before, nor even yet do I know all the rules properly. However it seems a rather easy game to me, but there is not an awful lot in it; except that it does make you run round quite a bit. Lately I am doing quite a bit of chess playing as well – but I fear that I much more often lose than win and I am rather slow at thinking my moves out which makes it somewhat uninteresting for my opposite number – and then I do such silly moves on occasion that I could kick myself over the moon!

I heard of Lord Halifax' speech this morning, and I think it is high time somebody tried to give high praise where it is due, and not to continually belittle our countrymen's efforts.

For the present I think I will conclude sending you all my very best love and wishes

From Your Most Affectionate Son,
Philip

P.S. I am coming on leave on May 5th. – have just heard. If all goes as per schedule.

My Dear Mother and Father,

Your letter was received last Monday and duly read and digested; the first part seemed a catalogue of deaths and I was wondering how many more there were going to be – however I shall strive to answer your request by offering up some prayers.

I am afraid that I gave you the wrong date for when I am coming home on leave; it is a week later than the date I gave, i.e. May 12th. Still I hope the days will soon slip round and that old Tchaikovsky can last out that long.

Spring is certainly here now – and to stay I hope! It is a great pity when you think of all that Spring should be and mean to people, with its gay sunshine, brighter flowers, blossoming trees, lighter evenings allowing all to disport themselves after the long dark days of winter, then to think that it will also be the signal for the mightiest and most ferocious clash of arms in history. I should be facing the next few months on a blithe and carefree note were it not for that spectre that must ever lurk in the back of one's mind.

We can only hope and pray that the sacrifice that the world is making of its very self, will ultimately be worth it and cause men to see things in their right perspective, that riches are not all we imagined them to be, that 'progress' means much more than merely constructing new and powerful and unthought–of machines which are hardly progressive when they prove so self destructive. In the past the emphasis has been too much on materialism, let's hope that all will now see its futility in the present catastrophe and base their hopes and ambitions on more permanent and certain spiritual grounds.

I suppose that I automatically write in this strain, as such sentiments echo most of the thoughts which have been running through my mind of late – for the truth is that in our billets here there have been furious debates on different things touching the war and the *Daily Mirror* (`a propos Mr. Morrison's threat)[1] so I have been in my element as I always am in such discussion especially as they all boil down to Christianity in the end. This is where I often manage to score heavily, because I do at least know what I believe but others who might oppose or question it, don't even know where they themselves stand.

Today has been such a nice day that as coming down from the camp I was longing for my old bicycle – and I think it would be a jolly good idea if I bring it back with me after I come back from leave. Most of the pilots here have bought second hand cars – some looking quite respectable, others more like a rather elaborate rag and bone man's cart. But in any case I am not too keen and I don't think you should waste petrol on such pleasures when others are dying to get it here; on the other hand my two pals and I have come to the conclusion that it would be ideal to try and buy or hire an old sailing boat (of which there are a number doing nothing in Ramsey) and have it moored just at the bottom of our 'front garden'. One of them even says that we could easily cover all expenses by occasionally fishing in the bay and selling it to the Sergeants' Mess! Then as I have observed, we could, instead of walking two miles of road or rough beach, sail in majesty and state into Ramsey harbour (for generally speaking the water is very calm within the bay). Anyway it would certainly be very refreshing after a day or night of flying, to go all nautical for an hour or two and it would seem a very cheap form of recreation! This Island ought to be a wonderful place in the coming months and now that I have borne the cold of the winter I want at least to see a little of its bright side.

I have played one or two more games of squash, but my pride has been laid low, for in another game I was beaten just as decisively. Still it is very good fun and maybe it will help to keep me from getting too fat; I shall have to try and get some tennis in this summer as well.

Fancy Bernard being home! I wonder how he has wangled it?

I have been flying most days this week but it has only been in bits and dabs and round about the islands. I had a little excitement yesterday when one of my props (propellors) refused to change pitch – however that is a comparatively small thing when you are quite near the aerodrome and I only had to come down again as quickly as possible and have it seen to.

This afternoon for the first time I had to carry out an air test on my own machine. Each aircraft has one of these after each occasion that they go into the hangar for servicing. At the moment they are constructing runways on the aerodrome which makes it more tricky for landing as such a large portion of the aerodrome is cut off.

The war does not seem to be making much of a change just now. I am not prepared to make any more prophesies about the Japs as they let me down badly about Singapore! The Navy has just shown that they lack none of their traditional dash and daring in their latest exploit in the Mediterranean – let's hope that the Japs will soon feel what it is like to oppose the British Navy as well! And now I fancy that I had better conclude or this letter will not reach you in time, so once again sending you all my love and best wishes, I remain

Your Most Affectionate Son
Philip

---

1. The threat of the Secretary of State for the Home Department to suppress the Daily Mirror's critique of the war

Dear Mother and Father,

Today clouds are down to the deck (as they say) and for once I am pegged down to the ground. The flying I have put in recently has tired me to a terrific extent and I am more than ready for this short respite. Last Saturday I was down over the Midlands again. I circled Bromsgrove two or three times but the industrial haze over all that part of the country makes visibility very poor.

On our way back from Brise Norton I reckon that we must have actually passed over the outskirts of Birmingham (on the west side) as we eventually landed up over Birkenhead with its silvery balloons glistening far below. However I was flying at 11,000 feet and didn't see anything below us at all when over the Midlands. And was it cold! I hadn't any of my flying clothes on except for helmet and Mae West[1] (which is supposed to keep us afloat if we find ourselves in the sea) as I wasn't expected to go that high. However frantic appeals from the wireless operator (who had all his togs on) 'that the cold wasn't even funny' gave me good excuse for losing a few thousand feet, even if it didn't suit the Navigator, who by the way was a Flight Lieutenant.

This coming Saturday I am going down to Cheltenham where I will land for dinner and return here in the evening. One of these Saturdays I shall try and get permission to land at Elmdon and see if I cannot see you for an hour or two; however don't bank on it but if it ever did materialise I would be pleased if you would give me the phone numbers whereby I could make reasonably quick contact with you either at Lucas's or at Pitt's.

I have this week received an assurance that I am to be posted back to Navigation Flight at the end of April or thereabouts. I seem to have a very good friend in one of the Officers in station flight who on his own initiative has done this for me. Not only that, he has put in a good recommendation for me to the O.C. flying and the Wing Commander to the effect that I should stay here – I was apparently on a list for posting to an Air Gunnery school in England. By the fact that I was a little on the slow side at first in picking up the flying again, and the fact that through no fault of my own I had done practically no flying, apparently some quarters had formed the opinion that I was not quite what I should be as a pilot. That seems to have been the reason why I was taken off navigation work – though they were certainly rather late, and only decided on that when I had eventually started serious work there.

However the Flight Commander in my new gunnery flight has also apparently put through some very good reports about me, and it seems as though they are going to put me back again in Navigation flight as before. I am particularly pleased as all this seems to have happened from outside sources and I have got what I wanted without any effort on my part, and in fact I was ignorant of most of it.

I have been enjoying myself lately, especially when I have been on bombing details. I always love the coming down from after finishing high level bombing exercises. From 6000 feet or 7000 you can make a wide half circle of the top part of the Isle of Man as you lose height, which always seems a very restful form of flying after the other, with the engines much more quiet and no bother of careful watching your instruments. Low level bombing is also jolly good fun; for this we generally skim just above the sea at about 300 feet, align the aircraft with the target then a snappy turn round to see how far the bomb was from where it should have struck.

By the way I forgot to tell you the most important results of my going back to Navigation Flight, which should be that I should have my leave at least very near to the pre–supposed date. At any rate I hope so and it won't be my fault if that will not be so.

I do not know whether Gerald will still be home now, but I would like to ask him whether he knows anything, or has ever heard anything of a new British made aircraft called the Mosquito. I think that we will be hearing much of them sometime in the summer. They are replacing Blenheims which I believe are becoming obsolete in England though they are still first line aircraft in the Middle and Far East. Anyway I have heard quite a lot about this Mosquito which is revolutionary in many ways and rather in the nature of an experiment, as they rely on speed for safety and carry no guns (unless used for night fighters).

Have I ever told you of the blitzes that the I.O.M. gets very frequently from British Bombers? When they do come the air is simply resonant with a terrific buzz which seems to come from every direction. It is totally different from German blitzes, for they seem to get the whole thing over in about 1–2 hours, but when they are on I imagine they must be mighty unpleasant. These often take place when you hear that heavy raids have also been made on Germany, so there must be no lack of organisation or aircraft .

Did you know as well that they have ceased taking more recruits for pilots, as they now have such a big reserve in hand, and already in the schools of England and Canada? I suppose that as well they are relying on America. When you fly over any part of the British Isles nowadays it is amazing how many aircraft you see; they seem to be in all directions and I believe that in the East of England whole squadrons are seen in the space of minutes.

Looking back over this letter, it is all I see to do with flying or the Air Force. But what about you, how do you find life these days? I often feel sorry that you cannot see all the freshness of spring as I do with all the radiant daffodils and other flowers whose names I know not, and all the new verdure on tree and bush; and then the sea of course can never lose its appeal.

Has my allowance come through to you yet? I think it should have done by now. How are Lorna and Monica looking these days – it would be nice to think they will never have to hear another air raid siren again wouldn't it?

And now I think I had better conclude this letter in the normal way by sending you all my love and very best wishes from

Your Most Loving Son
Philip

---

1. Cotton skull cap

Sergeants' Mess
Jurby, I.O.M.
Wednesday 1st April 1942

My Dear Mother and Father,

Thank you very much for your last letter which arrived on Saturday after I had posted mine to you. I am hoping that my mistake about the date of my leave will not cause you much inconvenience and that you will be able to arrange it all accordingly.

Yes, it is a very good idea of Father Boland's for Monica's First Holy Communion – I wonder does Monica appreciate it? Well it is Easter Sunday in four days time but I don't think I will be able to attend many of the Holy Week Services which I like so much – what a difference from three years ago when I would already have been in retreat! However with the lighter nights I have been able to make some visits to the church in Ramsey – especially this week in connection with the week of prayer. Last Sunday evening when I was able to go to Benediction for the first time since I have been here, I was wondering what you would think of my walk there along the wild sand dunes in and out of patches of ragged shrubbery with the low thud and slap of the water as it lapped against the shore, while the evening sun sunk in splendid majesty and slowing tints.

Maundy Thursday

To think that here I am in my ordinary room writing you this letter tonight as I did last night when in the meantime I have been within twenty miles of home! For this morning I flew right bang over Kidderminster on my way down to a little place by the name of Burford (some few miles west of Oxford). It was most interesting seeing so many places from the air that only a few years ago I used to cycle through such as Droitwich, Stourport, Worcester etc. Visibility was pretty bad and I am afraid I discerned nothing of Birmingham, not even a stray balloon, though I was wondering whether I could see some of the industrial haze.

I am very pleased this week as I have a new fellow for my wireless operator who not only seems very efficient at his job but is also from Eire, and a Catholic. I think we should do jolly well together.

Well I am certainly looking forward to my coming leave and it will be a real treat to be home with you all again. But I imagine that the time between now and then will see some pretty hectic hours or days; somehow I have a feeling that Germany will almost rock the world with this coming spring. However if this should prove true we will all have to steady ourselves and 'be not dismayed' for it may be the last throw which if held, may well prove the last phase of the war. It's rather selfish I know, but one cannot help feeling pleased that England will not have to take alone the full fury of Germany this spring.

How do you like this new wholemeal bread? What we have here is quite acceptable, but I am not certain whether yours would be the same.

By the way I have not heard from Bernard yet, except for a letter he wrote while entrained for Halifax in Canada – that one arrived here last Monday I think, and he said something about his getting a commission as an Officer for regional control – but it was all uncertain.

Good Friday

I have just heard that tomorrow (our normal day off) I have to fly so I shall have to get this finished tonight. Tomorrow, I am taking two Officers on a Navigational trip over Scotland and North England, and in the afternoon I may be coming down over the Midlands again.

And for now I think I had better conclude until next week when I will try to write at greater length. In the meantime then I send you all my love and best wishes from

Your Most Affectionate Son
Philip

My Dear Mother and Father,

Before I go on to anything else in this letter I will have to get off my chest some very disappointing news, namely that you cannot rely on my leave coming as early as May 12th I am very sorry to have to tell you this because I know that you will have been looking forward to, and making preparations, for that date. However just as I was getting into my stride in Navigation Flight I find myself suddenly posted to gunnery flight which is in itself another keen disappointment to me, not to mention the fact that the entire leave rosta has been ruined as far as I am concerned. It looks as though I shall have to wait AT LEAST a month before I will be able to tell you anything more about it, but believe me I shall leave nothing unturned in my efforts to get it as quickly as possible after that time.

Meanwhile there is a war to be won so that I shall have to set to by doing my best in my limited capacity – it wouldn't do to enjoy one's duty too much, as I am afraid I might have done had I remained on navigation work.

You should have seen all I saw last Saturday morning as I was flying at 8000 feet over the highlands of Scotland – I was just skimming the tops of a terrific white blanket of a cloud and had the sun and blue sky all to myself; while there could be nothing more thrilling than riding over huge rock like masses of dazzling cloud, then as you come over the other side seeing a sheer abyss into which you felt you must certainly fall. Then on Sunday there was the contrast when in dull grey weather we flew from near Dublin at not much above sea level, waving to the little coasting ships as they rolled and battled their wearisome way through heavy seas and driving rain. But now just when I seem to have tasted the pleasures of this Navigational flying I have been taken off it – and to make the pill more bitter there is the trouble about leave which concerns me most.

I hope that you will not be too disappointed; perhaps Lorna can pray that if at least I cannot be home before that time, I may at any rate be at home for her birthday.

By the way you might be pleased to know that as regards those girls to whom Auntie Celestine referred me, as I intimated at the time, it has all come to nothing and I have heard no more about it.

I have put that allotment through the official channels now, but will send you £1.00 this week pending such time as it comes through to you.

Friday

I still feel a little glum over this leave business – if we could only get a few weekend passes it wouldn't be so bad would it? Today it has been a lovely day for once, and it has already had its effect on the trees and hedges which are beginning to shoot out their green leaves.

I expect that you are pleased to have Gerald at home for a time, and as the nights seem rather peaceful of late I don't suppose he will be displeased either. Yes, I have been over Ludlow but as I told you last week I have even been nearer still to Birmingham. When we went over Ludlow we were somewhat off track; we were supposed to be going direct to Hereford. I am hoping that on occasional Saturdays I shall still be able to do a few Navigational trips.

Last night I saw a very good film called *The Great Awakening*, which is a portrait of Schubert and his music. If you get a chance I would advise you see it as it interesting and is full of very enjoyable music.

So now I think I will conclude once more by sending you all my very best love and wishes, hoping that the time will not be too far away when I shall be home again.

From Your Loving Son
Philip

Sergeants' Mess
Jurby, I.O.M.
15th April 1942

My Dear Mother and Father,

Thanks for your letter which I received last Saturday. I am sorry to hear that Mother has not been so well of late, but I hope that she will soon be well again – I hope Mother that you are not overworking yourself (This seems a funny way of addressing you, first as 'she' and then as 'you', but between you both I don't know quite how to put it!)

The weather today has been wonderful again – and with these peaceful evenings I am afraid I look forward to my leave even more – which I imagine should not be too long delayed after the first week or two of May – certainly not if I can help it!

This gunnery work is quite a strenuous type of flying, and after two days of it my left hand is quite sore with the continuous opening and shutting of the throttle. You have to fly between 110 and 120 miles per hour or else the drogue which is towed by a Lysander will recede into the background miles out of range. This afternoon I have been helping in Bombing Flight as well, which I enjoy much more than gunnery. For this work you go up from 6000 – 9000 feet (weather and clouds permitting) and make your runs as best you can. I was very pleased on my effort for the pupil (who was an Officer) with me, who told me that they were the best results he had obtained – for which I think the pilot is entitled to some self-congratulation. On Saturday I am down for two Navigation trips, so I am hoping that perhaps I might be coming down your way.

I am almost getting out of touch with the war news lately, I haven't heard it once these last seven days. I see that Russians expect Germany to be defeated this year. I hope that they won't prove to be like Hitler's promises last spring and summer. What do you think of the budget? That seems to be the most topical question! All the poor old people of Mainland seem to have been stunned, and I must admit that the doubling of the purchase tax will cause me to think not twice but three or four times before I buy my next record – if I do! I am hoping that records will somehow be exempt but I don't quite see why they should be. Whether you will like these snaps that I am enclosing I don't know but anyway there they are for what they are worth.

Friday

It is Friday evening again so I am settling down on the beach to finish this letter off as the evening is so wonderful. I am feeling quite weary with all the flying I have been doing these last few days, yet tomorrow, my day off (!) I am down for flying Navigation trips all day. I think that one of them is up to the Hebrides (where you said Michael is). I received your letter this evening; I am sorry you have been let down about my leave, but it cannot be helped and I suppose that these days we should be thankful that we have not much more to grumble about. Talking about A.T.C.[1] and Gerald, he may be interested to know that lately I have taken a few A.T.C. chaps up on our details – they all seem to think it great! I wonder would they if they had to do it every day!

By the way, I was wondering if you could get my grey flannel trousers pressed and cleaned without causing yourselves too much trouble. I don't want Mother to go washing and ironing them herself though, because if I thought that would happen I wouldn't have made the request, and whatever they might cost won't hurt me. But I would rather like to get out of uniform when I eventually do get home on leave. However don't let it put you to any trouble if it cannot easily be done these days.

And now I think it about time I finish this scribble and let you have this for Tuesday, so here's sending you all my very best love and wishes and hoping that Mother has made the most of (or is making the most of) her short respite from work.

From Your Most Affectionate Son
Philip

---

1. Air Traffic Control

My Dear Mother and Father,

I am snatching a few minutes to jot down on this small piece of paper which I've had to 'cadge' what I hope to be part of my letter for this week.

I have no definite 'gen' about my leave but somehow I sense that I should be home again sometime in May. I have swapped flights again and am back on navigation work though I am attached to a different flight. They have almost promised me leave in the middle of May, but I take nothing for granted these days and will not believe it until I have set foot in England (not in flying kit!) Last Saturday I spent a very pleasant afternoon in Cheltenham which I thought was one of the nicest little towns that I have come across. I had dinner and tea there and then flew back here in the evening, arriving in time for the 9 o'clock news. The moment is hardly opportune for me to ask to land at Elmdon yet, as one of the pilots stayed at his home town last week, because his battery (for starting the engines) had honked out – it was quite genuine as well, but it was naturally frowned upon by various authorities the next day when they were one aircraft short.

The weather has been excessively bumpy for flying lately and several of the observers have been sick – and for one brief moment the other day I too felt mighty queer around the region of my tummy but it soon wore off. As a pilot you always seem to have your attention so fixed on the flying that you don't have time to feel sick – and I have never heard of one yet who has been. In this windy and gusty weather it is most unpleasant taking off and landing and these last two days it seems that you almost have to fight your way in to land – there has been a 50 m.p.h. gale on!

What do you think of Hitler's speech the other day? I'm jolly glad that Mr. Churchill doesn't make speeches like that to us or I'm afraid even the stubborn English people would begin to wonder. Our raids seem to be extremely successful but I'm glad I'm not a night bomber pilot for I would rather not see a burning town below me and know that I had helped to make someone homeless. I suppose that York and Canterbury and Salisbury and Lincoln and such other places will come in for German bombing now. By the way, in the blitz on Bath (one of my pals was there on leave) all the German raiders flew over at only two or three hundred feet and made a terrific noise all night. He said that they were often quite visible, and that it is much more frightening. Anyway you have your balloon barrage and I hope you will have no more bother. If you ask me, I think there is a touch of desperation about this latest policy which is a very good sign. However I won't attempt to do any more forecasting, for this war seems to take the most unexpected turns whether the news is good or bad.

I haven't had much time, but I have good news – my leave will be on May 15th (if it doesn't get cancelled again) so it isn't so bad is it?[1] I have received your letter and thanks for the phone numbers which I hope to be able to use sometime.

This month I have got over 72 hours of flying in and must have flown over 10,000 miles. I'm very much looking forward to a real day off this next Saturday (my first for a month), for this continuous flying as in the last fortnight makes one quite fatigued. The other day one of the pupils I had with me completely lost his bearings, we were supposed to be coming up North to Carlisle over the Lake District and he told me to alter course the wrong way with the result that after some time we had gone right beyond Carlisle and were somewhere amid the bleak Scottish hills – so you see a pilot can ill afford to go to sleep when such things as that happen. However it is not really hard once you have become familiar with the coast line, and in the present clear weather the lakes and river mouths provide excellent land marks. Next Sunday I believe we are going down to bomb the ranges at Abingdon aerodrome (in Oxfordshire) and the whole trip has to be done at only 200 feet above ground level. I believe it's for cooperation between Operational and Training commands in the event of an emergency.

Well at this point I think I will bid you farewell for the present hoping that you all remain well and happy and that Jerry will not pay any more visits, so here's sending you all my love and best wishes,

From Your Most Loving Son
Philip

P.S. Just my luck, D.R.O's out tonight state that I am posted to my former NAV flight. Still I am always told 'Be not dismayed' by one of my pals when in a tight corner in chess, so I had better apply this same maxim here – I shall still endeavour to be home in May.

All love, Philip

---

1. In the margin there is a pencilled note to the effect that leave has again been cancelled

My dear Mother and Father,

I don't know what you must have thought of my last letter which must have seemed strangely contradictory on the subject of leave. However I have not wasted much time in this flight and I think I should be coming home somewhere around Whit Monday, Tuesday or at least some time that week, and I hope to see you all very well and in good spirits.

Twice on Monday I was over the edges of Birmingham both in the morning and the afternoon, and strangely enough I was also returning from Abingdon via Leominster, which took me slap bang over Ludlow[1] on both occasions, and yesterday I did even better for I was definitely over the west side of Birmingham, Kings Norton I should say, and up over Smethwick. The visibility was the best I have ever known it in England with the result that from my point of vantage 7000 feet up. I had quite a good view of this side of the city, but I couldn't make out anything definite where Handsworth should have been, and I didn't succumb to a surging temptation to come down much lower for a more detailed reconnaissance – but it was very painful to have to continue my way without so much as a wing waggle to give you.

Half an hour later brought me almost over Liverpool of which I had my best view yet – all the balloons were fully up her as well; some half hour after that saw me losing height over the small and tranquil town of Ramsey, and so to Jurby.

Friday

I received your letter tonight just after I had come back from a 600 mile trip, so that it was very welcome to my rather tired spirits. Yes, I do seem to have been a trifle unlucky as regards my leave, and I think it is a jolly good job I had some at Christmas, or else I would have had none since October. There is one chap with me in that position so I am not the worst. Still as I say I hope to be home this May, and perhaps for Lorna's birthday.

I hear Mr. Churchill is speaking to us again this Saturday, so I hope that things will soon begin to go forward. It is inspiring that up to the moment there has been hardly a move from Hitler; he is later this year than ever before which I hope is a good sign for us. I don't think that all is quite well beneath the surface in Germany, and I rather fancy that there must be some rifts widening in their High Command on vital military decisions. They certainly seem to be losing their heads when they definitely set out to destroy our Cathedrals and other places of historical interest.

Things are also being said on their radio which would never have been said on the B.B.C. in our darkest hours of agony.

This postcard which I enclose is a photograph of where I am billeted. It hardly gives you an idea how nice the surroundings really are, but you can see that it is a good place. The photo must have been taken from the edge of the sea–shore.

Well now I shall have to finish once more sending you all my best wishes and love, and hoping that this letter will find you in the very best of health and spirits.

From Your Most Affectionate Son
Philip

---

1. This is where brother, Gerald, was evacuated

Sergeants' Mess
Jurby, I.O.M.
11th May 1942

My Dear Mother and Father,

Today it is Monday, but I am Duty pilot and the weather is none too good which gives me some respite and a little leisure of which I hope to make some use.

I suppose that you heard Mr.Churchill's speech last night, and that you thought it very optimistic in tone. If the German people hear anything of it, it is to be hoped that they notice that Churchill could salute the British people, whereas Hitler was able only to offer his new threats. Otherwise I find it hard to catch on to his glee over the bombing of German cities, though at the same time if any people deserve it the Germans must certainly take the first place; and after all, I think that it is perhaps the quickest way in the end, and we do not seem to be doing it out of feelings of revenge, but only in so far as it will dislocate German industry, which we seem to be doing with very great success.

I am afraid that I very much dislike bombing, except regards strictly military targets as battleships and aerodromes, and I certainly find it very difficult to glean any joy from what must involve countless human tragedies. It seems as though it is the terrible price that nations and the world as a whole are paying for their waywardness and evils; let's hope that at least people will learn the obvious lesson that their selfishness and the exclusive pursuit of happiness, at any cost, is not even the best way of making this life a profitable venture. Fortunately there do seem to be signs that people as a whole are beginning to realise it.

Friday

After all I didn't seem to write so much in my time, though I do admit that my time wasn't so free as I thought while I was also Aerodrome Control Pilot during the night.

I hope to be coming home (this time I only say 'I hope!') on Wednesday 27th May. If I have to get the boat it will not be until late in the evening, whereas if I am fortunate enough to get a flip over I should be a little earlier.

I received your letter tonight and was sorry to hear that Leslie is so soon on the job and I will remember to pray for him all the more; it must be very worrying for his mother as also for Mary. I have never seen a Lancaster and in fact don't know much about them except that they are glorified Manchesters.

I haven't done too much flying this week on account of my other duties and also the poor weather. On Sunday I was down again so near home and yet so far, but it was raining and the weather was very bad so that I was flying quite low (only about 1000 feet) but it was most interesting riding over the rolling countryside I have cycled through so often – and getting to places so quickly! Trains and motor cars are passed by with the greatest ease; one minute you can pass over Cannock Chase while in the next one or two you can be over Kidderminster or some such place – perhaps a good two hours or more cycling.

Yesterday I was also over Ireland in appalling weather – a leaden murky pall of smoke haze and fog; in fact I was very near the island on my return journey and missed it altogether, whereupon I realised that I was all alone in the inhospitable Irish sea, and so made for Scotland where I was fortunate enough to quickly come across an aerodrome, which I did not use however as I came back to Jurby on wireless bearings – the first time I have need to really use the wireless. Actually I still had 200 gallons of petrol with me so that I should have been O.K. On the other hand it is extremely useful to have the help of the wireless at such times.

The day before yesterday was an industrious one for me as I got down for business and darned five of my socks – and quite successfully as well, though I imagine it was at the cost of a severe headache! and also only after about two hours work. But at least I have some socks of which I needn't feel ashamed now, which is a great burden off my chest.

Well at this point I think I will conclude as I will otherwise have little time to get it posted, so here is sending you all my very best love and wishes and hoping you are in the best of health.

From Your Most Loving Son
Philip

It looks like Philip got his promised leave

Sergeants Mess
Jurby I.O.M.
Postmark dated 27th June 1942

My Dear Mother and Father,

Please excuse this pencil but I must have left my pen at home. I am hoping you are still quite well and happy. As you see I am back here once more quite safely and find it as attractive as ever during this nice spell of weather.

But I am afraid in other respects a bombshell awaited me on my return. For I have been taken off duties as Pilot and recommended for a Navigation course presumably as an observer. I should also have been recalled from leave but the authorities here refused to do so – in fact they have fought the whole issue and say that it is all ridiculous. Anyway I have been encouraged by all those above who have anything to do with me to fight against it. My Flight Commander and the O.C. Flying have put at my disposal good reports for me to use as best I can, and they all seem intent to help me.

Anyway I am having an interview with the Air Vice Marshall this coming Monday and I am hoping to veto that order. I think it will all be to my advantage because I have been told that I shall continue flying at this type of place for the rest of the war, if I do wangle it.

It is all most mystifying, and I cannot help thinking that I am singled out for some most peculiar trials and tests of perseverance. However everything happens for the best, and there is nothing that I can ever regret, while I have a clean log book to show.

Anyway I shall tell you more next week, and I shall not let this episode worry me, and I am already much better after the first shock of hearing the news.

Let's hope and pray that the war will not last long, and that my leave will soon be unlimited. Meanwhile I hope the children are OK and I will remember to pray for Gerald during his exams.

Did you have a raid the other night? The Germans claimed so didn't they?

Well for the present, here's sending you all my love and best wishes,

From Your Most Affectionate Son
Philip

Sergeants Mess
Jurby, I.O.M.
Thursday, 2nd July 1942

My Dear Mother and Father,

It is now about time I thought of next week's letter so here I am making another start.

I hope that you will like all these snaps which have all come out quite well – I think Monica looks very well in them all. There does not seem to be much chance of any more films so those may have to do for the rest of the war. If you want any reprints just tell me and I'll have them done, or if you like I can send you the negatives, and then you can decide more to your liking.

As you can see I am still here, but I'm expecting to be moved any time now as I am going to a place called Carke (or Karke!) on the Cumberland coast for an A.O.S. night flying course on Ansons. Several of our pilots are there at the moment. It will only be an attachment for about a month, after which I shall return to Jurby. I saw the A.O.C.[1] of my group last Monday who quite conveniently happened to come up to this station. At least I have managed to hold off the evil day, and I have already this week done a little flying, and I am hoping now that they will not try interfering with me anymore, though I am learning now to be very cautious in my hopes and fears.

Well I certainly enjoyed my leave very much and I only hope that it didn't directly or indirectly cause you too much trouble, and that you were well able to put up with the general nuisance I must be in many ways. That might easily go for Monica as well!

One thing, wars may come, wars may go, and in all the changing circumstances they bring, and with all the travelling far and wide attendant on servant life, it is very consoling to go home and find it just the same as it always was; and so long as we win this war nothing can change that.

Well things are going very badly out in the Middle East, and if I judge correctly there is a crisis of battle at the moment which I hope and pray we shall survive. I wonder whether Hitler would have been in this position but for Japan – somehow I do not think so. Sometime ago the largest ever convoy reached India – but for the Japs it would have reached the Middle East. The Australians would still have been there, not to mention many of our own troops and perhaps General Sir Archibald Wavell, and much larger units of the Fleet. Yes the more I think of it, the more I cannot help feeling that Hitler owes a tremendous amount to the Japs.

Today it also looks as though Sevastopol may have fallen – well even if it has, they have certainly done a magnificent job of work of decisive value. Already I imagine it must have held up plans for an attack on the Caucasus for some months.

The weather has been lovely round here of late, and were it not for the fact that there is quite a breeze about I should have done quite a bit of bathing in the sea. By the way since I went on leave they moved us all out of our last billets and we are now in huts on the Camp – and not very nice ones at that; the day before yesterday one of our chaps shook over fifty earwigs off his tunic and though I cannot claim anything like such a number yet, they are quite a nuisance.

Last Monday (Feast of St. Peter and St. Paul) I was the only one on the camp privileged to hear Mass. There was nothing up about it on D.R.Os, so I asked our new chaplain about it, and he invited me to his room where he said he would say Mass. He is from Tasmania, where it is not a Holiday of Obligation.

And now I think I will conclude wishing you all my very best love and wishes,

From Your Most Loving Son
Philip

---

1. Air Officer Commanding

Sergeants Mess
Jurby, I.O.M.
Wednesday, 8th July 1942

My Dear Mother and Father,

Thanks very much for your last letter which arrived here on Monday – I am glad to hear all is well and that Jerry badly missed the mark that night.

I am afraid that my success of which I told you in the last letter was very short lived, for that Air Vice Marshall for some reason best known to himself, has changed his mind and I am now just where I was before – except that my patience is trying hard to become exhausted. Anyway in telling me that news the Squadron Leader, O.C. Flying urged me to go even one higher even than him, and to put in an application to see the Air Officer Commanding Flying Training Command – who is an Air Marshall on the Air Council. He gave me this advice strictly unofficially because as a superior officer he is not supposed to give such advice. Anyway as he urged me to, and since I have gone so far, and come so near, I thought that at least I have nothing to lose and all to gain and so yesterday my application was forwarded to the right channels. I cannot say that I am very optimistic or even that my enthusiasm is as great as it was – however it is playing for time and will be an interesting experiment.

It is all most peculiar for I have never heard of anybody else having the same trouble as I am having now and though I want to avoid trying to give the impression that there are no faults with me, yet at the same time I do think this action has been exceedingly drastic – and I cannot get any definite and concrete reason for it, in fact I don't think there is one that they could give. It makes it all the harder to bear when this station is now in the process of turning over on to Ansons which are relatively easy to fly as compared with Blenheims.

As for this Navigator's course, I am afraid I am not too very keen, and if there is a chance at all I shall try to get some other job. For one thing, it was hard for me to go against your wishes in the first place in deciding to undertake flying duties – and when I got my wings that was one sorrow that I had, namely that it would bring fresh anxiety and worry to you at home; there is also the fact that one feels one is more or less dead weight to the Air Force when one is continually training.

Yes, I might think to myself that I am singularly unlucky, but then I have only to look around the world where such things as Death and Terror and Starvation stalk about in search of prey – and then one is ashamed to even attach any importance to the minor setbacks that confront one. And if we in England have so great a desire for peace, how must the tortured peoples of Greece and Poland and all these other countries which have <u>real</u> cause to be impatient, how must they long for this day?

This summer, as I really expected, is showing a grave crisis in the turn of military events. For the moment our forces in the Middle East have rallied in a splendid way – now it is the turn of Russia to face a great crisis. One thing, Russian generals will not have to look over their shoulders because of Kremlin debates with all their nasty remarks, as our generals do with parliament.

By the way, they are making use of me for Duty Pilot most of these days and that is where this letter is being written now so it all gets put down in fits and starts. It is quite a bit of a job these days however for it is a twenty four hour duty and you are Aerodrome Control Pilot during the night as well – you have one day on and one day off.

The other evening as I went into the Y.M.C.A. at Ramsey, the girl behind the counter, no doubt surprised to see me after so long an absence, told me she had been making enquiries about me, and I was apparently referred to as that 'small Catholic'. Anyway I was rather pleased if that was my most obvious characteristic. And yesterday I was talking to this chap here who reckons he is a materialist or some such thing – and at the end of our conversation he told me that he had discussed the same topics over with certain other 'ministers', none of whom could present such sound reasons against his points as I, which again makes one feel very thankful that one's own principles are founded on such sound and reasonable arguments, as everything is in the Catholic church.

I am afraid that this summer is in no way comparable to that which I enjoyed this time last year in Canada. Tonight I drunk two cups of tea, and could have easily made do with one, but I can guarantee that on the evening last year that I would have gulped down perhaps five or six cups and not to mention all the other cold drinks, water and oranges which I took daily.

Friday 10th July

Well I don't know there is very much I can add now to what I have already said, except that I would like to wish that Dorothy DID have a very happy birthday, with all the attendant returns and etc. – as I'm sure she must have done with so noble and distinguished guest to tea!

And for now I think I will conclude sending you all my very best love and wishes

From Your Most Loving Son
Philip

P.S. Is there any interesting news of Leslie lately?

P.P.S. <u>Friday</u>

My Dear Mother and Father,

Just before I post this letter I do want to acknowledge your letter which came here tonight, and to thank you for it.

Well as you see total disaster has not taken over me yet. One thing, this little crisis has shown me how many good friends I have on this station which I would have never realised before. For some reason or other which I do not know I seem to be thought very well of. I'm afraid I should be very sorry to have to leave this station now especially as I find that Blackband (in my form at St. Philip's and with whom I often used to come home) is also here as a Sgt. Pilot and in my flight. Since he will be one of the few Catholic Pilots on this station and one whom I know so well, it would be a pity not to see him again. He was quite a pal of Bernard Coakley as well.

Thanks for your prayers which of course I always highly appreciate, and will return. The news from the Middle East is this afternoon a LITTLE BIT better which is a good thing.

So for now here is sending you all my very best love

From Your Most Loving Son
Philip

Sergeants Mess
Jurby, I.O.M.
Friday, 17th July 1942

My Dear Mother and Father,

Today there are a number of 'big names' on the camp including the Under Secretary of State for Air – it all seems to centre round the opening of a big cinema on the camp, built entirely by our own personnel. Still one wonders how this will help us to win the war.

As for me, I am still waiting here, at time casting envious eyes on the many aircraft landing and taking off. It is a funny thing that I never realised how much I had grown to like flying until now. However I am still a little hopeful, and meantime I am being left very well occupied in the Duty Pilot's office. I am wondering whether the reason why that last A.O.C. changed his mind was because that group of which he was in charge split up and we are now in the other half. Consequently I have now to see our new A.O.C. before I go before the Air Officer Commanding Training Command.

I received Auntie Kathleen's last letter this week which I shall include for you if I get chance to go up and get it in time.

I heard Tchaikovsky's 'Pathetique' Symphony early this week on one of the 'Prom' concerts and enjoyed it very much.

I suppose Gerald's exams are now almost over; I hope that he has done well. Congratulations to Kitty too, on her very great achievement – she was the only one to get it wasn't she?[1] I don't seem to have much to say this week, and at present I think I am rather tired, with the result that my thoughts and ideas are a little slow in coming, so if you don't mind I will bring this to an early conclusion and endeavour to do much better next week. So here is all my love and very best wishes,

From Your Most Loving Son
Philip

---

1. This was the Eliza Avins three year scholarship of £150 per year – extended for a fourth year – for piano and organ. Kathleen had only played the organ for six months, her audition included Bach Trio on organ and Mozart C minor Piano Fantasy and Sonata. She showed exceptional promise. She went on to become a concert pianist, and organ recitalist, often broadcasting on the BBC.

Sgt. P.J.Hermolle
Sunday night (undated)

My Dear Mother and Father,

I don't know whether you will believe me when I have to tell you once more that at the eleventh hour my leave has to be cancelled again – however that is what I learnt about two hours ago, and since then I have packed my kit bags ready to fly over to the mainland tomorrow to some other station where I have just been posted. As yet I do not even know where, as it has all been done in such a hurry; however I believe it is somewhere in the South and nearer home, so perhaps there will be a chance of some weekends at home!

Anyway don't worry! I shall write to you as early as possible with all the 'gen' which I am as anxious to know as you.

I'm sorry I hadn't written before this week, but I have been flying late, and also I have landed at Wrexham aerodrome which threw me out somewhat, (I got in some very bad weather while on a trip down south).

I'm ever so sorry about this, but there you are, it cannot be helped and perhaps in the long run it will all be for the best. I'm losing some jolly good pals and leaving a very good station.

Well for the present I will bid you farewell, hoping to see you soon all well and happy and full of good cheer, so here's wishing you every best wish,

From Your Most Affectionate Son,
Philip

P.S. Latest news shows I am still only attached – still hope to see you soon

CHAPTER TEN

BLACKPOOL THEN BRIGHTON

'I cannot grumble, because outside the camp life, I have been having a feast of good music such as I have never known before'.
(24 September 1942)

Catholic Club
Blackpool
Wednesday, 22nd July 1942

My Dear Mother,

This letter is primarily to wish you a very happy birthday and to convey to you all my very best love and wishes for this great day.

Unfortunately I am now on my way to Brighton so this may not reach you on the exact day – however I am getting it written while I have a chance. This morning I was held up at Fleetwood on account on something that seemed to be puzzling Jurby – anyway the net result was that I missed the train and was told to get a billet in Blackpool. However that order (the R.T.O. tells me down here) has also been cancelled and tonight I am to proceed on my way.

You will guess by all this that all my efforts have been fruitless, and what the future holds in store for me I don't know. I cannot deny that it has been a bitter disappointment, yet on the other hand, it helps to bring home to me that I am still only the same Philip Hermolle as I have always been, neither more nor, I hope, less.

I will try and write soon from Brighton and let you know how things go, and give you my address – I shouldn't expect (although I don't know) that I will be there long.

And now before I conclude I want to re–iterate all my very best wishes for the 25th and above all don't work too hard! So here is sending you all my very best love and wishes,

From Your Most Loving Son
Philip

A.C.D.W.
R.A.F.
Brighton
24th July 1942

My Dear Mother and Father,

As you can see I have arrived ok. I was very fascinated with what little I saw of London as I was taken between Euston and Victoria stations in a taxi cab, and I recognised Buckingham Palace as we drove right up to it.

Things don't look too promising here, but I see that <u>all</u> the chaps who were at Hullavington[1] with me are here and have been for some month or five weeks, though two of them were even there, assessed as 'above average' while one poor chap has done 500 hours on Bothas, and only yesterday heard he had been made ACii Aircraft hand. He is on leave at the moment. Two others have just written direct to Air Ministry (which they are not supposed to do) so you see I am not the only pebble on the beach by a long way.

Bombs have wrecked another part of the pier about half a mile away the night before last; we had an alert early this morning.

This afternoon the dentist is going to start hacking with one of my teeth, but I hope that will not be a terribly long job.

Well please excuse writing (as I am doing it on my knee) and don't forget to have a right good time tomorrow, so once again wishing Mother a very happy birthday, I'll send you all my love and best wishes,

From Your Most Loving Son
Philip

---

1. Wilts. – no known letters sent from

My Dear Mother and Father,

Thanks very much for various letters which I have received this week which include those from Jurby.

I have no more news whatsoever to give you yet – I believe it takes a week or so for documents to arrive at the different stations, and that is probably the reason. The weather is lovely here today, and most people seem gay and in festive mood with the holiday season in full swing. However even Brighton seems a little lonely when there is no–one you really know. Actually I have a job on one of the allotments just outside the town which the R.A.F. is helping to look after; it is not a bad way of passing the time at all.

Last Saturday I saw *As You Like It* acted in the open air and with the help of the Royal Pavillion Orchestra. I enjoyed it very much. Otherwise there is not much scope for music down here at all.

Well, the news doesn't exactly get much better does it. However I suppose it was to be expected that Germany would produce almost wonders this summer – but I only hope that the 'wonder' won't go too far and knock Russia out, or even gain the full control of the Caucasus. Unless the cost of such gains was absolutely crippling, it would increase our difficulties no end, and I suppose we would then have more bombing to contend with.

Talking of bombing how did you get on last Friday night? I hope all is well. I was pretty abruptly brought out of a semi–coma the other morning when a stick of four bombs dropped in the neighbourhood – fortunately I believe they were all on the beach. That would be the same time that you had an early morning alert.

You occasionally see large flights of Spitfires round here – I am not quite certain whether they are off to France or not.

Well, at the moment I cannot think of much more to say, except to thank you for your prayers and sympathy, and to wish you all the very best of everything and send you my love,

From Your Most Affectionate Son
Philip

1st August 1942?
Saturday Tea–time

My Dear Mother and Father,

I am at present having tea in the very comfortable C.W.L.[1] canteen next door to the Cathedral (Westminster). In fact I'm here on a 48 hour pass – there is a travelling ban on the Forces for the present few days so I wouldn't have been able to get home and I have taken advantage of a bus up to London. I was able to go to Mass and Communion this morning in the Cathedral and will go again tomorrow. I have had a busy day today and find London extremely interesting, but I am no doubt missing a great deal.

Tonight I am going to a 'Prom' which should be good. Will this ration card be any good to you? It is not for me.

I shall try and get home when I can but won't make any promises.

Meantime here is wishing you all my love and best wishes,

From Your Most Loving Son
Philip

---

1. Catholic Women's League

A.C.D.W.
R.A.F.
Brighton
Thursday, 6th August 1942

My Dear Mother and Father,

Thanks very much for your last letter which I received this morning – I remember now that in my last letter to you I did not even mention to you the air raids on Birmingham; that fact occurred to me immediately after I had posted it. I am sorry that it slipped my memory to that extent, but I can assure you that it had by no means gone unnoticed by me. I have heard of none since, so I trust you are as well as can be.

I was rather surprised at your saying 'don't take is so hard', since I had been thinking to myself that I had not given way to my feelings so very much – especially in my correspondence. However you seem to have gathered somehow or other the depth of my disappointment; that is a strange thing about me, because small and apparently ordinary things can give one intense pleasure, and in the same way they are capable of having the reverse effect. On the other hand I simply don't know how I could have taken it any easier – had there been a way I would certainly have tried it. The point is that nearly eighteen months in the Air Force I have been waiting and preparing to do a job of work which would actually help the war effort – and then after all that hard work and effort, with a crash I find that far from helping, I am more of a hindrance to it all. I think that is my greatest disappointment of all, and I think you would have to agree that it is one to which one could hardly resign. There are several other aspects as well, not the least of which is the blow to my natural pride, which I suppose is inevitable. And again although you comment to me only of the destruction wrought from the air, my mind flies to the innumerable pilots who are preventing it, such as night fighters, and all those who are cooperating with the Navy to bring in our very food.

Of course I had realised that Divine Providence has decreed otherwise, and I have tried without stint to enter into that spirit; I have in my prayers said that I accept it all, and whatever more is to come, but that has not ameliorated what I have had to go through one little bit. But lest you should worry even now, I can certainly tell you that I am not giving too much thought to it. When I see the Spitfires returning from France, and some of the Bostons crossing the sea, I have to admit that I become exceedingly envious, but then that again is very natural I suppose.

There is one consolation that I have, namely that I have not tried to tread 'the primrose path of dalliance' through this war; I would feel terribly ashamed if my only thought and idea had been to survive whilst others fought and died that I might reap the rewards and fruits. I can never say either that it was not fine fun while it lasted, and though in the crew rooms we would all often talk of 'dicing with death'(!) it was always an unfailing source of mirth!

Anyway the fact that I did not write during last week was precisely because I did not wish to pass on any of my worries, and there did not seem much else I could say. I am sorry it had the reverse effect.

I am trying to get home this weekend but I have strong doubts as to my ability to do so – I have already put in my application and I shall now have to see how things go.

By the way in London last weekend I heard the B.B.C. Symphony Orchestra under both Sir Henry Wood and Sir Adrian Boult. It was very good indeed (in the Royal Albert Hall). On Sunday I heard the London Symphony Orchestra and they played Tchaikovsky's *Fifth Symphony* (the last two movements of which I have at home). It was very good.

As I was wandering around in Westminster Abbey Sunday dinner time an American Corporal came up to me and asked me where 'Poets Corner' was. This made me terribly ashamed because not only could I not tell him, but I was not even aware that there was a 'Poets Corner'. He said he wanted to see Shakespeare's grave; I did not dare tell him that I did not know that he was buried there.

However I remember now I would have been quite O.K. as 'Bill' was buried in Stratford. It was all most interesting indeed. The choir in Westminster Cathedral was excellent, but it only consisted of about seven or eight men (some of whom had to take falsetto parts – if that is the right word!) I presume they sang Palestrina, for it was not the bare plain chant.

Yes London is a wonderful place; I see the *Dream of Gerontius* will be performed next November at the Albert Hall.

I shall post this letter tonight and perhaps I shall see you this weekend; but don't count too much on it. Meanwhile here is all my love and very best wishes,

From Your Most Loving Son
Philip

A.C.D.W.
Brighton
Thursday, 13th August 1942

My Dear Mother and Father,

Well I don't think there is much I can say at the moment, because things are only the same as usual, except that the Luftwaffe has been unnaturally busy this week. I arrived back to Brighton just in time for quite a sharp blitz, during which quite a bit of damage was done, though I haven't actually seen any.

I will be unable to come home this weekend, but I have put in for some leave due to start a week next Saturday. Whether I will get it or not I don't know, and if I don't I shall have a good try for a weekend again.

Did you enjoy that concert last Monday at the Town Hall? By the way what do you want for your birthday Mother? To buy records appears like an excuse to add to my own pleasure. Anyhow it would be a good thing if you tell me. Also as Mary will soon be twenty one I would be more than grateful for a hint from her.

For the present then I will now conclude sending you all my very best love and wishes and hoping I may see you all again soon.

From Your Most Loving Son
Philip

A.C.D.W.
R.A.F.
Brighton
Friday, 15th August 1942

My Dear Mother and Father,

This will be a different kind of letter to my usual one, for I have what I think will prove some surprising news for you. I have this week written to Mary Gough (sister of Jim, who is now in South Africa) with the idea of seeing her some time during my next leave, whenever it will be. When I tell you this, it will be bound to make you wonder a little on quite a number of things, and I suppose the fact that I find it rather hard to express myself and tell you of most of them is my fault. However with regards to Mary, there is but little that I can tell you save that I met her when she went up to Blackpool to spend a week with her brother, and that since that time on very few occasions I have written to her. From what I know of her she seems a very nice girl, and certainly she comes from an exemplary family. She is the youngest of six (or seven) and having the name of Mary should auger well shouldn't it?

Anyway I just thought I would like to take advantage of a leave to see her again and am just awaiting her reply.

You will notice that I write this on the Feast of the Assumption which seems to me very appropriate, because is telling you of such matters as this I cannot divorce them from their spiritual significance. Naturally I know that you will inevitably ask yourself, and would wish to ask me, 'And how does this affect your attitude to the Priesthood?' And for my part, I do not know what I would answer. I have given the whole matter very much time and thought, and it seems to me that if I go on as I am now, I shall end up similarly to Pat Brady (with all respect to him), but which to me seems neither here nor there. I desire to exercise caution in all that I do, but feel that if I do not cease to pray for help, everything will come much clearer by my following my inclinations where quite permissible.

I hope that what I tell you will not disappoint your ambitions for me too much, because I know that you see things differently to me. I have long asked the help of Our Lady on this question, and I do not feel unsatisfied. I am naturally anxious to know your reactions to this, and I hope that you will never find your son too wayward, nor seem too certain of himself to ignore any advice you may have to offer.

You will see that I have just taken advantage of this rather small occasion to try and tell you one or two things which maybe I should have said before. It is difficult for me to explain all I mean, but I'm sure you will understand most of it. There is no other definite news, so I will conclude in the usual way by sending you one and all my very best love and wishes,

From Your Most Loving Son
Philip

A.C.D.W.
R.A.F.
Brighton
Wednesday, 19th August 1942

My Dear Mother and Father,

Thanks for your letter which I received this morning. And what a morning this morning is! I suppose you have already heard the news! What a thrilling spectacle we have continuously above our heads. I have never seen anything like it before. Formations roaring out to sea, and more passing them homeward bound – yet I suppose that I can see only a fraction of our actual fighters being used. The drone has been almost continuous since dawn.

Today I only have a limited amount of news – which is not entirely good. For the first place I cannot have my seven days leave; I am only allowed four days (if I can fit them in before September 1st). But in the meantime I am one of about nine chaps who have to have an interview with a 'Pre–Selection Board' presumably about my future in the R.A.F. Until I have seen these gentlemen I cannot even get away for a weekend, so I shall have to hang on for a bit.

And now to answer your various queries as far as I can. When I spoke about it being 'surprising news' I was referring to my own action and thoughts of which I was going to tell you. Actually I was far from assuming her assent, but I told you notwithstanding, because I did not see why you should not know that I had asked her, even if without success. As a matter of fact I have her reply in which she thinks it a grand idea.

I thought you knew all about Jim – they don't live in Birmingham, but in Bloxwich which is just outside Walsall. I suppose it is not too handy to Birmingham, but on the other hand it would be no more inconvenient (or very little) than Kings Heath would be. Anyway up to now there is no question of my spending part of my leave away from home. As the present arrangement has been agreed I don't suppose you will mind my taking perhaps one evening off – I had never thought of anything more than that.

Perhaps in my last letter I seemed a little bit too serious about it all but I think that was because I wanted to take advantage of it to explain to you how I felt in regard to the Priesthood.

At any rate I don't know enough about Mary Gough to know whether you would approve of her; I only know her rather superficially and my first impressions may not be what I thought. What I do know of her promises quite well, and if she is anything like her two brothers whom I know, she will be very good; but in any case it is some time since I have seen her, and it was mainly from a feeling of companionship that I asked her. I am uncertain of her age but I think she is nineteen.

I suppose I must be a 'Funny Mick' and hard to understand; however nothing will give me very such pleasure if it does not also please you, so in the long run I hope I won't even persist on a path which is not also agreeable to you.

I have to break off from this line of thought now because I have just witnessed (from a grandstand view) a German aerial attack on some assembling shipping just off the coast. The barrage our boats put up was simply terrific! I think all the bombs missed their mark – but they certainly make a noise don't they! And one of the Jerries has crashed into the sea. I bet they give us a good night tonight!

Last Monday I saw Eileen Joyce with the Western Philharmonic Orchestra and a very good programme too – including Schubert's *Unfinished Symphony*.

Well at this point I think I will finish in the usual way by sending you all my love and very best wishes,

From Your Most Loving Son
Philip

P.S. Have you seen that in the papers about all weekends being cancelled altogether? I hope they won't do that. Anyway I will try and come home as soon as I get a chance and hope to see you soon.

Following home leave

A.C.D.W.
R.A.F.
Brighton
Thursday, 3rd September 1942

My Dear Mother and Father,

I wonder where I will be when I get my next leave and even this weekend what will I be doing, and who will be my new pals? It is a peculiar life isn't it when you know so little about the next item on the programme. However here I am back for the moment with still nothing to report to you, save that this morning for the first time in my R.A.F. career I found myself on a charge for absenting myself from a guard duty last night – it was a great surprise to me because the whole business arose from a mistake of the Sgt. in charge of us, who told me to report to the wrong place. Anyway the case was dismissed because I had a witness to prove that I turned up at the other place, and they could not prove anything particular on either side.

This week in Brighton the Carl Rosa Opera Company are here. I have just missed seeing "*La Boheme*" and "*Il Trovatore*" but saw the "*Barber of Seville*" last night, and I hope to see "*Madame Butterfly*" on Friday and perhaps "*Faust*" on Saturday – for I don't think for a minute that my weekend leave will come through.

I am sorry that in spite of my leave I didn't make the birthday purchases I should have done. If you are going into town I wonder whether you could get that book (cooking didn't you say?) for Mary; and if you buy for yourself whatever you would fancy I will make that my birthday present to you and 'on my return will repay thee'.

Well today is a day of prayer and you might be interested to know that all the airmen have gone off to some place of worship which seems quite a good thing doesn't it? First thing of course I went to Holy Communion – I don't think I told you that one advantage of Brighton is that I can go every day. However this morning the Church was quite full.

You seem to be very anxious that I do not go again as air crew and I can hardly blame you. But I think that if it weren't for you I would be ready to go in the capacity as air–bomber. However I shall try and get out of it as it is, but if I should have the chance again to fly as pilot whether in the R.A.F. or the A.T.A[1] I think I should like to do that. Actually if I could but get out of the R.A.F., I could soon get in the A.T.A. where there is some very interesting work and a shortage of pilots. I suppose that you will find some relief in knowing that the chances of the above are very slender, and I don't really expect to have any luck that way, while I do not want to create too much of a disturbance about the business because I feel I might be only tempting fate to do its worst with me when providence has so far been rather kind. If I am meant to fly I am rather apt to think that the chance will come my way without my going too far out of my way to look for it.

There is one part of my having been a pilot which I can never regret and that is that I have been given the chance of buying so many of those records I now have at home – they even echo through my mind when I am away from home and at this moment that 'Nimrod' variation of Elgar no. 9 rings as plainly in my ears as when the record is on (or it seems to).

In the train down here by the way I did get a seat at Rugby, so I wasn't standing all the way.

I don't think I told you on Tuesday that in the course of that morning when I popped into St. Chad's Cathedral I met Canon Manion![2] He told me that he was 'delighted to see me' which rather made me think of all the occasions he certainly appeared to abhor my presence! Especially in his Greek classes! He is a peculiar character and even now I don't quite know how to sum him up.

Well I will now conclude by sending you all my very best love and wishes and the best of health,

From Your Most Loving Son
Philip

---

1. Air Transport Auxiliary
2. Headmaster of Cotton, retired in 1941

My Dear Mother and Father,

Thanks very much for your last letter which I received yesterday. Yet another week has gone, and still nothing has happened. Had I written to you about last Tuesday I would have informed you that the Selection Board was about to commence and that I might be moved from here any day. However we have been informed that those of us who came here before August 15th are not going to see the board, but are being dealt with directly from Air Ministry. This puts me at a great disadvantage I imagine, but I am becoming rather accustomed to these little things now; the board seems to be doing some good work for one or two as well, but one of the chaps in my room off flying for medical reasons is reduced to AC! With prospects for a commission a little later.

This week is Brighton's musical festival week and should be a very wonderful one judging by the artists and conductors who will be down here and I am hoping to hear it all if I can.

In many respects I am just beginning to feel I could settle down in Brighton – a sure sign I shall not be left for long – since I am just getting to know some interesting Catholics around here who have a large number of records! The Priest here is very good too, and has allowed me the free use of his library, of which I have already made use by borrowing one of Cardinal Newman's books called *Difficulties of Anglicans*.

In other ways though Brighton is not too good because it is much too expensive, and there are no amenities at our disposal on the camp to occupy one, as would be found in a decent Sergeants' Mess. Even when I write letters I have nothing to rest the pad on – which you will agree doesn't improve my writing does it!

I enjoyed those operas last week, but it is hardly fair on the artists when you have heard such good records of Gigli[1] beforehand. I am thinking of that one from Faust especially.

The Russians are doing well aren't they? I hope that they can hold on for some time longer, because it will be hard for the Germans to keep up this pressure too long.

Well I will conclude now by sending you all my very best love and wishes,

From Your Most Loving Son
Philip

---

1. Beniamino Gigli, Italian tenor

My Dear Mother and Father,

Before I know where I am, another week will have gone round, and unless something happens, with no more news, and meantime this station of Brighton does not seem to improve one little bit. They keep on taunting us with the threat that they will ship us if we don't do this or forget to do that – just as though we are not going to get stripped if we are not good! However I am getting used to most things these days and there must be many who feel worse than me. I noticed that a flight sergeant with a D.F.M.[1] and a bar arrived here this morning; I hope that he will not be treated so ungratefully. Just lately I have been finding out some interesting details about things concerning the likes of us and if there is one thing that seems absolutely obvious, it is that there is a great superfluity of pilots. At one unit there was a notice in the crew rooms warning pilots that 'Air Crew are no longer indispensable'!

In other ways though I cannot complain, because I am really happy enough trying to live in the present and not thinking of tomorrow.

Last Sunday at Benediction, imagine my surprise and joy when I saw a tall sailor walk in whom I straight–away recognised as Bill Murtagh[2] who was in my form most of the way through Cotton and was in the Rugger XV with me! I could hardly wait for the service to finish and I think that we both had one of our best evenings recalling old times in the light of the present. He is not stationed too conveniently to see me every night, but I hope to see him again tonight; in any case his base is of rather a secret nature and I had better not divulge too much in a letter. He is, by the way, engaged to Joan Garvey[3]. It happens also that he too has had a disappointment, not unsimilar to mine, except that his was in just missing a commission.

It certainly is most refreshing to meet one of your old school pals in these circumstances because it seems that you pick up a certain kind of spirit or sense of humour when at school which no one else seems to have or understand; then there is the other reason in that he is a Catholic which makes no end of difference doesn't it? He had to finish training for the Priesthood on account of a breakdown of his health – but then Mary certainly seems to have put that right.

Up to now we haven't even had an alert for at least a week, which rather makes me wonder what is brewing. Such quiet periods always appear ominous to me. Up to the present Stalingrad still holds, but one wonders whether it will continue so to do. The fighting there must be simply terrific, and I hope that most of the civilian population have been evacuated. The Germans must be paying dearly for all they do, and I cannot help feeling that the cost may already have proved too much for them. But I won't say much more in that strain now because if the English people have learnt one thing in this war, it is to guard against wishful thinking.

So far the Brighton Musical Festival has proved highly delightful. Last night Stanford Robinson (of the B.B.C.) conducted and I liked him very much. Eda Kersey played Mendelssohn's Violin concerto, and Schubert's 'Unfinished' was also played. Tonight there is Beethoven's 7th Symphony (which vies with his 5th) and Eileen Joyce playing a concerto by Saint Saens.

I have just heard of one of the pilots who was on my course being shot down in that Cologne raid in a Manchester. He and all his crew have just escaped by way of Spain and Gibraltar and are now back in England. Good work, isn't it?

Friday

Still no 'gen'. Thanks for that letter you forwarded on to me and which I received this morning. I also had one from Les this morning. He seems a little tired, but otherwise happy. I can quite understand what he must feel. I should imagine there are few things more tiring than long hours of flight, and especially in those conditions. I certainly hope that he will enjoy his leave and find it a source from which to gather fresh powers and stamina.

Before I conclude I will just apologise for my writing, which I can almost hear you say, seems to get worse and worse. I hope you can read most of it – I would be able to do a little better if I had a table or some such thing on which to write, but as it is, I have to sit on the side of my bed (the springs of which do not form an ideal seat!) and then try my best with my knee for a support. Anyway I will now take my leave of you sending you all my love and very best wishes,

From Your Most Loving Son
Philip

---

1. Distinguished Flying Medal
2. A relative
3. From the Garvey family in St. Francis' Parish

The following letter encloses a programme for the Royal Albert Hall dated
20th September 1942 for a concert given by Myra Hess (pianoforte) with the
BBC Symphony Orchestra, and conductor Adrian Boult, given for Lady Cripps'
United aid to China fund.

A.C.D.W.
R.A.F.
Brighton
Thursday, 24th September 1942

My Dear Mother and Father,

My address is still the same as you see, and I am wondering whether Air Ministry has lost all record of me – I think I would be rather pleased if they had, for then I might be able to make some headway.

However, I cannot grumble, because outside the camp life, I have been having a feast of good music such as I have never known before – I fear that I have also spent money at a pace unparalleled before as well! On the other hand I don't spend it lavishly on drink and such other things, and I feel that I may as well make hay while the sun shines and until such time as I become A.C.W.[1] I cannot.

There were very few of my favourite pieces that I did not hear last week; included were the 'Unfinished' Symphony, Tchaikovsky's 'Pathetique' Symphony, Mendelssohn's violin concerto, Beethoven's fifth and seventh symphonies, his 'Emperor' concerto, the famous Tchaikovsky Piano Concerto (with Moiseiwitsch as pianist – you should have got <u>all</u> the records to that work, because I cannot understand why only the first theme is so popular) and quite a number of others. I took a Catholic girl, whom I have bumped into at the C.W.L. canteen, to two of them, after I had spotted her at the first concert.

To wind everything up I threw all discretion to the winds last Sunday when just after Mass I read in *The Sunday Times* the full programme of the afternoon concert in the Albert Hall for the 'Aid to China' fund. Hardly before I had realised what I was doing I had set out for the station and soon found myself speeding for Victoria without a pass, nor having even booked out. I suppose you heard the first half on the wireless by the warmth of your hearth. I don't think that I have heard anything to approach the B.B.C. Symphony Orchestra for their precision, grandeur, and sensitiveness – and of course there is only one Myra Hess. That Schumann Concerto is one of her famous pieces I think, and the one we heard her play on the wireless about two and a half years ago. The orchestra's rendering of Elgar's 'Variations' was perfect (at least to my amateurish ears!) and I shall never forget how Adrian Boult was able to make use of all his drums and percussion instruments. I only wish you could have been down there as well, because when one has so much to enjoy on one's own one feels that it is almost too much to absorb without being able to talk to anyone about it.

There is another very good concert next Sunday afternoon but I think I had better draw the line as when I do get a chance for a 48 hours pass next time I want to have the money to come home with. There is not a chance this weekend, but I hope that the position will not continue so. There is so far no more news regarding my position – I still just hope and pray, and still try to grin and say 'all will be well' whenever my disappointment is brought home to me, as it is from time to time.

I feel a little hopeless at times and wonder what is wrong with me, but I realise after all we cannot all achieve the same measure of success, and at least while I am left in Brighton it is fairly easy for me to go to Daily Mass and Communion – I have to miss breakfast for it, but that does not amount to much – and I may as well prepare for more stormy days ahead while I have the chance.

How is Mary finding life with the A.T.S?[2] I think that she should settle down to it quite well, and she should be quite capable of looking after herself. Anyway I hope that she will be as happy as possible under the circumstances – it may make her appreciate home a little more, though she will have a certain advantage in being within reach of Auntie Celestine. Is Kathleen doing O.K. with her organ lessons at the Institute, and does she like them, and her teacher?

Well for the moment I will sign off, sending you in the usual way all my love and very best wishes,

From Your Most Affectionate Son
Philip

P.S. It is now September 24th and Stalingrad still stands! That is good news isn't it? P.P.S. Thanks for the letter received Friday and glad to know all is well. Did you hear *La Boheme* on the radio yesterday? I suppose you will hear Moiseiwitsch[3] this afternoon in that Tchaikovsky Concerto. I am NOT going up to London for it!

---

1. Air Control Wing
2. Auxiliary Territorial Service– the women's branch of the British Army
3 . Benno Moiseiwitsch

A.C.D.W.
R.A.F.
Brighton
Saturday, 10th October 1942

My Dear Mother and Father,

Thanks very much for your last letter which I received last Thursday. I was very pleased to hear that you were so much improved in health, and I hope that, as you say, you will continue to grow stronger.

I have left the letter a little late this week – because to tell you the truth I never expected to write it. I have done my best to get a 48 hour pass, starting from After Duties on Monday, but I was disappointed at the last minute in finding that it had been refused. However I am going to press the matter next week and I shall do my best to be home with you for a short while, but from your own point of view I should not place too much reliance on it, because I always may get posted or some such thing.

I have still heard no fresh gen about myself. I simply cannot understand it, and I am beginning to wonder if there is anything behind it, or whether Air Ministry is a little unsatisfied with some part of the business. I am definitely the oldest one here now, and no other chap has had the delay I have. There is many a one who has arrived since me, and who now is an AC ii (or i). However I am not going to be taken in by a false dawn to my hopes before, to speak metaphorically, the sun arises in all its majesty and clad in all its glory – if you can understand what I mean!

I am very sorry I forgot to write to Kathleen on the 9th. But I hope she received the (birthday) greetings telegram O.K. and that it didn't cause you too much of a scare. I am so pleased she is proving so capable at the organ and will be able so efficiently to relieve you – and I hope also that you will take full advantage of it.

You may this week be getting a receipt from Cotton for a postal order I sent them for The Cottonian. If you do, it doesn't matter about re–addressing it on here.

I am glad Mary is so fortunate, and so happy in her new abode – I haven't written to her yet but will do so at the first opportunity. It is at least a good send off to service life in having Leslie so near.

Yesterday I played a game of football – like a fool I volunteered for it! So you can guess how I feel today – just about as stiff as a poker. Still it was quite good fun, though I always feel a bit of a fool when I am playing football and not rugger, as I always seem to be off my balance or not quite where I should be. It makes me smile when I look back and think how high my ambitions used to soar with regards to football; in those days I thought how wonderful it would be to be a professional footballer, and of course in my wildest dreams I was always the star of the match before hundreds of thousands of people at Wembley Stadium! I even used to wonder how on earth people could be happy if they didn't play football – in fact those used to be my greatest anxieties about Heaven where I felt sure that the angels wouldn't play football!

Well I will not have much time to say much more – I hope you can understand what I have written, because I'm afraid that I have rushed along with it all very impulsively. I hope all will be well with you, and I hope too that I shall soon be doing something useful and worth doing to get this war over and done with. Yes I can still say that Stalingrad has not fallen and it is October 10th! There are some things that the Germans are saying and doing just now which I am blowed if I can understand. I think they might be becoming a little desperate, but it is also a kind of desperation which I don't quite like. It seems to me rather calculated to make a terrific fight of it. However as the P. M. once said: we must not flag or fail but go on to the end, all else we must leave to God in Whose hands we are.

Well now I shall send you all my love and very best wishes, so bidding you adieu,

From Your Most Loving Son
Philip

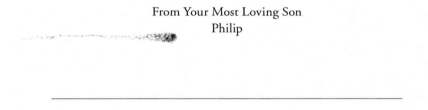

A.C.D.S.
Brighton
Wednesday, 21st October 1942

My Dear Mother and Father,

As you will see, I am going to make an early start on my letter this week. Together with an Aussie friend of mine, I have decided to hitch up to London next Saturday afternoon, and we both intend to hear what we can of the best musical concerts up there. I am afraid that Brighton, for all its happy go lucky spirit and its multitudinous forms of entertainment strikes me as being a rather soulless sort of place, and one is apt to feel very lonely even amid such throngs of people.

I think I would have had a pretty raw time down here if I had not met Bill Murtagh on the one hand, while I must admit too on the other hand that I have formed a friendship with a Catholic girl, of the name of Dorothy, who has also helped me to keep my head above the water, as it were. She is very fond of music and a helper down at the C.W.L. canteen down here, and on two occasions she has invited me to her home to listen to good radio programmes, and I have had occasional evenings out with her. However notwithstanding I shall be glad to leave

Brighton, for there is only one real advantage which I can consider worthwhile, and that is that the Church is so handy at all times, and if I cannot help the war effort in any other way, I am striving hard to do my little bit by making the utmost use of it.

Well I think it was well worthwhile going home last weekend, and though it was only of short duration, it was very happy. If it should happen that Christmastide should still see me down at Brighton – and at this rate it will! – then I shall do my very utmost to get home during that festive season, but of course if they have woken up by that time (i.e. Air Ministry) there is no knowing what to expect.

Friday

I shall have to make an attempt to finish this letter today so as to let you have it in good time. Last night we heard quite a lot of aircraft – I should now imagine that they were German bound. Did you hear that speech? Very good I thought, and I am very pleased to see that many of the things that I have always thought are his views too; and they all say that he is one of our greatest brains in this war. I was very pleased too, to see that he was one who gave Britain so much credit and praise for her part in the war; I think far too many people underestimate all that we have done and are doing. We all know how wonderfully well the Russians are doing – but all that they have done, and their very survival until now, has only been accomplished by the grit and hard work of our own country.

Was Leslie with those 94 Lancasters last Saturday? When I hear of such feats as that and the Augsburg raid[1] I certainly feel I would give anything to be in the air again. I certainly feel I would like to do my utmost to make this second front business much less costly for our soldiers.

By the way, they are beginning to panic down here about flying kit and they want to check up on it. I was wondering if you would mind dispatching it as freight down to me. Don't go to too much trouble about it, nor worry yourself about rushing it down too quickly. I should imagine that Gerald could see to it because there is not a great deal of weight in it. I am sorry now that I did not bring it last weekend.

Well I shall now conclude, sending you one and all my very best love and wishes,

From Your Most Loving Son
Philip

---

1. Carried out against large Schneider factory at Le Creusot,
300 miles inside France on 17th October 1942

3 Squadron
R.A.F. station
Brighton
Tuesday, 27th October 1942

My Dear Mother and Father,

Please excuse my flying to pen and paper like this, but I feel I have to tell you that as last something has at least begun to happen. Like a bolt from the blue my name was called out for me to go and see the Selection Board this morning. The result is that they are 'strongly recommending' to Air Ministry that I be kept on flying and sent to an A.F.U.[1] course since it is so long since I have flown. The old Group Captain there has warned me however that Air Ministry is a hard nut to crack, and that he may not prove successful in getting me this.

I had no trouble at all in persuading the board in my favour. They were extremely pleased with those two reports I have from July and all that is in my log book, and they even ventured to say that they could not understand my position at all.

You see I am hoping that this third interview will prove more fortunate. At any rate I am as pleased as punch that some part of officialdom thinks I am at least worth another chance.

It is a most happy thing that only this morning I put in for nine days leave which I hoped might commence next weekend – however this latest event makes me think they may have to put the tin hat on that.

I had a most enjoyable weekend in London, and heard Moiseiwitsch and Ida Haendal and Janet Howe in two concerts both conducted by Sir H. Wood. My Aussie pal took me as a guest to Australia House where we joined up with quite a number of Australian air crew personnel (there was even a Wing Commander amongst them!) and we all finally invaded new Zealand House before going to our various abodes. I like the general fun of Australian chaps very much.

Anyway for now I shall conclude sending you all my very best love and wishes,

From Your Most Loving Son
Philip

---

1. Advanced Flying Unit

There is quite a gap in Philip's letters here, for reasons unknown. It looks as though some may have been lost. There is a letter (appendix 3) which is from Philip in an RAF camp in Gloucs., after Brighton, so we can assume he had been posted there before Bicester.

Summer days before the war – the Hermolle family all together. Left to back row: Mary, Father (Gerald senior), Mother (Norah), Philip; middle row: Lorna, Kathleen (Kitty), Monica; front row: Gerald

Happier times and still together – Hermolle family from back row: Mary, Father (Gerald senior), Mother (Norah), Gerald, Philip; front row: Monica, Lorna, Kathleen (Kitty)

Philip at Cotton College (front row third from right)

Hockey team at Cotton College (Philip back row second from left)

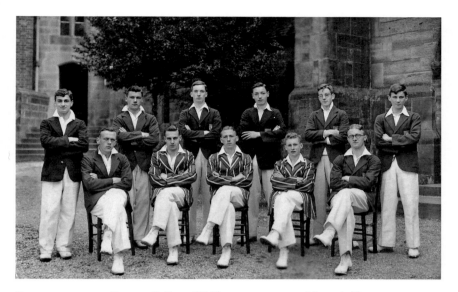

Summer sports at Cotton College (Philip top row second from left)

Philip's rugby team at Cotton College 1937–8 (front row on right)

Still there – Philip's rugby team Cotton College 1939. Philip middle row on right

Final form photograph at Cotton College – Philip front row fourth from left

Portrait of Philip in civilian clothes

Just called up – A young Philip dressed in RAF uniform, including coat

A portrait of Philip in RAF – now with wings

Philip's wings

Philip in RAF – on duty

Philip ready to fly

Philip enjoys a cup of tea in RAF

Out on the town – Philip as a young man (on right)

Happy days in the RAF (Philip front row third from right)

BUCKINGHAM PALACE

The Queen and I offer you our heartfelt sympathy in your great sorrow.

We pray that your country's gratitude for a life so nobly given in its service may bring you some measure of consolation.

George R.I.

G. A. Hermolle, Esq.

Telegram from Buckingham Palace

Philip's grave in Ortona, Italy

CHAPTER ELEVEN

BICESTER, OXFORDSHIRE

'I am afraid that at last I have gone the whole hog and completely written off a whole Blenheim and a lorry as well'
(Saturday, 1 May 1943)

My Dear Mother and Father,

I expect you are wondering what I'm up to since I have come back, but there is nothing terribly sensational. It seems that the weather was far better than I had estimated down in Oxfordshire, and the previous course finished more quickly than at first anticipated – hence our recall. Meantime we have been moved to Finmere in Buckinghamshire but this is only temporary until March 31st. The mail will all be forwarded the same day so that you may as well continue writing to the above address. Whether I will be home for a day or not I am hardly in a position to say just now, because although we will probably have a day off per week, I do not know whether we will also be allowed the night off before, and I have so far not the vaguest idea of how best to get on the way home from here, which is miles from anywhere as far as I can see.

I had an hour or so in the air yesterday. It was a lovely day and proved very enjoyable.

The Germans seem to be making far too good a rally in Russia for my liking, and I only hope that it doesn't prove successful. Everybody seems keyed up with a sense of expectancy as to what is to happen next, and still we wait, I wish we could get cracking somewhere.

Tomorrow (Saturday) Kitty is going in for her theory exam isn't she? I hope she knows all her stuff by this time, and will take all well within her stride. I shall remember to pray for her success, and hope that she will take no notice of the date.

What sort of a birthday did Gerald have? And how is his Wellington coming on – if so?

By the way the food is much better up here at Finmere, and on Ash Wednesday we had lovely roast pork! The Sergeants Mess is also much warmer and more comfortable but in other respects things are not so good, as everything is so far dispersed and inconvenient to reach.

Well I will finish now hoping to see you again in the not too distant future. For the present then here is wishing you all my very best love and wishes,

From Your Most Loving Son
Philip

My Dear Mother and Father,

I am sorry that I am so late in writing this letter, but I am all in a spin this weekend from my hectic flying of the last three days. On Good Friday we became marooned in the stormy skies of Norfolk, Lincoln and perhaps many another county. Anyway I was thankful to put down at Bircham Newton (very near Kings Lynn) where we remained until yesterday. And just this evening I have arrived back once more after a rather unsuccessful flight, in which I am afraid that my Navigator made a very big mistake somewhere. Anyway, here we are again better for the experience, for at least we did ultimately find ourselves back here.

I arrived back quite O.K. on Sunday last, and the light was so wonderful that I came up from Oxford in good time. I have also had some most enjoyable rides around here in the evenings, and my bike has enabled me to go down to the village church for Stations of the Cross and Benediction nearly every night last week.

There were some other things that I had been saving up to say to you for this letter but for the moment they seem to have floated away and I won't delay any longer. One was about this income tax business, and I am sorry that last week I brought up that part of it about after the war. Straight afterwards I felt that I had been very mean. You know that I would be only too pleased for you to have all that allotment, and if I am causing you extra income tax I do ask you to take whatever you want from it, for that is only fair to you, and otherwise it would be better for me to stop making it. However perhaps I can talk to you a little later on about it, and I am certain some better arrangement can be made.

Romeo and Juliet is on the radio just now (Forces programme) and it is lovely isn't it?

The news is good isn't it? There is no question about it, Germany and her satellite are in a very bad way especially internally, and I only hope that the rot will soon set in, in earnest.

Well I shall now conclude for this weekend, just to let you know that I am in fine fettle and find life very pleasant just now. (The food we had at Bircham Newton was wonderful – lovely bacon and eggs on Good Friday! – and was I hungry!)

Well for now, my best love and wishes to you all,

Your Most Loving Son
Philip

My Dear Mother and Father,

I am due for a trip this afternoon but I shall make a start on this letter now and then I should be able to finish it tomorrow in time for Sunday afternoon's post. It has been a very busy past week for me and I have been feeling dead tired once or twice, especially after flying through some of the bumpiest weather I have ever had cause to meet. For about one quarter of an hour last Tuesday evening we were tossed about just like a small rowing boat would be on a choppy sea. Yesterday with very bad weather and no flying, we paid a visit to the power plant at Northampton over which we were shown. It was quite interesting, but with my non–mechanical brain, there was much of it which I was unable to absorb. As the bus was not returning until 11 o'clock that night we all had an evening in Northampton –it was rather marred coming back by the state of several of the chaps who were truly far gone in drink.

By the way last week I forgot to thank you for the pyjamas which you dispatched so hurriedly to me. Thanks very much. Also before I forget, I remember that Mary should have been home as from last Wednesday, and she and Les will wish to see the two photographs which I am enclosing. I hope that she will have a very happy leave.

That seems a very good scheme that the government are getting out doesn't it, about helping servicemen and women after the war – I feel very pleased about it, though I haven't had time to look at it properly.

Saturday night

There has been a little excitement since last I was writing this letter. I am afraid that at last I have gone the whole hog and completely written off a whole Blenheim and a lorry as well. However I may tell you more about it when next I see you. I and the whole crew have not so much as a scratch, so don't worry. There will of course be a Court of Enquiry, but I am not worrying about it all, and feel certain that I did the right thing and am not at all to blame, though of course they always try and pin these things down to the pilot.

I certainly hope this will cause you no worry – it is rather a big thing for me not to mention at all, that is why I mention it, but you can rest assured that there is nothing at all wrong with me in any way.

The war news is still good isn't it? Tunisia is a hard nut to crack,[1] but it will be one of our hardest ones I think. Germany is undoubtedly in a bad way at home, and it cannot last too much longer I shouldn't think. The Russo–Polish friction is a bad thing – but one cannot admire Russia's part in it. If Poland's part lacked a little in wisdom, it was at least humanly understandable, for their plight is pitiable indeed.

Well I shall now conclude sending you one and all, my very best love and wishes,

From Your Most Loving Son,
Philip

---

1. The Tunisia Campaign: 17 November 1942 – 13 May 1943 (also known as the Battle of Tunisia) was a series of World War II battles that took place in Tunisia in the North African Campaign of World War II, between Axis and Allied forces

Sergeants Mess
R.A.F. Bicester
Oxon.
Saturday, 8th May 1943

My Dear Mother and Father,

Thanks very much for that letter of yesterday. I was sorry to hear of Mr. Sheehan's death but will remember to pray for him as frequently as possible. He must have had a troubled last few weeks, and I hope that his last moments were happy and peaceful.

On the other hand the news of that chap Jefferies was wonderful, and I should myself think that it must be true – have the War Office confirmed it yet? Anyway she should probably get more news now sometime in the future. Let us hope that he will soon be free once more. To be a Jap P of W[1] could not be pleasant at all.

Isn't the news wonderful this morning! Tunisia and Bizerte in our hands! I did not expect anything like such swift results. I'm afraid that Germany is finding it impossible now to hold our air power, which when combined with the British Navy and the Army has proved devastating. What an air force we have built up in less than four years. I suppose you heard what they said during the week about Mosquitoes – it is almost every pilot's one ambition to get on to one of those, they are certainly wonderful machines in every aspect.

The news that old Tim[2] is waiting to give me added welcome on my next visit home is also a very pleasant surprise. He should be fully trained by then shouldn't he? Domestically I mean! I hope so, because a dog howling for mercy always seems a little heart–rending!

I have not done quite so much cycling this last week, for the weather has not been quite so pleasant. However it is very handy when you haven't much time, and you want to pop somewhere quickly.

Last Sunday night while shaving I was wondering why my neck was stiff when I suddenly noticed that one of my glands underneath my chin had swollen up – one that I have never had trouble with before. I did not bother straight away, but on Thursday morning another one was a little sore, so I went to the M.O. He sent me to the dentist, who sent me yesterday to a place called Horton for an X–Ray of my lower set of teeth. There, a Wing Commander dentist took several photos, but I'm pretty certain that my teeth are not to blame. I think that yesterday and today there is some slight improvement, but they are still there. I asked the M.O. if it could be as a result of some sort of shock from last Saturday's affair, but he said No.

Actually, the shock was not half so bad in its reactions as at the time I thought it would be. I thought that by that evening I would have a violent headache and feel pretty sick. However, we went down into Bicester and ate a hearty meal and began to laugh at all the more funny side of it.

The other chaps on the course are now of course continually cracking jokes at my expense, but I smile and hold my peace, and remind them that the gremlins may strike at them in exactly the same way, and that they know not the day or the hour! – as a matter of fact I've thought of writing out a detailed report on the strategy these gremlins employed for the use of other pilots who have never been brought under their fire!

A Squadron leader gave me very great help just afterwards (one on our course) for he virtually dictated the report which I had to write out on the incident. You can imagine what a help that was because one's mind is not very clear at such times, and one certainly does not feel like concentrating on lots of little details, and making sure you don't leave them any loop–holes. He told me that he had made out hundreds of them and never been bounced yet!

I've heard no more of it since. The court of enquiry is still to come, but they seem to be very reasonable about it up to now, and there is nothing positive that they can blame me for. I have flown again during the week, but the weather has prevented a lot of it.

Well, there does not seem to be a lot more I can say just now, so I shall conclude, wishing you all my very best love and wishes and thanking you for your prayers,

> Your Most Loving Son
> Philip

---

1. Prisoner of war
2. New family dog

My Dear Mother and Father,

Thanks very much for both your letters which arrived yesterday morning. I shall have to be rather brief in this letter, for tomorrow I am due to fly at 7.30am and I shall have no time to catch the post if I do not get it written now. This morning I have done my longest trip to date of nearly 700 miles, so I have not had so much time today either.

It's all right, I am not worrying one scrap about this court of enquiry whatever way it may turn out. Actually the flight–commander has already half admitted that the machine was primarily to blame – and if he says that much without going into all the details, it is admitting quite a lot.

Only today I learned that the lorry driver (whose van we hit) had been taken to hospital. His troubles however are only superficial, but he was the luckiest of all of us. I am sorry I didn't know at the time for I would have popped in to see him.

The weather seems to be picking up once more – and the news! It simply baffles one doesn't it? The Italians are badly rattled, and I am not so sure that the Germans are not. It's so wonderful to have good news in plenty and to dare to ask oneself what new outstanding victories are hiding around the corner. Unfortunately tomorrow will be the first Sunday for some time on which I will not be able to go to Mass, but in my prayers I shall most certainly join in the nation's thanksgiving.

By the way I had a letter from Colin Doyle at the beginning of this week, and we have both determined that if we both come through this war okay we are going to Lourdes and Lisieux in thanksgiving, and for help in future. It would be lovely to see another pilgrimage there again, with everyone able to sing lustily and without constraint.

It seems that Tim should have another name! Still he must give you a few lighter moments on occasion, and I am longing to see his tail wagging at sixty to the minute when I come home. By the way, what kind of dog is he and what colour?

This last fortnight I have been getting in a lot of sport, with some very energetic games of tennis, some cricket, and some badminton in the gym.

It was very funny the other evening when I went down there for a game of badminton, for a real 'tough' airman came up to me while I was waiting with 'Hi Sarge, give me a bit of practice with the gloves . . . just a bit of a spar . . .' or words to that affect! 'But' I said, in an effort to find an excuse, 'Ah' he said 'Come on Sarge, I won't make it rough' and with an air of finality he told his seconds or whatever they were to put the gloves on me. With a look of helplessness I turned to my pals with whom I was supposed to be playing badminton but they only had sickly grins on their faces and made no effort to rescue me. Fortunately at that moment a table tennis game had finished, and a Corporal WAAF P.T. Instructor wanted an opponent, and I can assure you I literally bounded across in a way that must have surprised her. What my other more aggressive opponent must have thought of my hectic retreat to the shelter of a little WAAF I would not like to know, but looking back I think I scored a brilliant success, for I afterwards learned that a few years ago he had knocked out the German light weight champion!

For my pains however the WAAF showed me how table tennis should be played, and I only won one game out of six, which was a severe blow to my pride. At such times though, I always console myself with Daddy's motto that the 'game' is greater than the prize.

I cannot tell you when I shall get some leave. It may be very soon or a little while. Whenever it comes I am hoping that it will be long and with many extensions! At the moment I have still not done any night flying and we have to do a little bit. I am hoping to get it in very soon while the moon is coming up at night.

My glands appear to have got better now. The M.O. has done nothing and he said that it would be better for me to forget them unless they get worse. But they haven't been at all bad.

Well I shall now conclude sending you my very best love and wishes,

> From Your Most Loving Son
> Philip

Sergeants Mess
R.A.F. Bicester
Oxon
Saturday 5th June? 1943

My Dear Mother and Father,

Thanks for your letter which I received yesterday. I am pleased to know that in general all goes well, even if in much the same old way. This applies to me in the main part as well, though there have been one or two things of even more disturbing nature that have come to add a little variety to the usual course of events. First of all I discovered to my dismay that my rolls razor was missing from my attaché case just the morning I wanted it in a hurry and when we were just about to go on a parade.

It seems that it has been pinched and I don't think there is much likelihood of my getting it back again though I am keeping my eyes open and have done all I can.

The other more sombre note of the past week I am afraid started in the dentist's chair. After flying one afternoon I was summoned to that august gentleman's presence, and found I had the choice of two, whereupon I asked one or two attendant WAAFs who would be more sympathetic and more gentle about the operation! I was duly informed that the Irish chap in room four may be worth trying in preference to the other, so furtively crept in through the half open door, and asked him if he was ready and willing to do the deed. He appeared a very affable sort of chap, with a very raw Irish brogue, so I suggested to him it may be a good thing if he crowned my tooth instead, to which he retorted with a huge grin 'I'll crown you!'

Well to cut a long story short he made a very good effort that afternoon, and told me to report in a further 48 hours and he would see what he could do. Well, in just over 24 hours after that I had chronic tooth ache and so first thing that morning I presented a very dismal spectacle indeed, as I stumbled into S.H.Q. not bothering to apologise for my rather premature visit, but rather demanding that he should do something about it! However I can remember distinctly even in that awful moment how it still brought only the broadest of smiles from him! He was definitely amazed, and I suppose he must have thought 'That's shown him!'

Anyway he told me that it would be far better for me to have it out and done with, to which I readily agreed. He showed it to me after the extraction and pointed out an abscess which was on the end of it, and was apparently the source of all the trouble. It had only been dormant beforehand.

But now, this is where I want you to ask for a little advice. I made enquiries about having a plate put in. I cannot have it done it through the R.A.F. for simply one tooth. But he will do it as unofficially at normal prices between £1, and £1 and 5 shillings, if I go to him in approximately a fortnight's time. Would you advise me to have it, or not? He does not think that at my ripe old age my teeth will grow any more crooked!

Well there you have the story of my week's woes and sorrows! However things have not been bad otherwise. We still have not even had a chance to come home. I cannot make any plans as to the immediate future either, but naturally as you know I have only to be allowed but a day or so and I shall be off like a rabbit. This week I went with my navigator to see *Maid of the Mountains* in Oxford which proved very enjoyable – but we were fortunate to get there on time, and were mainly indebted to an army captain who gave us a very good lift.

As a whole, I think life is becoming much more enjoyable at Bicester – perhaps it is because I am beginning to know some of the chaps a little better, and also because of the better weather and longer nights.

Yes as you say the news is still continuing to be good from Africa and especially in the air warfare throughout the whole world. I think Germany is now doomed in this field altogether, and her future seems bleak indeed. Nothing short of an immense improvement in their U– boat warfare can restore their situation. However I suppose our main preoccupation is to get it over with maximum speed and minimum casualties.

I was surprised to hear that Mary and Les were planning a wedding so soon. Still we can only hope and pray that it will be blessed and crowned with many graces. I shall try and write to Mary soon.

At the moment I am in the crew room awaiting developments with many others. Naturally it does not help concentration to hear all this hubbub around you, everybody recounting their various experiences and generally talking shop with many humorous additions. So now if you don't mind I shall slide back once more into the oblivion with which Bicester is shrouded, and send you all my love and best wishes,

Your Most Affectionate Son,
Philip

TELEGRAM: *dated 16ᵗʰ June:*

LEAVE EXTENDED MIDNIGHT 26ᵀᴴ JUNE 1943 SUBJECT TO IMMEDIATE RECALL. AERONAUTICS BICESTER

Sergeants Mess
R.A.F. Bicester
Oxon
17th June 1943

My Dear Mother and Father,

As I shall be busy until I get settled down at my new station, I will content myself with telling you that I and my navigator are being posted to 60 O.T.U. wherever that may be. We are losing our gunner. It sounds to be like Beanfighters of Fighter command but I have no definite news.

Two others from our course are coming along too – all the rest, to my surprise, have already gone to squadrons. Please do not worry over me. It's little use saying that I know, but I hate to think that I am making things so difficult for you.

The wedding will be in full swing by the time you get this (I hope!) If I am not present in reality, I shall certainly remember to pray that God will bless this auspicious occasion, and grace it with favour.

Shall write again from new address as soon as possible – all my very best wishes to you all, and tell Lorna and Monica that I'll soon be on their tails once more!

All my love,

Your Most Affectionate Son
Philip

P.S. New address: Sergeants Mess, R.A.F. High Ercall, N. Wellington, Salop

---

Sergeants Mess
R.A.F. Bicester
Oxon
Saturday, 26th June 1943

My Dear Mother and Father,

Believe it or not we have been posted back again to Bicester, so what is going to happen now I don't quite know. There was one crew left at High Ercall but apparently the rest of us were not quite up to it, and I think they wanted chaps who had already had operational experience. I had done no flying since last Tuesday.

So now I do not suppose I shall be able to see you next Tuesday. However if ever the chance comes along I shall be popping home.

I am hoping that you Mother are now much better than you were and are enjoying some relaxation after the wedding. As for me, my cold has almost gone and does not seem to have left me any worse.

At the moment I cannot find very much more to say, since nothing outstanding has happened, and at the moment I am rather keen to get to bed after the strenuous business of travelling and changing trains; and I want you just to have this by Monday evening so that you will know that all goes well.

From the past week I at least have the satisfaction that I have completely flown the world's fastest and best aeroplane, and the knowledge that I could fly it quite ok. For the rest I suppose all is God's will.

For the present then here is sending you all my love and best wishes,

Your Most Loving Son
Philip

Sergeants' Mess
R.A.F. Bicester
Oxon
Friday, 9th July? 1943

My Dear Mother and Father,

Thanks for your letter of yesterday, and I was pleased to know you are well again now. We are still hanging around here, and the latest job thrust upon us is coffin bearers at a special new air crew cemetery in Oxford for Dominion personnel. However I was rather pleased to take part especially in those of two Catholic Canadian Sergeant Pilots. I was the only Catholic there apart from a Canadian Padre and while their own relatives were so far away I was glad that I at least would be able to offer up a few prayers for them when last homage was being paid.

The other side of this week's story is of a very different character, for the Carl Rosa Opera Company is in Oxford this week and I have been to the *Merry Wives of Windsor*, *La Boheme* and a 'Faust', all of which I have enjoyed immensely, though the tenor parts are all very weak after hearing those records of Gigli. In fact they have been outclassed every time by the leading lady who was Helen Ogilvie and who sings extremely well. Have you heard of her before? Or is she a well known singer?

There seems to be no news at all from this end as to my future whereabouts – but I expect that they will soon fish something out of the bag. My gunner was still here when I arrived back and had been crewed up with a Wopp/AG but he has now come back with me.

Did Mary and Les have a good time at Colwyn Bay? Has Les discovered any snags yet?

Well I don't seem in a letter writing mood just now – perhaps it is the desultory weather – anyway I shall conclude for now with best love and wishes,

Your Most Affectionate Son
Philip

CHAPTER TWELVE

FINMERE, BUCKINGHAMSHIRE,
THEN CORNWALL

'I am afraid it looks rather definitely that I shall have to go overseas'
(17 July 1943)

My Dear Mother and Father,

I am commencing this letter tonight though there is not much to say. I have not seen anybody special yet, but from preliminary reports it seems that there will be much less delay here than I thought. However, now that I am back here, I will not be sorry to get out there, so that then I shall at least be able to look forward to coming home again! – It is overseas by the way.

Anyway I hope you will not worry too much. Keep on thinking how good the news is, and how every day that passes is one day less to go through. Remember too, that while so much of the world suffers in a way that we can hardly realise, it is only right that we should be able to have a small quota to offer up, and up to this point in the war, I must admit that I have been fortunate indeed. Of course you will always know that wherever I may be I shall always remember to pray often and hard for you all.

By the way I have just remembered that I put that film in a yellow case on the mantelpiece above the gas fire, and forgot to take it down to Pocock's, I suppose you will be able to see to that. Well, since I know you will be looking for a letter, and as the postal service isn't too good from here, I shall conclude and let you have this one. I shall keep you as fully informed as I can. My very best love to you all,

Your Most Affectionate Son
Philip

Sergeants Mess
R.A.F. Finmere
Buckinghamshire
Saturday, 17th July 1943

My Dear Mother and Father,

Yesterday, after great pains I had managed to get permission for another 48 hours this weekend, but just as I was about to get the final signature from the squadron Leader, he said 'Hi, I want you!' – and he said that I was one of a number of others who would be posted to Finmere today. So I had to set to work packing, and later on I sent a telegram for Monica.

I am afraid it looks rather definitely that I shall have to go overseas, but I should get a leave first. I cannot grumble however because it is already July 17th and I can most certainly say that I have had a good innings in this country, and the war situation is such that we can at last look forward hopefully to far better times, and all the time the German opposition is growing woefully weak, especially in the air.

Did Monica have a good time on her birthday yesterday – I was thinking I should be home to see her, but as I have told you a last minute hitch prevented it, however I hadn't forgotten about her and remembered her in my prayers.

The weather has been very wonderful once more hasn't it, and I notice now that they are gathering in the harvest round here.

There will be a very good concert next Wednesday on the wireless consisting of works by Handel, and including two organ concertos played by Cunningham and the B.B.C. orchestra in a Prom, so don't forget to listen.

Last night we had a very good gramophone session here, in which was included the 'Kyrie', a part of the 'Credo', and part of the 'Agnus Dei' from Bach's *B Minor Mass*.

What a difference to this present moment when 'Never before did I believe my love could be so hard' are the preponderant sentiments of one of Henry Hall's artists.

I do not expect it will be very long before I see you again, and perhaps once more there may be an extension or two, who knows? Anyway I seem to be drawing to the end of my letter as far as this writing goes – I don't seem to be able to concentrate on letters lately – so I shall conclude and let you have it in good time. Here is every good wish to you one and all,

Your Most Loving Son
Philip

P.S. I am enclosing three of these little pamphlets with the accompanying prayer which appeals to me very much. I thought that you might like it as well, and you can dispose of them how you will, love Philip

Sergeants Mess
R.A.F. Finmere
Bucks
Thursday, 22nd July 1943

My Dear Mother,

Though your birthday is tonight some three days hence, it behoves me now to write you this letter to send you all my love and best wishes for very many happy returns of your birthday, otherwise it will be too late. I am hoping that Sunday will prove a very happy and pleasant day for you.

Thank you for your letter which I received last Tuesday morning. I had intended to acknowledge it before, but I am afraid that while the spirit was willing the flesh was a little lazy. However I would like to thank you so very much for your prayers and those of Dorothy, and all others whom you ask to pray for me, and I am sure that they are being answered and heard even now, and in any case it is very consoling to know that so many people are praying for me, and I shall always do my best to pray as hard as I can for all of you, for I know perfectly well that you suffer even more than I do on account of the war.

I imagine that I shall be home on leave sometime next week, but I cannot say for how long. However things are not really so bad, and I feel very optimistic about things in general.

I shall not mar this letter any more by talk of the war, but close once again by sending you all best wishes and every happiness for next Sunday, when I shall remember you especially in my Holy Communion.

Your Most Loving Son
Philip

Sergeants Mess
R.A.F. Finmere
Bucks.
Sunday, 25th July 1943

My dear Mother and Father,

Thanks for your last letter which came yesterday. I don't know whether there is much of interest or that is new that I can find to say. Life is not too strenuous here, we just have enough to do to keep us occupied, and this afternoon I have had just under two hours in the air, and as they don't seem too particular we just flit off to various places we think fit, do a couple of steep turns around them and then hop off to the next place on the list. This afternoon, although so very warm and sunshiny, was extremely hazy and visibility poor, however Northampton, Bedford, Bletchley, Oxford and Stratford, and Cirencester were all duly called at. I haven't told you yet, have I, that I am flying Bostons now? They are certainly very good kites and much better than the old Blenheims.

Did you hear that programme of G.D. Cunningham last Wednesday? I did and enjoyed it very much indeed. In fact I went down to the Education Office at Bicester to hear it, as I also did on Friday and last night.

Well there is not a lot more that I can find to say, so I shall now finish and let you know that with me all goes well, and I hope to see you this week or next. I hope, by the way, that you Mother are having a very happy birthday today, and as I promised I have offered up my Holy Communion for you.

Here's sending you all my love and very best wishes,

Your Most Affectionate Son
Philip

Had a short leave

My Dear Mother and Father,

As I want you to just have this little note for Monday morning I shall have to be very brief and walk into Buckingham tonight to post it.

Twenty four hours after I left you we landed at an aerodrome just on the outskirts of Glasgow, where we picked up our various kites, and flew down here again in the afternoon in formation. Today the weather has kept us all grounded but we have got cleaned and various other odd jobs done. By the way I was informed this afternoon that I am now a Flight Sergeant as from August 1st!

I want to send some money home if I can manage to register it before I go, but there certainly won't be an opportunity before Monday.

All is well with me, and after the initial shock of having left home I am settling down very well indeed, and though I know overseas sounds nasty, all is really for the best, and I look forward to the time when I can return home once again to see the black–out lifted and all the sand bags taken away.

Well for now I will conclude, hoping you are all well, and sending all my love and best wishes,

From Your Most Affectionate Son,
Philip

During a final home leave Philip is recalled and catches the train back on the morning of Thursday 26th August:

TELEGRAM 25TH AUGUST 1943

SGT HERMOLLE 128 FARNHAM ROAD HANDSWORTH BHAM 21 RETURN TO UNIT IMMEDIATELY = AEROS FINMERE

Finmere
31st August 1943
Tuesday dinner time

My Dear Mother and Father,

Thanks for your letter received this morning. The main thing I want to ask you in this letter is to take the enclosed money and bank it (or keep it if you will). The other envelope is what my navigator wants to be sent to his wife. We have one registered envelope between us and can get a pal to post it to you (for we cannot get out to the Post Office). So will you please have his letter registered and sent on to his wife.

Well I shall try and write again before we go, but we do not seem to have too much time. Thanks for all your prayers. All my love,

Your Most Affectionate Son
Philip

Sergeants Mess
R.A.F. Finmere
Bucks.
Wednesday, 1st September 1943

My Dear Mother and Father,

I am making another start on a letter just to let you know that on Wednesday evening the weather still keeps me here, but otherwise we are only awaiting the word 'go'.

Last night I wrote to Fr. Singleton, bursar at Cotton, asking him to continue sending the Cottonian to '128' etc. but I told him that you would forward the money since I cannot get out to a Post Office. Will you please do this for me, from my own money. Take your time for there is no particular hurry, (4 shillings for the year, by the way).

I hope that you also receive that attaché case okay. I have cut down my bag and baggage to a minimum, because there is not too much room.

If I cannot write to Mary in time will you please wish her many happy returns on the 7th of the month.

The mess is being darkened in a minute or two for a picture show so I must finish. Hope you are all as well and happy as I am. All my love

Your Most Affectionate Son,
Philip

P.S. During my (fuel) consumption test on Monday, twice I was very near home, but it didn't do me much good did it?

The following two letters had been put away unopened. It seems they arrived several months later. They were postmarked 4ᵗʰ and 7ᵗʰ September 1943:

Portreath
Cornwall
Friday evening, 3rd September 1943

My Dear Mother and Father,

This seems a very busy day, and I have found very little time to myself. However just a short note – probably the last before I go away – but I shall strive to let you hear as often as possible. I hear we have invaded Italy today, but have not heard the news properly.

I hope you will not mind my ending so soon, but as I have to be up at 4.30am tomorrow I shall now prepare to go to bed. For now then, all my love, good night and God bless you,

Your Most Loving Son
Philip

Portreath
Cornwall
Monday midday, 6th September 1943

My Dear Mother and Father,

You see I am still in England, even though only just. However the last two full whole days (Sat. and Sun.) have been very pleasant ones and relaxing. We have been down to the beach each afternoon, which opens into a typical Cornish cove with picturesque cliffs on three sides, and rocky mounds and caves along their edges. It is really a lovely place.

Weather has been detaining us thus long, but I don't suppose it will last much longer. When I say weather, I really mean unfavourable winds, for we have been graced with wonderful sunshine while we have been here as well.

Yesterday I served Mass in the little chapel on the camp.

This afternoon we will probably go out again (each time we do we say it will be the last!) – Yes it is a very nice holiday we are having!

I don't think there is very much I can find to say just now – beside my stomach beckons me on to what it considers more important tasks. So for the moment here is wishing you all goodbye, and all my love

Your Most Affectionate Son
Philip

PS Excuse writing, as I am sitting on my bed, with this pad on my knee.

CHAPTER THIRTEEN

AFRICA THEN SICILY

'Life is very rough and ready here and we are all under canvass'
(29 September 1943)

The last chapter of letters come in the form of Airgraphs. Some were very short single sheets so space was saved by abbreviations, lack of paragraphs etc.

No address
16th September 1943

My Dear Mother and Father,

Here is another short letter to let you know that all is well. We have not moved since last week when I first wrote as they have been working on the ——— (*here a name which is blacked out presumably by censor*). For that reason I do not know whether I can find an address to give you, but I will try and put one on afterwards. Already it seems a long time since I saw you and 'old blighty' as the chaps out here call England. I am also beginning to wonder whether there is not a lot to be said for so much cold weather and days of rain. At least the flies do not pest one so much.

The food on the camp is fair, but down in the local town, you can do quite well, grapes, oranges and eggs in plenty – but how I would love just an occasional cup of tea! Well we shall all have to keep on praying until all this is over and we meet again. How are the ramblers[1] settling down in the front garden, and how is Gerald getting on? All my love to you at home,

Your Most Affectionate Son,
Philip

---

1. Some roses planted in archways along the garden path by Philip during his last summer at home.

No address
Tuesday, 21st September 1943

My Dear Mother and Father,

This morning finds me still not at my destination, but at least a little nearer to it. The station at which I am at present seems a big improvement, and yesterday at tea time we were all (our crew) delighted with a large mug of tea while the breakfast we have just eaten would compare quite favourably with that of many home stations. We are sleeping under canvass and are rapidly becoming used to life of field conditions. The country round here is most uninteresting as regards its scenery, and from what I have seen one town is much the same as another. As you will have gathered, I am still quite sound in mind and body (if I can judge on such matters!) and I am hoping that all you at home are just as well and happy. When I get more settled I shall try to write a proper letter. Meanwhile I hope this one and the three before will help to tide over the delay. Goodbye for the present. All my love,

Your Most Affectionate Son,
Philip

Sicily
Wednesday, 29th Sept 1943

My Dear Mother and Father,

It is now just over a week since last I wrote, and I am feeling quite a little relieved now to have another chance. I am writing now under a blazing sun in heat wave weather, and looking around me, there are hills dimmed by the afternoon haze on most sides, the top especially of Mt. Etna peers down in disdain upon them all. From this you will guess I am in Sicily, but if you want to know my impressions I shall have to ask you to wait awhile, for I have only seen various towns from the air, and apart from an old farmer who came around this morning saying something about 'graves' – which I was informed meant something to do with grapes that he was selling – I have seen no others of the population. I was disappointed in the countryside which looks to be all brown and yellow, not unsimilar to Africa, and trees are mainly along the main roads.

By the way letter writing materials come to us mainly at the rate of one air mail per week (like this one) and one green envelope. So I shall have to wish Kitty many happy returns for the 9th in this letter. Up to now I have only been able to write to you, with the exception of one airgraph to Bernard. If we get issued with airgraphs again I won't be so restricted, but meanwhile I shall try and let you hear at least once a week.

Life is very rough and ready here and we are all under canvass; however I am not going to say that it is without its compensations. All the chaps seem a very good lot and there is a very cheery atmosphere. The radio that we have in the Sgt.'s Mess (just another marquee) is worth its weight in gold. We can hear London every evening quite well in their overseas programmes for the troops, and it makes you feel that you are not so far away after all.

Well it is now just about a month since I heard from you last, but I am hoping, praying and trusting that you are all still well and happy and making ready for victory. I suppose that there are lots of other things that you would like to ask me, but I had better be discreet and not anticipate them. I hope that you are not worrying about me at all because I can assure you I am in one of the best places I could be.

Has Gerald got fixed up in a job yet? And is there any more news of Kitty in her musical career? Lorna is still trying to dance and sing her way through life I suppose, with Monica still lending a helping hand.

By the way Fr. Boland will be interested to know my address, but I cannot write to him just yet until letters become more plentiful.

Most of the things I set out to say have now been said, and I find I still have some room left which I shall have to try and fill with a few casual remarks. One of the things which I have oftentimes wondered is whether those ramblers have died off or not. My navigator who is very proud of his own garden in London says that though they appear to die off in the autumn and winter they might easily grow quite O.K. in the spring. One thing looking at the soil out here I would not like the job of digging a garden in Sicily. It gets very dry and hard and is full of large cracks. Well I don't know whether this letter has proved very interesting but at least it is a letter and you can be assured of my good health and happiness. Here's sending you all my very best love and wishes,

Your Most Affectionate Son,
Philip

Sicily

4th October 1943

My Dear Mother and Father,

Today I am just taking advantage of these few airgraphs to let you hear again. There is not a lot of news, but just in case I find some difficulty in writing during the next week, I will feel a little more contented for having sent this one. The day before yesterday we had a terrific storm, which blew the tent down before we had realised it had come, and most of our kit was drenched not to mention ourselves, in fact chaos reigned supreme for the night, but I am glad to say the cook–house still came through with some hot tea.

I don't know how long these airgraphs take to reach you, but rather fancy there is some delay at this end. By the way I have bought two pairs of silk stockings for you Mother, which I shall send home in a parcel later on. It is rather surprising the things you can buy here, but prices in the main are very stiff. Of course wine is very plentiful and very cheap, but I have drunk very little up to now.

I shall now have to close once more, hoping you are all well and sending my best love and wishes.

Your Most Affectionate Son,

Philip

Sicily

9th October 1943

My Dear Mother and Father,

Out here one finds it a little difficult to keep a check on time, and so quite when last I wrote or on what day I do not know. However, I feel pretty certain that it was less than seven days ago and in any case I want to let you have another airgraph as a sort of stopgap and something to be going on with. I wonder have you received my address yet – if so I should be hearing from you fairly soon. Most chaps are out here about a month before they receive their first mail.

At the moment I am writing this at the foot of a hay stack, and clad only in a pair of khaki shorts, shoes and sunglasses. Perhaps to you I might look brown, but alongside old timers I am easily recognised as new to this clime. By the way it is Kitty's birthday today, so I hope she is having a good time. I am hoping too that you are all still very well at home, and seeing the best in everything. Touch wood but I have kept remarkably well up to now, and am finding many things of great interest to occupy my mind. I am looking around for an Italian grammar for I would like to learn a little while I have a good chance; 'poco bono' is hardly sufficient when purchasing stockings! Well I must end now, so to you all my best love and wishes,

Your Most Affectionate Son,
Philip

Sicily
18th October 1943

My Dear Mother and Father,

There has been a little more delay in writing this letter but I trust it will not have caused you undue anxiety, for it is not my fault. You have to write when you can out here but I think it should be generally easier than just now.

I have not heard from you yet, but in another week I shall be anxiously and expectantly watching each batch of mail directly it comes in, and meanwhile I hope you are all still very well and happy.

As for me, you will be interested to know that whatever my regrets are at being so far away from home there are many compensations, and I have been truly amazed at much of what I have seen of the Italians. The peasants, of which there are a very large number, are extremely simple and very primitive; they seem to live in the smallest of hovels, they carry everything on their heads (or rather I should say the women folk do, for the men more often than not walk alongside empty handed!) They plough their fields with a wooden pointed pike which is towed along by two oxen, and altogether they remind one of what it must have been like in mediaeval times. There are sketches of 'Musso' (or there were until they were splashed over with other marks) on almost every large building, and extracts from his speeches are everywhere.

How would you like a bottle of olive oil? I ask you this not because I can send you one but because I am the proud possessor of one. The bottle though is a large wine bottle and is full! The other day I went into an olive oil factory (about the size of Pitts) and watched the whole process from the olive to its oil, and then the chap in charge filled this bottle and gave it to me. He also gave me two casks of wine which I carried back in triumph to the other chaps.

You will probably be wondering if I have been in any of their churches yet. Well I am afraid that I have only been into one, which is a large Cathedral in one large town. It was very spacious and no doubt would have been grand, except that it has suffered a little through the fighting.

Well here comes the last page, and all too short you will probably think.

However we will not always have to rely on a short airmail to talk to each other and meantime we shall all have to do our respective jobs. As our time here is the same as yours in England I often stop to think what you will be doing at home. I made them all laugh the other Sunday when, at about 5.15pm, I remarked that one of my sisters would now be insisting that the Children's Hour be on! A case of where Lorna has been the source of a laugh, without her even knowing anything about it, which is a change isn't it.

I suppose autumn will also be well under way by now as well and the leaves falling – but over here there is little sign of anything like that, and the only sign that summer has broken up is the fact that the skies become overcast with clouds much more frequently; there is also quite heavy rain on occasion, but otherwise the climate is very nice.

Well I shall have to conclude once more now, but will try and write early. Here's sending all my love and best wishes and hoping all are well.

Your Most Affectionate Son,
Philip

CHAPTER FOURTEEN

ITALY

'The weather here is more harsh than it has ever been since I left England – a gale force icy wind has followed a Boxing day which rained from one end to the other. Talk about mud and its consequent evils, I bet Flanders' mud has not so very much to show us now'
(29th December 1943)

Italy
25th October 1943

My Dear Mother and Father,

It is now exactly seven days since last time I wrote you, so I shall have to look sharp. I am hoping that this will be the last letter I write without having one of yours to answer. I have now been here about a month with the squadron which is generally when chaps expect to hear from home.

There is one item of fresh news which I am allowed to disclose which is that we are now on the mainland of Italy, and so are already on our way home! Anyway from all that I have seen and heard, it is far, far better than the desert and there is a great deal to interest us. I shall have very many things to tell you when I come home again and the war over but in the meantime I cannot mention much in particular at all.

We are still having plenty of sun out here, and bathing proves a wonderful pastime – still I must say I envy you your frosty mornings and all the roads littered with leaves!

Well this long black line underneath tells me that I shall have to wish you goodbye once more though my thoughts are always with you.
All my love and God bless you all.

Your Affectionate Son,
Philip

Italy
Wednesday, 27th October 1943

My Dear Mother and Father,

Well as I have come in a little late, I have clicked for an extraordinarily large meal, with the result that I find it necessary to remain very still and quiet for some time to come! So, thought I to myself, what a wonderful opportunity to get in another letter to you at home, and to picture to myself how you might all be just now. Yes I can just picture a very chill evening and the merry fire you will have going, perhaps Kitty rushing to finish her homework, and telling Lorna to hurry up and finish her practice because she ought to have done it before; and as a woman's work is never done, I suppose Mother will be thinking of all the ironing she hasn't done etc., etc., etc., and then finally the inevitable question 'What's for supper?'

Yes it presents a very pretty picture to me as it does to every chap out here, but the continual good news makes us ever more certain that the days are rolling steadily nearer that will see our homecoming.

I still haven't heard from you, but there has been no mail in for some days now so I expect some with the next lot.

Just at the moment there is some very enjoyable music on the radio from C major Symphony of Bizet – the first I have heard since I left home on August 26th. – it is coming from England of course. I must say that the programmes as a whole are very suitable and put over very well for the troops.

Talking about music reminds me of how in Italian cafes there always appears a group (three or four) of minstrels who stand just inside the doorway and play and sing for all who are eating. They seem very fond of the violin and guitar (if that is how you spell it). And of course they do it all in a very affected and dramatic manner, but if you don't look at them and simply listen, it can be very entertaining.

When they pass the cap around, you cannot get out of looking for they will not let you – all Italians seem very good at begging for anything, but poverty is much more widespread than in England. From this don't imagine that I am always hopping in and out of cafes, because only on two occasions have I done so. They spoil what good food they have by doing it all in olive oil which leaves a very strong flavour. Apparently the 'Ities' like it, but our chaps cannot palate it.

Last Sunday I went to Mass at the local church, but there was no music. There are no seats or kneelers (except a few chairs which can be hired inside) and nearly all stand up throughout. The people are not half so reverent about it as they are at home – perhaps another case of familiarity breeding contempt.

As I shall have to finish just now I will just reassure you by telling you that my digestive organs have profited well by this short respite.

Now I really must say ta–ta, so here's sending all my love and best wishes,

Your Most Affectionate Son,
Philip

Italy
1st November 1943

My Dear Mother and Father,

A few more odd moments on hand so I am trying to whip off a short note, though I am not certain when I shall be able to post it. However I expect you will find them acceptable whenever they arrive. I happened to hear on the radio last night, as I was passing one of the tents, mention of the heavy rains in Italy hampering the army. It hasn't done much to ease matters for us either, though I must admit that for the most part we are managing to keep dry. I have been trying to get hold of something to send two pairs of stockings in for Christmas but unless I can soon find a means I will be too late. There doesn't seem much else I can send for the others, dolls are available when you can get to the shops, but the last time I was there I was very low on money at the time and couldn't quite make it, and there seems a rush on them as well; and I am not allowed to send tobacco, of which we get a plentiful supply. I wonder whether you will have any almonds this Christmas for they are in abundance out here.

In a day or two I shall try and write an air mail which should reach you before this airgraph. For the time being then I shall finish.

All my love and very best wishes,
Philip

Italy
Friday, 5th November 1943

My Dear Mother and Father,

I am sorry that this letter has been delayed two days over the week but it is not my fault. I wrote an airgraph three or four days ago, but have only lately realised that they are not nearly so quick as these air mails, so I am afraid that you will have found my correspondence very spasmodic, but I shall try to rectify that in the future. 'Ginger', my Wopp/AG was the first of the crew to hear from home the other day, but there is again some hold up in the post so there may be something waiting for me. If you could send out airmails occasionally to me instead or airgraphs (if those are what you are sending) they will reach me much quicker, and they are a lot more roomy, and cost sixpence, I believe.

Looking back, this appears a very dictatorial manner to commence a letter but I know you will realise I do not mean it in that way. At the moment I am feeling not quite my best for I have a chill on my stomach where big battles seem to be taking place! What amazes my crew is that I even seem temporarily to have lost my appetite and when meals are up they do not see me in the forefront of the queue as is my wont. However a day or two should see me O.K. and back to normal once more. We do not seem to hear a lot of news out here of the war as a whole, but whenever we do, the Russians seem to be doing exceptionally well which is a good thing.

Last Sunday I went into one of the churches in the local town, and a Bishop said the Mass and preached. I should imagine it was a very good sermon indeed if I could have but understood what he was saying. It was funny, for I was the only one in the church in khaki, and it was packed right to the doors with people, the only others in uniform being soldiers of the Italian army in their light grey blue – yet I didn't feel a bit strange. In fact someone offered me a chair to sit on though they nearly all were standing.

There has been one thing out here that has impressed me very much and that is the dreadful plight of a country in defeat, and they will need a very able Government to remedy most of the results of what for Italy has been a disastrous war. Why, it is the unusual thing to see children with shoes to their feet and the rest of their clothes are more or less rags and tatters. Nearly all the boys from the age of five upwards will pick up or cadge cigarette ends and puff them, and as for the men, they will do almost anything for a 'cigaretto'. In fact you can bargain better with cigarettes than anything else, for instance my Wopp has got a very good watch in exchange for fifteen packets of cheap cigarettes. And of course nearly everybody looks badly undernourished and hungry, and they are doing better than they have for a long time.

Well, I wonder how things are going at home now and what sort of Christmas they are going to let you have. I do not suppose you will be able to do much with regards to Christmas puddings and the like but I bet there will be something nice and tasty. How are Les and Mary these days and has Les got over his little term of punishment at Sheffield! I hope that all you at home are all very well and happy and keeping free of colds and the like. Remember me to Dorothy any time you see her and tell her to go steady with the fish and chips, for I want a few when I come home! Here's sending all my love and very best wishes

Your Most Affectionate Son,
Philip

Italy
Monday, 8th November 1943

My Dear Mother and Father,

I intended to write to you today in any case, but now that I have received your first letter of October 21st it seems much more opportune.

Well I cannot tell you how welcome your letter was after so many weeks without word at all. As a matter of fact I was boiling a tin of water in which were some of my underclothes in the mid–afternoon just outside our tent, when looking across at the Marquee I saw a chap with a big bag across his back. Could it be mail, I wondered and without more ado I left my washing to try my luck – with what result you know!

I am very pleased you are all so well, but it seems to me my mail to you has not been too regular. Did you not receive my first letter which I posted (wrote) on the 10th or so of September? and which I gave to a chap who was flying to England that night, asking him to have it censored at his station and sent straight on to you. You should have had that within about two or three days. I was also surprised at that air letter taking three weeks or so to get to you, for I believe that they should do it more in the region of ten days. However, perhaps things will gradually get better now. Today I have just written out my Christmas card which I am hoping will reach you by Christmas – if it doesn't you will know it is on the way.

Mary's 'rights' regards leave made me laugh a lot. So she thinks she can play about with the army does she! Pity the army won't play! Yes I had occasionally thought about the *Dream of Gerontius* which will be on about this time – and I hope you are going, or have been as the case may be, even if it costs you two pounds, twelve shillings and sixpence! Congratulations to Gerald on his good S.C.[1] and I am pleased he is fixed at the Reference Library.

No, I don't think there is anything I want out here. Razor blades are more plentiful than in England. Fancy Victor being back so soon! Has he a commission in the R.A.F. now as well? I know he was anxious to get one. What does he think of his new son?

There is a distinct touch of autumn in the air these last few days and we are all turning out our kit bags for our great coats and other warmer clothing.
However I suppose it is still much warmer than in England.

---

1. School Certificate

This letter was interrupted yesterday as my crew and I were given free tickets for a concert in . . . just remembered I cannot say where! There was a very good tenor, Andrew Reid, who sang some enjoyable songs. In other respects too it was a very welcome change. On the way I received my second letter from home (Daddy's) for which very many thanks. I also came across an issue of '8th Army News' a daily paper out here, and it was doubly interesting as it was the same day's paper! I liked particularly a part from Joe Stalin's speech saying the German fascists are nearly finished! I hope he is right.

That letter you mention from Gregson – he is that Australian chap I met at Brighton; he writes an awful scrawl doesn't he?

I believe that Hitler was supposed to make a speech yesterday. I don't know whether he did, but it would be very interesting to know his thoughts just now!

It is very good of you to remember me so much in your prayers, and I thank you and all the children, especially Kitty very much. In a short time I have got to go down for a bath and believe me I certainly need it now. And now it seems I might say goodbye, so here is sending all my love,

From Your Most Affectionate Son,
Philip

November 8th 1943

TELEGRAM: Greetings from the Royal Air Force Italy Christmas 1943:

'AIRGRAPH TO MAKE SURE!' LOVE, PHILIP

My Dear Mother and Father,

Two days after the first letter, I received another batch, one from you dated November 1st and which I received on the 8th November! Not bad at all was it! There is nothing like a letter or two to send one's spirits soaring. It was very laughable that afternoon as we all brought our letters back to the tent to see how suddenly all faces lit up in radiance, and how all throats burst forth into song! Yes, mine included! Pity we were not all singing the same tune though, for the net result hardly did credit to our feelings! However I am pleased to know that you are all well and working hard.

We have all been counter checking on our various letters home, and it seems rather clear that about three which we posted from Africa did not reach you. While there it was very awkward for us, and we were held up much longer than we should have been. I was not too keen on Africa at all, and though we had a few days leave in Constantine which was supposed to be a good place, I was not very thrilled with it. Most of us seem to prefer the Italian people as individuals to the French.

Anyway this is all rather old news now, or at least so it seems to me, for although time does not go too slowly here, there is so much that one has seen in such a short while, that much of it takes on the air of being a long time ago.

Yesterday was pay day for us, and the first time I have drawn since I have left England. I decided I would buy a small radio for the tent to help brighten up the winter evenings, and now the crew have all decided to buy it between us. We haven't got it yet, but hope to in a day or two.

During the next week I am also hoping to lay my hands on a very good selection of photographs which will prove a very good memo for when I go home. I am very sorry I haven't brought my camera out here, and I was even wondering whether it would be possible for you to send it out here safely. However I shall leave that for you to decide.

Have just returned from dinner and another three letters. One airgraph from Mother (dated Oct.28th), one air mail (dated Oct. 29th but subsequently finished on Nov. 4th!) and an airgraph from Bernard. The air mail letter cards seem much quicker than the airgraphs (which seems contrary to your opinion at that time). To settle that little argument, none of your letters has so far been censored, but of course they are all liable to be.

Thanks for all the news and especially for the books which are coming. When I spoke of an Italian grammar it wasn't a hint by the way, but I still have not got hold of one, and it should prove most helpful. I haven't had much chance to widen my knowledge of Italian in recent weeks and I only know a few isolated words. Yes, the Sicilians are Italian to all intents and purposes, and very Catholic. Shrines are at numerous points along roads in squares (of which they are very fond) and on the walls outside farmhouses especially. Religion is born and bred very deeply in them, though I fear they take much of it for granted, or many of them must have elastic consciences. Their towns are for the most part very scruffy and dirty, and even smelly and they are content to live much more lowly and unambitiously than English people. Of course at the moment they are very undernourished as well.

I must now bring this to an end, thanking you very much for the latest letters (I have heard from Mary Gough) and hoping this will find you all well and happy,

Your Most Affectionate Son,
Philip

Italy,
Saturday, November 20th 1943

My Dear Mother and Father,

I am writing this letter without reference to your latest letters as I am in rather a hurry. I received your latest one last Monday morning and it had only been written the Monday night before that, so it was very quick, wasn't it? I remember you saying then that you had not heard for some eleven days or so but I hope that has long since been rectified; I am writing now with a fair regularity and I hope that there will not be many long spaces between your receiving them.

We are feeling much better now in our tent as we are gradually becoming organised. Last night I had my first sleep on a decent bed which I have purchased with two others from an Italian carpenter. It folds up very handily and is not very heavy – what a lovely night I had last night! I have also made good friends with an army sergeant on a nearby gunfight, who has had delivered to me a number of bricks from which we hope to construct a fire. I have not been so fortunate with the radio I had hoped to acquire, but as the mess is now also rapidly becoming more organised, that will not be such a drawback.

Yes, as you say in your letters the news these days is very wonderful indeed. There must be a very different spirit among our troops from that over the other side of the line. It's rather funny that both sides are getting nearer home yet the poor old Jerries must be very reluctant to do it! I'm afraid our chaps are not – judging from the numerous sign posts along 'Monty's Highway' which tell you, with a touch of humour, to turn left or carry straight on for London and various other British towns which are only 900 or so miles away! In many cases it is worked out to half a mile! Talking of sign posts there are many which make you smile. Some time back when passing under a partially wrecked bridge was a cautionary word of advice saying 'Drive slow, Musso's bridge nearly finito'.

I think you asked me in one of your letters how I found conversation with the Italians; well I can get on a little better perhaps than some others, with the help of a little Latin occasionally which will often give them an idea of the word, but for the most part it is rather difficult. However I think we are improving gradually.

I don't seem to have said a great deal in this letter, but if it lets you know that life in Italy is not doing me any harm, then it will have served its main purpose. Meanwhile I am hoping that all you at home are bearing up quite well and happily, and not doing too much worrying. Thanks for all your prayers which I am certain will be heard and which must be helping me very much. I hope that Wilfred Woods will be okay and if I should see him out here, I will let you know how he is looking, and tell him all the latest news of 'Blighty'. All my love and best wishes,

Your Most Affectionate Son,
Philip

Italy,
Wednesday, 24th November 1943

My Dear Father,

This may make you smile, but I really cannot recall whether the other day I wrote you birthday greetings or not. However not being willing to risk this notable occasion passing without a congratulatory word from me, I have resolved to write a very hurried note to wish you a very happy birthday with all the familiar greetings and wishes. I fear this will arrive a little late, but you will, I hope forgive that.

Life here is still brimful of interest if you call it interest. Anyway it is not so bad. Well at the moment I must fly so please excuse the brevity of my wishes which are none the less sincere. All My Love

Your Most Affectionate Son,
Philip

My Dear Mother and Father,

This letter would have been started about an hour ago had not one of these most annoying Italian whirlwinds suddenly sprung up in a matter of seconds, sending us scuttling along to our tents to try and save the position and keep most of our kit intact. While some of us were holding on like grim death to the canvass, others hastened hither and thither, beating down the tent pegs and fixing up the ropes. All now is calm (calm as regards the weather perhaps I should add) so here I am trying to write this letter. The above incident will probably be of interest to you in that it is typical of our little worries out here, but of course it is far worse when such things happen in the middle of the night, and when at last you are forced to leave the warm blankets for fear the tent will be blown from over you, leaving you exposed to the wind and the rain. What a life, isn't it? I shall never want to join the Boy Scouts after this war is over!

I received your letter dated Monday 15th yesterday, and I saw with a rather sad smile how you referred to one of my letters, in which I was suffering from the ill effects of too good a meal! Like most other things out here, the food has its ups and downs, and only recently we have been deep in one of the furrows, however things seem on the upgrade again and it is not so bad just now.

This last day or two we have heard a little about the bad nights that Berlin must have experienced this week; perhaps at home it is the main item of news and discussion. I rather imagine it is bound to have profound repercussions.

I am sorry that Kitty has not been so well, but I hope that by now all is well again. How are the others making out with the violin? Next Sunday in the local town there will be a Symphony Concert by an Italian Orchestra, but I doubt whether I shall be able to go, though it is especially for the troops. Talking about entertainment, they cater very well for the troops out here, and most of us are able to get to the cinema or a concert once a week and the ENSA[1] parties seem of a much higher order than they were in England, though I hardly ever attended them then. The Army chaps out here all seem a very good bunch of fellows.

I suppose that you have heard the good news from the front line out here tonight, it's very good isn't it? So Les thinks a lot of the Yanks, does he? I must confess that I too have to own to have a greater admiration for them since I have been out here.

I am sorry that you do not seem to have had two of my earlier letters – perhaps I said too much. Actually there were one or two things I mentioned about local towns and which I afterwards discovered oughtn't to have been referred to, so maybe there is the explanation.

I have just written an airgraph to Mary, but haven't heard from her yet.

I was telling her how, if she were an Italian girl, she would not be very concerned about finding a house after the war, for in this country of clear blue skies (!!!) you see any amount of huge families living in three or four rooms. I couldn't say whether they are different generations of the same family, but they all seem very easily satisfied as regards housing conditions. Apart from farmhouses, which have no rural beauty or picturesqueness about them, as so many have in England, I have seen no detached houses, nor any gardens. Washing is hung on bands outside windows, or up to odd trees and posts in the streets every day of the week and more often than not Persil could not have been used, which is perhaps a good job when you see how the passing traffic can soil it all.

As you can see I must now say farewell so here is sending you one and all my very best love,

Your Most Affectionate Son,
Philip

---

1. Entertainments National Service Association

Italy
Wednesday, 1st December 1943

My Dear Mother and Father,

There are two letters for which I have to thank you in this letter, the latter an airgraph from Mother, the former the usual fire–watching letter of Monday 16th[1] (or have I already answered that one?) Anyway thanks very much. I did not know whether I could detect an anxious note in the airgraph, but I do hope you are not worrying too much, as things are going very well for me.

You say also that the weather has been terribly cold. Here it has been cold, but we have had no frost up to now, and as it is December there must surely have been plenty at home; cold, rain and heavy winds are our main enemies and they spoil many a night's rest.

Just this minute four air letters have come in to me, two from both of you and one from Mary, one from Grove (who left Oscott about a year ago) – all dated Monday 22nd Mother you must not take too much notice when I mention a bit of tummy trouble, for everybody gets it out here, and in fact I have got off very lightly indeed. In the heat of summer are the greatest dangers of these ailments, but we are all well instructed in symptoms, preventive measures etc. etc.

As for your advice about food, well it would be all right if you had as much choice as that. There has been very little variety, but you have to eat what you can get. At the moment we are not doing too badly, but fresh vegetables would be very acceptable, though we always get them when we can. But in any case I can certainly put up with all this until such time as Jerry has received his final knock out, and I bet that we are doing much better this winter on the south side of the front than he on the north.

Yes I have heard from Mary Gough (once, nearly a month ago!) however I seem to have had a fair amount of other letters from chaps at Oscott, Bernard, Fr. Boland etc.

Just in case this letter is the last to reach you by Christmas I want to wish you a very happy and pleasant time; and don't think that it will be too hard for me, because there are turkeys and Christmas puddings on order not to mention a few other extra items to add to the festivity. In fact if you were to take a walk around some of our tents you would see a number of the said turkeys strutting about feeling quite at home in blissful ignorance of the fact that they are being fattened(!) for the slaughter. However I intend to write again in time for Christmas, so I hope this will not be the last mail.

I'm sorry to hear of Dennis being off again, but perhaps it will not be for so long this time. Funny you mentioning Auntie Kathleen, as I only dispatched an airgraph (full of apologies) to her yesterday. Have you heard from her recently?

Thanks for all the parcels that are on the way. You say I don't smoke cigarettes, but I am afraid that I have been while out here. By the way please excuse this scrawl, but I'm writing with my silk gloves on. Outside the wind howls and causes the tent to flap and shake in an almost terrifying manner.

I'm glad that Gerald is settling down very well now, that he has a job and I hope that he will soon find his feet properly and settle down to the sort of work he really likes.

From Mary's letter it appears she has now had all she wants of army life, but still I don't think she will have too long to wait now. Well I don't think there is much more I can say in this short space, so shall bid you farewell, and send you all my best love and wishes,

From Your Most Affectionate Son
Philip

---

1. His father was on fire watching duty during the war and if he was able, used the occasion to write to Philip

My Dear Mother and Father,

Well I have a few moments to myself just now, so I thought it would be a good idea to write off another letter to you particularly as this one will probably be the last to get to you before Christmas. You may be interested to know that just now I have had to rub my eyes because of all the smoke that has poured out of one of our experimental fires that we are trying to make in the tent. What a good job it is that we can all see the funny side of it, and are so full of mirth. That is one of the things that has amazed me since I have been out here, for I have noticed that although things are often hard to put up with, and although difficulties are many, and there are so few things to occupy one's mind, yet we get just as many laughs if not more than we used to in England. Chaps seem to come into their own a lot more, and find enjoyment from innumerable small things which they would not have noticed before.

This change is all the more noticeable with those chaps who before they come out here, could think of no other place than the pub in which to spend their evenings and which had to be the atmosphere for all their merriment. We have no beer out here, but apart from a few odd wishes or grumbles, I don't think that it is missed any more than (one) would miss the few opportunities of having fish and chips. There is very little wine drunk in spite of the fact that it is very cheap, so the net result is that nearly all of us are quite sober all the time.

I have heard some 'gen' this last few days of a big Conference between Joe Stalin, Churchill and Roosevelt but nothing definite. Apart from this theatre of war, I do not really get much news at all, but if it is all going as well as it is out in this country, it cannot be going badly, can it? Perhaps by the time you receive this letter, it will be even better – I certainly hope so.

I had a letter from Mary the other day and she said that she feels sure that we will all be at home for Christmas 1944 – what a lovely thought that is! I can hardly visualise what it will be like to be at peace once more.

Today we caught one of the most curious species of insect I have ever seen. He was something like a beetle only with terrific armour plating on his back. His size was such that he filled a whole match box, and we were all keen on giving him a rather wide berth. It was Ginger (my Wopp) who finally dared to catch him in a match box and then we heard little squeals coming from the inside! Talking about these curious things that seem to thrive on Italian soil (not counting the odd creatures of Mussolini's calibre) I wonder whether I have ever told you about the snakes that I have seen and killed about here! Oh yes and most horrible of all are the long brown centipedes which never fail to send a shiver up the spine of even the most dauntless among us. However I think that winter is rather curbing (though not stopping) the activities of both snake and centipede.

And now I have reached a point in this letter where I invariably take stock, and ask myself what I have written and then what I should have written; then of course there is the additional question of what would you like me to write and could I have obliged, or is there time and space to make up for it now? Anyway, all this time, space is getting shorter and I have come to the conclusion that I have just rambled on without giving you much consideration, but on second thoughts I imagine that it will give you a more intimate insight into our activities out here and the atmosphere in which we live.

And if I have not mentioned much about you it is not because I do not think of you, for that would be very hard for me to do. I am always wondering what you can be doing and the only times I can be pretty well certain are at 8 o'clock on Sunday mornings, when I know that you will all be remembering me as well. I hope you are all in very good health and spirits, and as I am now going to settle in bed, here is wishing you good night, very happy Christmas and all my love.

Your Most Affectionate Son
Philip

Italy
Friday, 10th December 1943

My Dear Mother and Father,

At the moment of penning this letter, there is no more mail in but I hear that up at the P.O there is another full bag, so there may be something in from you. The letter Daddy generally writes on fire–watching night seems to arrive here on the Wednesday nine days later, but this time it seems to have proved an exception.

It is a funny thing, but at the beginning of a letter like this I am nearly always looking for something to say and wondering how I shall fill up the other two pages and a half, yet by the time I am approaching the end there are always a score of things which I find I could say or continue talking about. So it is just now, and I am all set to tell you that this week there is very little to say and my brain has run dry. However I must set to and make whatever I do say as interesting as possible. I don't think it would be of much use if I told you that I was the happiest boy in the world, because it would only make you think that I must be thoroughly miserable and fed up with life, but I will at least discount the latter view and assure you that I am enjoying life on the whole, and am certainly bearing up as well as the majority of chaps.

Actually what one might almost class 'home comforts' have cheered things up a great deal and made everything far more tolerable. For instance we have now a fire in the tent, and found means of keeping most of the smoke going in the right direction (i.e. going out of the tent flaps). This week has also seen fresh progress in the lighting at night time, for now we have an electric bulb, whereas before the whole period of darkness, which as you know is now very long, was brightened only by two very crude makeshift oil–lamps, which gave barely enough light for one person to read by and which succeeded mainly in spreading around their not sweet smelling odours. In fact with Bill Shakespeare we might have complained that our noses were full of indignation!

It was at that time I made strenuous efforts to acquire a radio, but I never brought it off. But in this respect too we are better off once more, for the Sergeants' Mess has just managed to get its radio on again and there is no doubt that it adds great warmth to the atmosphere and gives one a real link with home. It comes through very clearly most of the time as well and if it were not for an occasional fading, one could almost persuade oneself that it was the B.B.C. Home Service and that one was back in England. The only time I really hear the news is at 7 o'clock and 9.45pm both on the African services. You can easily hear those yourself, for our time is the same as yours.

By the way, Jimmy (my navigator) told me the other day that his wife had received that registered envelope from you – the one I asked you to send last September. Talking about money reminds me that I have made a remittance to you of £6. 15d. today. It is money that I do not want out here and which may as well be banked. I think you will have notice of it in about a month or six weeks. I may make several more, so do not be surprised if they suddenly come through.

The day before yesterday I sent a green envelope (sea–mail) to Fr. Boland, so you can tell him a reply to his air–letter is on its way. I cannot write airmail to anyone else but you, apart from very occasional ones, for instance I sent one to Aunty Kathleen a few days ago and one to Mary Gough a week ago. I have had another letter from her and she says that there has been a great deal of illness among some of her nephews and nieces next door but one, and now, or at that time, her Mother had also to be confined to bed; but it seems that things are gradually getting better. I hope that in this respect all is very well at home, and that all your faces are bright and cheerful. You see I <u>have</u> managed to fill most of this air–letter!

Well, all my love and very best wishes,

Your Most Affectionate Son
Philip

Italy
11th December 1943

My Dear Lorna and Monica,

Just now while I write I bet you are being urged to hurry up and get to bed; the 9 o'clock news will just be starting, and supper will be being prepared. So just before you go upstairs I want to say 'Good night and God bless you from this far off land of Italy'. I am sorry, Lorna, that you have not been well, but I hope that by now you are much better, and that you, Monica are making the best of this time when you are not being teased by me!

It is now Sunday morning, a night later, and just now you will be preparing to go to Benediction, but I am not because I am unable to. In Italy they do not have evening service. Will you tell Daddy that I have just received a letter from him, and please tell Kathleen that I am very sorry that she has been sick again. I shall try and write to her soon, and Gerald too. I should love to be at home with you this Christmas, but I am afraid that I shall only be able to do so in my thoughts.

Mary told me in a letter how well you are both getting on with the violin; you will have to play 'Ave Maria' for me when I come home, and maybe I shall even try to accompany you on the piano.

Will you give my love to all at home and keep a little for yourself,

Philip

Note – this letter sent by sea and not received until mid January:

R.A.F. Squadron
C.M.F.
Italy
Sunday, 12th December 1943

My Dear Mother and Father,

As to how far I will get with this letter tonight I do not know, but I thought that an extra letter by sea will do no harm, and it does not cramp me for space. At the moment there is a programme on the wireless that Gerald may well have switched on – in fact I can readily imagine that even now he may be sitting in the corner laughing his head off at the antics of Mr. Lovejoy and Enoch in 'Happidrome', for this programme is on the home and overseas service.

Today I have just received a letter from Daddy which has taken much longer than usual (nearly a fortnight) but I will answer that in my usual air letter in a few days time.

Christmas is fast approaching and quite naturally my thoughts tend evermore towards a home which grows more dear with every day which passes out here. Not that I am walking about miserable and forlorn, for I am very pleased that I can be out here with so many of the other chaps who have fought steadily from long before El Alamein. Furthermore we all seem to enjoy ourselves very much more than we used to in far better conditions in England, and there are unlimited horizons in the realm of thought. Out here one comes across human nature as one never did in England. I have spoken to soldiers who a few days ago have been up in the thick of it, to others who have not seen war—time England – others who have been away most of the war and who have even had the most initial disappointment of having had their engagements broken off (how common this complaint is with poor chaps who have been in the desert three or more years) in fact they seem to expect it after two and a half years! Then, it is a revelation to see how all the troops out here look forward to their letters from home, and how they seek for every bit of news from England as it is nowadays. No—one tries to hide their hopes and fears as they would have done in England.

The 'Tommy' is just the same as ever in company with the Italians, his soft heart seems to get the better of him and he will forego his own rations or some of them when he sees the plight of so many of the Italians. He is always very much at home with the children, and even as he talks one can almost read his thoughts to which he will give occasional utterance. 'This d. . . war was none of our making, and yet what else what else can we do?' – I do not know how much of its catastrophic results Hitler has seen, I'm sure he must have seen lots of it in Poland and Russia and I can only deduce that he must have a very hard heart indeed as he contemplates his own handiwork and still forebears to have done with it. There is no doubt at all that much as England has suffered she has been spared much more, and I always thank God that this has been so. I hope that after the war with all these experiences fresh in mind people will turn with great sincerity with help from God to wipe away this curse.

This morning I was able to get to Mass for the first time for a month, and had a chat with the Padre whom I found very nice and helpful. He gave me a medal of Our Lady and the Immaculate Conception which he blessed, and he said that he liked all pilots to have them. Out here we can receive Holy Communion without fasting, and they are trying to arrange evening classes for us. Talking of medals reminds me that I have acquired many in my short sojourn in Italy. Nuns often make a point of giving them to British troops, and when I have paid visits to churches I have also been given them by other visitors.

I see that I have well nigh completed four pages of what would seem to be a gloomy picture indeed, or at least I have allowed my thoughts on some of these things to run away with me and I have dwelt mostly on the grimmer side of what I have seen.

However there is one consoling thing about it all, namely that the greatest and most prosperous eras are borne of sorrow and for my part I am very optimistic regarding the post war period, now I hope not too far distant future. As far as the Allied nations are concerned there seems to be plenty of generosity and sound planning.

Does it seem long to you since I left you on Snow Hill station that Thursday morning? To me it seems ages and yet I cannot say that the weeks have dragged or that I have forgotten what England looks like. I suppose that so many places have been passed and so many new experiences crushed into a small space, that it seems so long. I remember as I took my last glance of England just after dawn on the morning of September 7th with grey mist before me and my feet feeling terribly cold and I thought to myself 'So this is the beginning of, well, what? . . .' And on we went for four long and weary hours occasionally catching glimpses of the wide wastes of sea down below, but mainly of the limitless oceans of white cloud below us, which merged on the horizon with the greyer cloud above us. How awfully lonely it made one feel, and how small in all that vastness, and how powerless as we ploughed our way through occasional rain storms not being able to see a thing in front but a dark sheet of murk! What a relief when at long last we finally saw land, and saw Lisbon lying far below on our left. And then how suddenly hot and oppressive as we went on thirsty and hungry and what a thrill as we jumped down from the cockpit in another continent! Yes all that happened in one short morning of September 7th and yet I think to describe it adequately I would have to write at much greater length. And that is, I suppose, how life has become this last three months and the explanation why August 26th seems so far away.

Nevertheless, the time is going quickly and I hope I shall not find it too long in getting home once more, and in the meantime I hope you are not worrying much, because I repeat what I told you before that I am exceptionally lucky in this posting. I cannot give you more concrete grounds for this confidence, for I might have to exceed the bounds of military security to do it, but I repeat that I am very fortunate, and in any case our Lord will look after me whatever I might be doing if that is His will, and for my part I am asking no more than that I fulfill it and that your prayers will be heard.

And now I think I have written enough for one letter, but before I close I will ask you to give my best wishes to all friends and relations, thank them all for their prayers which are very comforting – especially Dorothy for I have a feeling that she prays harder than most others. For the prayers of you all at home and of Kathleen, Lorna and Monica I am also particularly grateful and I try always to return them to the best of my ability.

Here then is sending you one and all my very best love and wishes and a peaceful 1944!

Your Most Affectionate Son
Philip

Italy
Wednesday, 15th December 1943

My Dear Mother and Father,

Thanks very much for the letter of Monday 28th which I received last Sunday. The mail situation seems temporarily to have deteriorated so I may have to wait a few more days before receiving your usual ones, but I am glad to hear that the latest news from home is that all is well, but I am sorry to learn that Kitty has been down ill again.

Last Sunday I wrote off a sea letter to you, but I do not suppose you will receive it for a month or so after this one. It is in one of those green envelopes that you must have become so familiar with in the last war. In this letter however I can answer some little things from your last one to me. I am glad that you say Northern Italy is far more like Western Europe, because in that case it should be much better than it is down here in Southern Italy. I should very much like to visit some of the Northern towns like Florence, Padua, Genoa and Venice and of course I do not want to leave Italy without having a good look round Rome.

There were a few places of historical interest in Sicily, such as Augusta, Syracuse where there are old Roman ruins, but I am afraid I had not sufficient time to see them properly. Indeed most of the ruins I saw were of a much later period! The mainland of Italy is much better than Sicily, for it is far more like England while Sicily seems to have more akin to the barrenness of Africa. Yes, the Italian one sees round here with a fair complexion is the exception – nearly all are dark brown or black, and the womenfolk seem extremely fond of black clothes and shawls and I don't think they could all be in mourning! Those men who are not what one would call shabbily dressed, seem fond of what we in England would term 'cheap and showy' clothes. I'm afraid their ties would disgust any English chap who considered himself a connoisseur in them! Of course there is pretty well no industry about in the South, and I could not think what most people find to do beyond making vino, ice cream and cutting hair (I should think one shop in four is a barber).

You mention my trying to purchase a radio. Well I have not got one yet, but it is mainly because I want a small battery set, and I cannot get one in our present locality. Ordinary radio sets are available, in fact it is surprising how many things one can get at some places, but prices are going up by leaps and bounds. It can generally be said that the further away from the front, or those parts the longest occupied, are the most expensive.

There is one thing I have noticed out here which strikes me as most peculiar and that is Italian cemeteries. They are most wonderful and elaborate affairs. Each gravestone is more like a miniature palace or castle, and without exception more ingenuity is shown in building these, than there is in keeping or making the homes of those who still live. In this country one seems to fare much better by dying, and the other day I noticed a funeral which was being led by a small band playing a brisk march tune! The atmosphere of rejoicing seemed complete when the hearse rolled by, a masterpiece of decorative art, and enlivened by all the most brilliant colours of the rainbow.

What a curious people they all are and even after allowing for different nations outlook and way of life, I often think that they are all most laughable, especially when you think that they pretended to have such wonderful military prowess..

It will now soon be time for me to say goodbye and I see I have said nothing except of one or two things I see and think out here, but I am in good health and spirits, and telling myself that Victory is just around the corner, and that soon I will be able to come home – who knows it may well be! Anyway until next time, all my love and a very happy New Year,

Your Most Affectionate Son
Philip

Italy
December 21st 1943

My Dear Mother and Father,

I received a letter from you dated Dec 6th and one 1st Dec some few days ago, both of which were very welcome. I cannot quite remember which day it was that I wrote to you, but I do not think it is a week (ago). I am glad that things at home are going on fairly well, and if the flu has been very prevalent I hope that it has not prevailed on any of you. Thanks for your Christmas wishes and all the other good things that you tell me are on the way; I will endeavour to save those photographs for Kitty as you ask, that is when the camera arrives.

It will be Christmas Day next Saturday and yet the weather at the moment seems anything but Christmassy. During the daytime it is often quite warm and sunny, though it becomes very cold with the advent of evening, and so it remains until the sun comes up next day. We have not had so much rain of late which has been a good thing. Anyway the weather that we are having seems a lot better than you have been having at home. As Christmas is at hand you will probably want to know what I shall be doing, but apart from one or two details there is not a great deal that is definite. There will be lots of good things to eat, including turkeys, pork and Christmas pudding. There will also be Midnight Mass for us in a large church in the local town, which is something you will not have. There are stacks of Christmas cards and letters coming in these last few days, and nearly everybody is keeping a good look out for things for themselves.

Somehow I cannot make headway with this letter, and I imagine you may be thinking it a rather poor effort, but there are a group of chaps just nearby who are talking and laughing with extraordinary zest, and I am finding it extra hard to put my mind on it properly.

Fancy Mary is still talking about her 'rights' in the A.T.S.! It doesn't seem to agree with some of her earlier and loftier ideas about it. Of course to me seems more laughable than ever after seeing so much of the grimmer side of war, but it does not do any good to take the attitude so often expressed by chaps who have served a long and arduous time in this theatre and who tend to condemn all the more fortunate ones still in 'blighty'. But to me it does seem a very small thing to adopt such an attitude even if it were correct.

As you remark in your letter the Germans will not spend a very pleasant Christmas this year! The sooner they realise the game is up, or the sooner they can get rid of their present ruthless gang at the top the better it will be for all concerned. However it rather looks as though Hitler will do almost anything to hold them down and retain power, but he could not be a happy man these days. What a terrible condition he has put Europe into – no wonder he dreads the consequences!

And now I am approaching the end of this letter once more so I shall conclude in the usual way, by wishing you all at home a very happy New Year, and that you will have had a Happy Christmas. All my love,

Your Most Affectionate Son,
Philip

Italy

24th December 1943

My Dear Mother and Father,

Just at present it is about 9 o'clock on Christmas Eve – I am on duty all night and so isolated from all the festivity, the strains of which all seem to meet at my table here, for from one side (the airman's mess I think) that wonderful melody 'All through the Night' can just be heard, while if I listen hard I can discern the coarser notes of 'My eyes are dim, I cannot see' from the Sergeants' mess. Up to the moment the Officers must be retaining a dignified and more austere joviality for I have heard nothing from their quarters! However being on my own on this most wonderful of all nights makes me more reflective than ever, and of course my thoughts at such times always fly back home to all of you and I cannot but think how wonderful it would be to be with you all, to sing those carols which are now echoing through the countryside.

I am hoping you will have a very happy time and you can be sure that I am; I am writing an air letter as well. All my love,

Your Most Affectionate Son,
Philip

27th December 1943

My Dear Mother and Father,

In this fair land of sunshine and blue skies, I sit frozen to the marrow so if this letter lacks any of the usual points, good or bad, which you expect, you will know the reason why. Actually there is an icy wind blowing and since it comes after a day of continuous rain we are not in the best of positions for dealing with it, nor can we evade it by scurrying between good solid walls or cramming round a fire, so as I say here I am making the best of a bad job taking what cover I can in the tent. I shall be very glad for the drier season to come again, for everywhere you go, you are slithering around in mud and it is hard going if you want to walk any distance, as for instance I did yesterday when going to Mass. A distance of a mile or so took me best part of an hour, which you can readily understand when you realise that each leg has to pick up about twice its own weight in mud, and the fact that often you cannot put your foot down with any certainty of its staying put.

However I started off with the idea of answering two letters which arrived yesterday, Boxing Day. One was written on December 9th. (Mother's – and continued over the next weekend) and one on December 13th. Thanks for them both.

I should not bother about the camera as it is so much trouble and uncertain. We may get one out here. I am very sorry you have gone to so much trouble with it though. Yes I have heard before that chaps in the army can say where they are, but it seems that the R.A.F. are more particular, which I can understand in a way. However places which I have seen, and in which I have been, include Catania and Messina in Sicily, Taranto, Brindisi and Bari in Italy. The last town that I have seen so far is Bari which I believe is where King Victor and Badoglio hang out, but I have not been visited by them yet so I cannot give you all the latest inside information! More than these bare facts I am afraid I can tell you but little until later on, when we get Jerry back into Jerryland.

I had a very good Christmas Day, although I was on an all night duty that prevented my going to Midnight Mass and I had to go in the morning. We had a very good dinner and served the airmen to their meal. There was a toast which the S.W.O.[1] gave us in the mess which I liked very much, that next Christmas Day would see us having our Christmas dinner in our own homes. What a cheer went up and mine were as loud as anybody's! In the evening I laughed more than I have ever laughed before at some of the goings on in the mess. There were plenty of choice Italian wines and a small amount of beer and best of all some wonderful turkey sandwiches.

I am trying to send you two copies of our *Daily* out here, *Eighth Army News*. I notice that in one copy is news of Monsignor Griffin's new appointment to Westminster. That is a great honour for Birmingham and Cotton isn't it? Will you please keep both these copies for me, as they will be good things to have as memories after the war.

Well I am frozen and cannot write very well just now so please excuse my finishing like this. I am very well and happy and hope you are. Here is sending you all my love and very best wishes.

From Your Most Affectionate Son,
Philip

---

1. Station Warrant Officer

Italy
29th December 1943

My Dear Mother and Father,

Well Christmas is now over for you at home I suppose, perhaps it was this morning that you started work once more, or perhaps I do you wrong for maybe you started yesterday. Anyway I hope that you have all enjoyed yourselves very much and that the girls have helped brighten up the time with all their carols round the piano. For me Christmas has lacked most of its usual atmosphere, save for the good will and 'Merry Christmas' salutation accorded to all and by all.

The weather here is more harsh than it has ever been since I left England – a gale force icy wind has followed a Boxing day which rained from one end to the other. Talk about mud and its consequent evils, I bet Flanders' mud has not so very much to show us now; snow has been in evidence on the hills but so far we have been spared it. However I am looking forward to the summer coming once more, though even then I suppose we shall grumble about the mosquitoes who give us no rest in the very hot weather – perhaps the war will be over then, for I have been reading a number of the papers from home and there is a lot of talk about it being over in the next six months.

Talking about these papers, it is with a very critical eye that we read some of the articles on Italy. It seems to me that many of the commentators (especially in the political field) would do much better to come and see things for themselves before making sweeping statements of what the people feel and think. There was an article I read in the *Sunday Express* which also expressed this view. A good instance of this is the way they talk of the King of Italy. Whether or not he is good or bad, he certainly seems to have retained popularity with the Italian people. Besides things are too grim for irresponsible talk of the type one so often reads.

I have never told you, have I, of some of the ways we amuse ourselves when left on our own some evenings in the tent. Fortunately 'Ginger' who is my Wopp is adept at making laughs, sometimes with reminiscences that date from his school–days up to the present, sometimes with the silly things he does when acting the fool. He used to be a brick layer in civvy street and from there too he can give us most humorous stories.

Sometimes we often burst into song, and Ginger will start 'locks, bolts and bars' – (four semi quavers) which I in turn take up in a slightly different pitch, all of which we both repeat, and then (quavers for two voice parts, 'rifle, rob' sung by different singer) 'when we rifle, rob and plunder' we both sing and repeat. I am sorry I have missed the central part out which is 'will fly asunder, when we rifle, rob and plunder'. Anyway the refrain gives us infinite pleasure, and is even becoming well known with other chaps in the squadron. There are many variations both in the theme and movement and I am sure that at times we must even attain to operatic heights.

Of course our biggest laughs as they always do among air crews, come from different little experiences to do with flying. I often think what a pity it is that the concert halls could not reproduce some of these, although it may be that the general public would not see them in the same light that we do. You will see from what I tell you that our pleasures are mainly very simple, but they are also very stimulating, and I think that I can say I get more fun out of ordinary life than I have ever done before. If it were not for the fact that we are not much further away from home I would much prefer life in the field to that at home, for everybody seems more helpful and more noble in spirit, and I will even add, more religious. Certainly there is more tolerance of religion and its principles – and how all to a man loves to think of going home once more! And how they all love their mail from home! Really it is a revelation, when used to standards in England.

I see space is getting short once more so I had better prepare to bid you adieu. This morning I had a letter from Mr. Duffy and he says you all are well for which I am pleased. Will you thank him and tell him that an airgraph will soon be on its way. It is time now to wish you Good night and to send you all my love and very best wishes,

From Your Most Affectionate Son,
Philip

Italy
2nd January 1944

My Dear Mother and Father,

I don't know whether you will be able to see the marks of a recent storm on this letter when you receive it – but this valuable air letter was nearly lost and ruined as a result of it. I would have written yesterday had it not been for the fact that we had all our work cut out in pulling ourselves together, re–strengthening the tent and generally sorting things out.

However there was one bright spot yesterday when I received a letter dated December 20th so I can reply to that as well. You will be pleased to know that last year I received your parcel and another air letter from Mother dated December 23rd which took eight days inclusive – that of course was the day before yesterday 31st

December! When I was reading your letter then, I was going to tell you not to feel so sorry for me as things were well under control, but I'm afraid I received a slight check to this complacency when the New Year came in like a roaring lion – I only hope that now it will go out meekly as a lamb handing a peaceful heritage to next year.

Thank you very much for the parcel and all your letters and Christmas cards therein. Those of Lorna and Monica were very good indeed and I must say it was like a little bit of home to read all their letters and their little pieces of news. Thank them all very much will you please, and I shall endeavour to write as well when I get a few more airgraphs. All the presents inside were very acceptable, especially the boot polish which has been very hard to obtain for some time. The dictionary settled an argument that same evening, and I am very pleased with the Italian grammar which seems a very useful one for my purpose. Thank Mrs. Sheehan for the shaving soap. I shall try and get in an airgraph to her as well.

I am pleased that Gerald is going on so well now – I expect he will seem quite changed when next I see him; as I picked up my plate to go for breakfast this morning I wondered what he would think if he had to use my plate which had been clean the night before, but was then muddy, grimy and smelly after being the night's playground of the numerous mice we get round here.

Yes most of those turkeys have now had their day – and very nice they were too. I will let you have our Christmas Day menu card when I write you another sea letter. Incidentally I am going to try and write you a few more sea letters. We have been allowed a few extra air mail letter cards for Christmas time, but I have almost come to the end of the surplus ones now so I shall only be able to write once a week by this form of letter. I should have written to you much more except that our conditions are rather against prolific writing. Will you keep all these letters please, as they will be interesting to re–read in better times ahead and will perhaps recall many of the things I would put in diary form if I were keeping one. In a sense I think letters are better, because they bring back one's feelings and reactions much more vividly than a series of happenings listed each day.

It is rather unfortunate really that some of the highlights have to remain obscure, but it will not matter much.

My Italian I'm afraid is still very poor indeed. We do not get an awful lot of chances to learn or improve it, and when we do, gesticulating seems to be the best form of conversation. When you go into a barber's shop, you are shown very politely to your chair and the operation proceeds with him occasionally nodding to see whether his handiwork meets with your approval – which it always does because otherwise you would be all day trying to explain and even then would not be successful.

Well I must conclude now, so here is all my love and very best wishes

Your Most Affectionate Son
Philip

Philip was reported missing following air operations on 4th January 1944 in Ortona, shortly after the eight day Battle of Ortona, in December 1943. Although Philip could never allude to military operations in his letters (due to censorship), he must have been aware of its destructive force. The whole town had been reduced to rubble and its San Tommaso cathedral physically torn in half in the run up to Christmas that year, the symbolism of which will not have been lost on Philip. The Allies, including many Canadians, fought the Germans in Ortona in what has been described as the most ferocious, bitter, bloody battle of the Italian campaign; day after day fighting had continued with artillery, air strikes, and for the first time in the conflict, hand to hand combat, leaving over 3,500 dead. The Germans retreated on 27th December, having been warned that carpet bombing of Ortona was scheduled the next morning. Engaged in a continued show of strength, Philip's plane and crew was one of those reported missing.

APPENDICES

APPENDIX 1

LETTERS OF SYMPATHY

From Philip's brother—in—law, Leslie. He addresses Philip's mother, as 'Mother' as was often customary:

R.A.F Wellesbourne
Mountford
Warwickshire
12.1.44

My Dear Mother,

I had a letter from Dad this morning telling me that Philip was missing. It was a terrible shock to me and I know how much more so it would be to you. I know it must be a terrible worry, but don't give up hope. Look how many pilots in that part of the world have been reported missing and yet got back to their base.

I certainly won't forget to pray hard for him and I know everyone else who knows him will do so too, and if the worst does come to the worst and you do not hear from him, first remember this, I personally never knew anyone who was more fitted to go straight to heaven. But put all that talk aside, I think it is highly probable you will hear from him soon. I hope so please God.

I am at the moment at a convent school of all places, tell Kitty that and I bet she won't believe it. I have at last managed to get on one of these 'Sword of the Spirit' leadership courses, and it really has done me good. I have put Wellesbourne's address on the top because I will be going back on Friday.

Please let me know if you hear anything, if you can spare the time.

God bless you.
Fondest love
Les xxxxxx

Ps I have of course told Mary.

From Philip's sister, Mary (now married to Leslie):

646 (M)H.A.A. Bty RA
Bawtry Road,
Bainsworth
Nr. Rotherham.
14th. Jan

My dear Mother and Daddy,

I was shocked to get a letter from Les this morning with the news that Philip is missing, the news took so long to get here. I feel at a loss to know what to say, I just hope and pray that he is safe and well and that you will all get news soon. Keep <u>hoping</u> and <u>praying</u> won't you? I will write to Fr. Holoron tonight, and get him to say a Mass for him.

I am moving from here (Alley Beeches) tomorrow and we expect to go to Chapeltown, and go mobile for some time to come relieving batteries so please write to Brinsworth as it will catch me up pretty quick.

I am wondering how you are feeling yourself, I hope the shock has not upset you too much. I wondered whether to ask for any time off, but I don't feel it would help much, especially after this time. If your nerves are bad or you are ill, be sure and let me know and I will get some time off. When we get to Chapeltown there is a chance we may get some passes as there are none here unless we have got good reason.

I am not going to make this a long letter, but remember to look after <u>yourself</u> and <u>keep hoping.</u> I will pray hard.

God bless you all
Love Mary

From Philip's Aunt Celestine:

35 Berners St
Leicester
Jan. 18th 1944

My dear Norah and Gerald,

We are all terribly sorry to hear the bad news and only hope that before long you will hear that Phillip is safe and well. In the meantime you may be sure that we shall <u>all pray</u> for his safety. Thank you for sending my photograph. Thank the children for the nice little letters they sent me. Tell them Mr. Dunn often asks about them, and he says that Pony is as naughty as ever. Sister Loyola was asking how they were getting on the other day. We liked the Christmas cards very much. They were beautifully done.

Try and not worry too much, though it is easy to talk I know.

When are you coming to see us again, it's your turn you know!

Best love from all here
Celestine
Xxxxxxx

From Philip's schoolfriend, Tom Gavin:

Oscott College
Sutton Coldfield
Birmingham
18.1.44

Dear Mrs. Hermolle,

It was only last night that I heard the very sad news from Jack Hartley that Philip is missing. I find it difficult to say how much I sympathise with you and your family. If we who were at Cotton with him loved him so much for all his great qualities, then you must have loved him very much more. I can only say that I shall pray for him in the future as I have prayed in the past – please God we may yet see him safe and sound, or at least you may hear from him.

We were particularly friendly during his last year at Cotton – I had to stop on for another year – and he used to write to me fairly regularly. I've kept all the letters he wrote to me since I came to Oscott including his last Airgraph at Christmas and I'll send you most of them if you like, as I know how much I prize the letters of my own relatives. I have a photograph of him – taken in Canada – but I should like one taken from rather less distance away, please, if you could possibly spare me one.

Whatever Philip did, he did with the knowledge that he did it because it was right. If Philip does not come back, though God may grant that he will, then you may rest assured that he met his Creator with the clearest conscience that anyone can have. The trials that he underwent to attend Mass when in the Forces filled us all with greatest admiration, and I am sure that all of us here who knew him are praying hard for him and for you and your family.

Yours very sincerely
Tom Gavin

St. Paul's High School
Vernon Road,
Edgbaston,
Birmingham 16
19.1.44

Dear Mrs. Hermolle,

I am so sorry to learn of your anxiety and I assure you of my sympathy and prayers.

Thank you for letting me see your dear son's letter. It is a beautiful one, full of trust in God and love of his home. Our Blessed Lord will surely look after your son whatever has befallen him and you have the consolation of knowing that he was faithful.

He is in God's Hands but it is a great trial for you and you have my deepest sympathy.

The children, too, are praying for him.

With all kind wishes and regards,

I remain,
Yours sincerely in Jesus Christ
Sr. Veronica Marie

From Philip's school friend, Colin Doyle:

S/2148087 Sgt. JC Doyle
The Hall
Great Bromley
Nr. Colchester
Essex

Dear Mrs. Hermolle,

I am afraid that no letter could ever express how much regret the sad news about Philip has caused me and how much sympathy I have for you in your present trial. I know how my own Mother worries about me, so I also know what a big blow this has been to you.

Philip and I were great friends at Cotton and were on the Lourdes pilgrimage in 1939 together. During our letters to each other since we have been in the services, we have promised to make a pilgrimage to Lourdes as soon as possible after the war is over. Therefore, I suggest we offer our prayers to Our Lady of Lourdes.

I have made arrangements for a Mass to be said for our intention and no doubt the merciful God will answer our prayers. A blow, like this, only makes us in the Forces more determined than ever to finish the job and kill the Evils we are fighting. That Stockport address is correct and I will always welcome any news you get of Philip.

Once again, my deepest sympathy to you all, and assuring you of my humble prayers for Philip's safety.

Yours very sincerely
Colin Doyle

Air Ministry
(Casualty Branch)
73–77 Oxford Street
W1
25th July 1944

Sir,

I am directed to refer to the letter dated 20th January 1944 from the Department notifying you that your son, Flight Sergeant Philip Joseph Hermolle, Royal Air Force, was reported missing as the result of air operations on the night of 4th January 1944, and to inform you, with regret, although no news of your son has come to hand, a report has been received from the Base Personnel Office, Royal Air Force, British North African Forces, stating that the body of Sergeant R.E. Blair, a member of your son's crew, has been recovered by Army personnel at Caspel di Sangro, Central Italy, 22 miles south east of Sulmona.

I am to add an expression of the Department's sympathy with you in your anxiety, and to assure you that you will be informed of any further news received.

Telegram

3 AUG 1944

PRIORITY CC GA HERMOLLE ESQ 128 FARNHAM RD HANDSWORTH BIRMINGHAM=
FROM AIR MINISTRY KINGSWAY PC 432 3/8/44 DEEPLY REGRET TO ADVISE YOU THAT YOUR SON 1354399 FLT/SGT PHILIP JOSEPH HERMOLLE IS NOW REPORTED TO HAVE LOST HIS LIFE AS THE RESULT OF AIR OPERATIONS ON 4TH JANUARY STOP THE AIR COUNCIL EXPRESS THEIR PROFOUND SYMPATHY STOP LETTER FOLLOWS SHORTLY STOP UNDER SECRETARY OF STATE STOP

Buckingham Palace

To G.A. Hermolle, Esq.

The Queen and I offer you our heartfelt sympathy in your great sorrow.

We pray that your country's gratitude for a life so nobly given in its service may bring you some measure of consolation.

George R.I.

From Colin Doyle's mother:

Trigo
South Drive
Poynton Park
Stockport

Dear Mrs. Hermolle,

It grieves me much to think of your sad loss. Pray bear up as well as you can. Colin had told us of Philip's death, also your letter, but do excuse him, because he took the blow so hard. Colin is somewhere in Europe, I have wrote and told him of your letter and card, and told him I will keep the card until he comes home, as I have placed it amongst his most treasured possessions.

Yours sincerely
Mrs. Mary Doyle

From Dorothy, Philip's young lady friend in Brighton:

94 Stanmer Villas
Brighton 6
Sussex
24th October 1944

My dear Mrs. Hermolle,

I received your letter on Saturday, and would like once again to express my deepest sympathy with you and your family in your dreadful loss. I sincerely wish I had been able to write before, but as I explained, I had only that afternoon come across the address which Philip gave me while I was stationed in Brighton.

I expect you'll be pleased to know that I am a Catholic. Actually I met Philip in the C.W.L. Canteen in Brighton where I used to help a few times a week. He was, I'm sure, the staunchest Catholic I met during the two years I was at the Canteen, and he was very well liked by all the elder women who ran the Canteen. I missed him badly after he left Brighton, as for the three or four months at the end of his stay here we were together almost every evening. I was proud that he should give me his companionship, being so much younger than him, both in year and disposition, and it is due mainly to Philip that I learned to appreciate really good music. When he came back for these two 48 hour leaves, music was definitely our main topic of conversation, as by then I had acquired a small record library of my own.

I have one photo of Philip which he sent when he was at Bicester. I believe it was taken when he was stationed at the Isle of Man. I first saw it when he was showing me snaps of his family, and also his stay in Canada and I had always admired it. It isn't very big, only a small snap actually, but it's very like him, and to me is an ever constant reminder of a most delightful friendship.

I too, would very much like to meet you Mrs. Hermolle, and will take advantage of any opportunity to call and see you.

Before he left England Philip told me he had asked St. Teresa to be his patroness whilst he was in the Forces – I've never forgotten and will continue to pray each day to her that Eternal Happiness for Philip will not be long delayed.

In deepest sympathy I am
Yours very sincerely
Dorothy (Geerts)

APPENDIX 2

The following are a selection of letters found with Philip's war letters. Some are from his family to Philip at Cotton College, his boarding school. Perhaps the two most touching letters in the collection are the ones that describe his decision to give up the priesthood, and his mother's response.

128 Farnham Road,
Handsworth
25.1.33

My dear Philip,

Thanks for the two letters and card. I think Philip that your sore throat is due to home–sickness. I don't mean that it isn't genuine – it is, but I think that you must 'look up' get plenty of sleep (if you can) and then enjoy yourself during the day. If you have no temperature I don't think it would hurt you to go into the sea but mind '<u>not</u> with a temperature'. Try and shake it off and don't get thinking of me too much. I told you if you got bad not to eat but Philip you might be making a mistake by not eating especially fish which is very <u>light</u> and ought not to hurt you at all. Use your own judgment about eating (if you feel like it) it may help to throw the sore throat off. So <u>do</u> try and shake it off there's a good boy. Enjoy yourself to the fullest. I am sending you some lozenges, suck one occasionally (not too often) and then if you don't feel otherwise bad go on as usual doing anything – swimming and eating. Remember <u>good</u> ice cream will relieve a sore throat <u>and don't starve yourself</u>.

Thanks for birthday wishes – give me a happy birthday by getting better and having a good time.

All my love
Mother

128 Farnham Road
Handsworth
6th March 1938

My dearest Philip,

May you be very happy this day and may God give you happiness always, even in your trials. This is my biggest prayer but of course I pray for other things too.

Daddy and all the others will send you their greetings. I will think of you a good deal you may be sure. I wish you many happy returns. And much love from

Your affectionate
Mother

My dear Philip,

Just a line to wish you many Happy returns of your birthday.

I notice your last few letters were in more cheerful vein, so trust you are taking a brighter outlook on life. Perhaps you find it better having a bigger variety of things to do.

Anyway I hope you are keeping well and happy and no matter how things go, always try and take a cheerful view, I think that is the best wish I can give you, so cheerio

Love from Daddy

Cotton College
N. Staffs
undated – February 1939?
(tearstained – difficult to read)

My dear Mother and Father

Thank you very much for yesterday's letter.

I'm afraid however it has brought matters to a head. Your mention of the ..Mass now compels me to tell you that I am still unsettled in my vocation.

Having said this much, I want to apologise for having led you up the garden path with hopes of my future; and now to have to spring on you this . . . and very bitter disappointment. However I can both assure you that it is not my fault, and that it is quite as big a sorrow for me to have to tell you this, conscious of the way I have as it were played around with you, as it will be for you to learn it.

At any rate I hope that this will now clear the air to some extent, and I will now endeavour to reveal my thoughts to you as clearly as possible. I have felt, and do, it to be very hard to live a celibate life and a good Catholic married and family life quite about whatever course is mine, but I think that I will sooner or later have to see my confessor, for I cannot keep on when I am made so restless during the holidays, without finding out whether all this is something real which I have to follow, or a mere temptation.

Well this is but a very imperfect exposition of what I feel, but I hope it will help you to understand me, and not take it for granted that I have parted this period – although I must admit – and apologise for it – that I have been responsible for your thinking so. Perhaps this quotation from my book might help you to understand, and to console you God's call is a mysterious thing. 'He calls one and not another, and after our surprise at those he calls comes our own still greater surprise at those he does NOT call'.

There can be little more to say I'm afraid, I could say much but it would be to no use, all I can say is that honestly appeals to be more than the priestly. This however I regarded as totally inadequate reason, and was rather ashamed to give up on that account. Secondly there is another consideration which I feel, but thought would hold no water and that was just an ideal that would get nowhere, namely that I have a special calling to live a long life as perfectly as possible. In that case it seems that providence has led me to Cotton simply to prepare me in the best possible way for this.

I might add, that if I have even since continued in my efforts to try and keep my dispositions for the priesthood, during term time I can generally succeed in reconciling myself to this, but each holiday always produces the most disturbing effect. One thing, it has driven me to prayer, for I have prayed ceaselessly now for

18 months, and last holidays, although I regularly paid visits to St Francis of over an hour duration and frequently went to benediction or holy hour there.

So really, there is nothing to fear. I would very much appreciate your prayers and ask you to accept this cross in as cheerful manner as possible – I myself do not mind suffering on account of it but I hate to think of yours. Remember that you will have special consolations either way, and for my part, I will do everything to increase and multiply them.

Yes I will certainly pray for Kitty and wish her every possible luck. The Pope I hear is dead, and must pray for him very hard too.

Well finally don't let this spoil your weekend at all, it's better you should know, so with my very best love

I am Your Most Loving Son
Philip

Ps I can give you more unimportant reasons later. Actually I would have told you all before only I have not felt it so deeply till lately. I certainly have not made up my mind against it yet but am rather battling against it.

My Dearest Philip,

It is with such a heavy heart that I write to you this morning. I am sorry that your letter was not posted in time. Philip! I simply don't know what to say to you! I myself am suffering from a terrible lot of remorse. I feel that I'm the cause of your feelings. I've made you feel how expensive you are to us and how we have to go without on your behalf. Oh! Philip! I would go without twice as much if God would restore your former feelings. I will <u>never never</u> again mention the expense you are to us. I shall be longing now to keep the expense and for it to grow harder. I complained bitterly of the burden God had given me although he offered me such a glorious reward so now he is taking the burden of the prize from me. Oh Philip!

What am I to say?

I know that it is your duty to give up if you feel that you haven't the vocation but —————————————————oh Philip in my heart I feel you <u>have</u> but I've made things harder for you. Is it lack of courage on your part? Please don't come home too soon because I think it may be just a fleeting doubt. Stay as long as you can praying and hoping for courage. You may be sure of my prayers and I am having a Mass said to help you.

I shall try not to miss one Holy Communion for you, and I shall pray to St. Theresa as you ask.

Don't do anything too hurriedly – take a term even a year to consider it in case God restores it to you. I feel unable to write about anything else now so please forgive me.

Your affectionate Mother

FAMILY LETTERS TO AND FROM PHILIP

To sister, Kathleen:

Postmark 10.10.40
c/o 38 Banks St.
Blackpool

My dear Kathleen,

Fancy to–day is your birthday and I find to my amazement that I have not wished you a very happy birthday. Well I am ever so sorry and all I can do now is to hope that you did have a wonderful time and were not kept in the air raid shelter too long. I was wondering what I could do when I realised quite suddenly that I could at least offer up a little prayer on your behalf, and I hope it has done some good. For the present however will you be content with this letter, and I shall then go and hunt around the shops to see what I can buy for you.

Tell Mother that I think I will be in Blackpool for another week or so, though the larger part of the squad will be off tomorrow, I know I am not going tomorrow.

Well as I say, I hope you have had a very pleasant birthday and that you will be a good girl!

So with all my best love and best wishes, I remain

Your Most Affectionate Brother
Philip

From Philip to brother, Gerald:

Christmas 1941

My dear Gerald,

You are finding things more peaceful I hope now, but I bet you will feel a little lonely this Christmastide all on your own and separated from Kathleen, Lorna and Monica and Daddy and Mother and Mary. However, I too will, I think be on my own 'somewhere in England' – at least I hope I will be in England, and Blackpool will be a better than a camp.

Anyway the real purpose of this short note is to wish you a very happy and merry Christmas, and so with these wishes I will now conclude, so best love and wishes,

From Your Most Loving Brother
Philip

1354399 AC PJ.Hermolle
4 Flight, 2 SQUADRON
10 I.T.W.
GRAND HOTEL
SCARBOROUGH
19.1.41

My Dear Gerald,

You are I suppose feeling a little lonely out in Ludlow by yourself in this wintry weather and would welcome a letter. I am afraid I have not heard much about you at all since you left home, so I don't know whether you have good billets or whether you have Gordon Hearne with you, or how you are going on. Have nearly all of St. Philip's gone up there? How do you go on at night and in your free time at weekends? Is there much you can do or are there any good walks around there? I hope you did have as happy and cheery a Christmas as possible, and that the landlady found you something good to eat. In the meantime how is your work going down? Let's see you ought to be in third form now oughtn't you? And next year you should be taking your S.C.

Well I bet you are glad to be out of Birmingham now and in a fairly safe area and able to sleep in peace, but you must not forget to pray for Mother, Daddy and Mary who are still there, that they may all be safe and sound. Have you seen our new house yet? I have seen it from the outside, but I have not been home yet since I last saw you.

Although I am now on my pilot's course, I have not yet been inside an aeroplane; however I should leave Scarborough in about seven or eight weeks and should commence flying soon after if I pass all my exams here all right. The course is very interesting and we have to learn how to recognise all British, German and Italian planes from any angle; there are 88 types in all including the Fleet air area so you can guess how much we have to learn. I can tell a few British planes, but that is all for the moment.

Scarborough is a very nice place, and I recommend it if ever you want to go on your holidays in more peaceful times. We often see big, large convoys pass very near in, sometimes with coastal command aircraft zig zagging above, and warships in front and behind. It is hard to see the warships because they lie so low in the water and are camouflaged to look like the sea. The main thing that gives their presence away is the spray churned up from their propellers and the flow as it cuts its way through.

Well I shall have to finish now, wishing you all the very best,

From you affectionate brother
Philip

Ps If you do wish to answer, send it to Mother to send in her letter to me – it will save a stamp.

To sister Kathleen, now evacuated to Herefordshire, from Philip at home on leave:

128 Farnham Road
Handsworth
Birmingham 21
8th October? 1941

My Dear Kathleen,

Well fancy my having to WRITE my birthday greetings to you from home. Anyhow I have to, and I wish you a very happy and bright birthday. Mother told us that Mrs. Roberts was going to give you a birthday party; well, you know, you're very lucky aren't you? Gerald will be very lucky too since you are sure to invite him, and I bet he will not be like the men in the gospel of today who, being invited to the marriage feast, refused to go because they had plenty of work to do. Even if he should have plenty of work on hand I could not imagine Gerald finding it more important than going to a party, though I doubt whether he will think too much of his 'party frock'.

Mrs. Downy[1] told me that she saw you pushing a baby in a pram the other Wednesday while she was there; was that Michael? Do you often take out babies like that?

I see that you seemed a little sorry that the war was going to last a long time. Well, you know, the Roberts might perhaps be wrong and you may not be away too long, you will have to say a few prayers that it will be only a short war.

Are you still playing the piano as much as you were at home? I do not suppose that you will be able to do so, for you have to go next door don't you? And how do you like St. Paul's now? In your next letter you had better write a bit of French just to show us that you have started it, and if you are not better than Gerald well, you cannot be much good. Do you know that I put a simple French sentence in one of my letters to him and he replied saying that he could not understand what I had said – at least that is what I suppose he said, for he replied in French . . .of a sort! And if I remember rightly he asked me not to write any more in French. It does not look therefore that you are likely to receive much aid from him.

To conclude, you had better tell me what you would like for your birthday – within limits of course – then I shall see what can be done about it. So now sending you once again my very best love and wishes for your birthday,

I remain,

Your Most Affectionate Brother
Philip

---

1. Neighbour, Tony Downy's mother

From Philip's father, Gerald Hermolle Snr to Philip:

128 Farnham Road etc
3.3.42

My Dear Philip

Well to start with I want to wish you many happy returns of the day and I hope by the time your next birthday comes round again that the war will be over. Things look pretty black at present but I suppose the present state of affairs can't continue indefinitely and things will take a turn for the better one of these days.

Well you have had some changes since your last birthday. I think you could do much worse than remain at your present station while the war is on.

Fancy you starting a trip over the Midlands and having to turn back on account of the weather. I daresay you would like a view of Birmingham from the air.

The weather has turned a bit milder this afternoon but it has been very cold these last few weeks.

Auntie Eileen is now at home and although improving is still in a pretty bad way. She can manage to walk a few steps with someone to help her, but has not got much use in her right arm yet. Still she is talking much better and seems stronger in herself.

Glad you received that letter which I readdressed. I was sorry after that I hadn't put it in another envelope.

Well I don't think there is any further news this time and I expect Mother will be writing to you so Goodbye for the present and best wishes for your birthday

Love from all,
Father

From sister, Lorna to Philip:

128 Farnham Rd

etc

Wednesday 3rd March 1942

Dear Philip,

I hope you are very well and that you have a very happy birthday. I hope, also, that you will come back to us all soon. We have not got you a present yet, because we don't know what to get you, but we hope to later. I hope you receive this letter on your birthday but it is doubtful. I cannot think of anything else except that Monica has had a tooth out yesterday and that I had to go to school by myself. It happens to be night now, and I will have to be going to bed soon so

All the best of love

Your loving sister Lorna

Ps May God bless you and bring you safely home.

From sister, Kathleen (aka Kitty) to Philip:

128 Farnham Rd

Handsworth

B'ham 21

3rd March 1942

Dear Philip,

I hope you are still keeping well and happy, and also that you have a very happy birthday. At home we are all very well and just settling down. I hope you will get this letter in time but I quite forget the time until quite late last night. I have rather a lot of practise to do lately for I play for the youth club's country dancing and also the choir's opera songs I am playing for, and then there's Mrs. Payne's work. I'm in school at the moment, and I'm going to try and post this at dinner time. Do you like flying up at night? We sometimes hear aeroplanes over here but they're English. I am in a hurry to get this off, so I hope you'll have a really happy birthday, with all my love

XxxKittyxxx

128 Farnham Road
3rd March 1942

Dear Philip

I hope you have a happy birthday, also I hope you are well. I haven't a birthday present now. I hope the war will be over soon. Philip I hope I can get you a birthday present.

With lots of love
3xxxfrom6xxxxMonica9xxx
12xxx15xxxx18xxx
21xxx24xxx 27xxx
to Philip
Jesus will bless you

A letter from Philip's Auntie Kathleen in New Zealand (encl. with letter of Friday 17ᵗʰ July 1942):

c/o Flax Mill
Leeston
Canterbury
New Zealand
April 20th 1942

My Dear Philip,

I received your nice long and newsy letter last week although the postmark was 22nd December 1941 and six days later I got one from your Mother and the Birmingham postmark was 28th February 1942, so you see how disturbed the mail passage must be. However I was delighted to get both letters after a long spell.

Yes I was surprised to know that you went to Canada to complete your training but it would be a great experience for you and a rest from the strain felt in England. Fancy your Mother back in the old home again. They must be getting on with the job of repairs and that is a very good sign. I also hope that those days, or nights I should say, of raids are over for you all. I have to be very careful what I write now for fear of 'giving information to the enemy' and as things have so changed on this side of the globe.

Thank you for the information re the different positions in the R.A.F. Yes quite a few people here think that St. Chad's (Cathedral, Birmingham) was down but I am glad it is not so. Before I got your letter I was talking to a man who keeps a paper shop and he said it was down, but neither of us could remember the name of it and concluded that it was St. Joseph's, so when next I see him – I can correct this. It is peculiar how one forgets the names of places and streets which we knew so well at home. I had forgotten the name of St. Philip's also until you mentioned it, but I expect after the war there will be a lot of new places and new buildings, it should be a nice city.

Yes I expect you would meet some of the new Zealand pilots in Canada, they would be able to tell you something about Christchurch. Did they tell you it was the Garden City but I may say all our gardens are put to another use for the time being – I hope they will not be required.

You say you have been buying records for the radiogram – I cannot understand how you work them for are they not connected with the radio – you cannot have the air as well can you? I cannot imagine the radio at all in some of the houses at home – for I feel sure it would be heard in each other's house if it is put on like some of the folks out here use it. The houses out here are all well away from each other, you know that don't you? Yes we heard all about the 'mysterious' voice on the air, I could not imagine the English people being anything else than amused at such tactics from Germany.

By the way, the boy Humphreys (Flight Lieutenant) who has just won distinguished honour lived a short distance from Stanmore Road and is an R. C. but he has been flying in England since 1939.

Well Philip, take care of yourself as far as is possible and I pray to God that you will be spared – I am always thinking of you and hoping that you are out of danger. Thank you for saying a prayer for me – I need it but don't expect you to find time for me. May God bless and protect you.

Lots of love from your affectionate
Aunt Kathleen

APPENDIX 3

Correspondence between Philip (known here as Yipe) and school friend Fr. John Garvey, aka Gargoil. The first is a letter to Kathleen, to whom he sends them.

1 Bridge House
Dorchester–on–Thames
Oxford
OX9 8JR
22nd February 1979

Dear Kathleen,

You must have given up all hope of hearing from me and of receiving Philip's letters. I have at last got round to sorting them out from a box containing many other letters of the war years, mostly from my sisters and brother – in – law. Yesterday was an enforced day of rest for me, for on Tuesday I had a minor operation to have a couple of cysts removed. For a priest on a parish there is always work to be done and it is only at times of sickness that one feels easy in conscience to ignore the demands that are always there. So yesterday I spent a pleasant half day indulging in nostalgia.

I had not read through Philip's letters since the time when I received them, but some points have always stood out in my mind. On re–reading them I was confirmed in recollection of him as being a young man of deep faith and holiness and of having a wisdom above his years. Though he refers to some of the letters being confidential I am sure that at this lapse of time he will not mind his own family knowing their content. You will gather that over a period I was experiencing difficulties and temptations concerning my vocation, and his very firm and sound advice, plus his prayers were a great help and encouragement to me. His idea of the standard which a priest should set himself makes me feel very humble now. Had he lived he would have been an inspiration to us all in whatever vocation he found to be his own.

I assume that from his letters to the family, you were well aware of his virtues and strength of character, but I am sure you will find these letters throw extra light on your brother, of whom you must be justly proud.

I did not cash the cheque which you kindly sent with the request for Masses. I should have told you this before. I am glad to offer the Masses for your intentions, but do so as a very small token of thanks for the many helps I received from Philip. God bless.

Yours sincerely
John Garvey

1354399 L.A.C. P. J. Hermolle
Yeadon
2nd May 1941

Dear Gargoil,

Thanks very much for your letter of today – it came at a moment when I was thoroughly down and out, and in a sense struck by the very stings that are causing the most pain at the moment. That was when you spoke of your sister Mary's extreme heroism – and your Mother and Father's too – in taking such a hard decision. You see, I have just heard too, that I am for posting abroad, which is going to prove a very nasty pill to swallow under the present circumstances when all the blitzes are on. However we are all to remember that in sorrow shall we bring forth fruit, and I have always protested in my prayers that I am never to be far from God's feet on the cross, that I shall only be certain that I could not be very far from the right track when I can see some dark clouds of suffering and trouble about me. In this sense I therefore welcome what is to come, but it takes great willpower to try and see it in this light, and it affords me but little consolation from a physical point of view.

Firstly I could never do what you say your sister is about to do; I fear I must be far too attached to the things of this world, and my strong love of home is perhaps greater than it should be. I remember that it was a dreadful ordeal for me to have to return to Cotton in those old days – yet then I was so certain of my vocation that I stuck it out no end! I hope that with changing circumstances and older years I am not falling too much away.

I often get this feeling, especially because I do not pray half as much as I should do. Mind you I am caused much suffering in a way because I have nowhere to go and pray, and go pour out all my troubles to Our Father who used always to be so sympathetic and helpful and handy when at school. As you can well imagine things are very averse to prayer in conditions as I am in now, I fear too that they will not improve abroad. How welcome it is to go into Leeds, there to hop into the Cathedral if only for one day per week! Do you know that I am prepared to make all that excursion for no other reason, and I therefore have to choose to go alone, but it is worth it. How I long too, for days to arrive once more when I can go to meet my Maker in daily Holy Communion, and take my orders from him!

Does this affect you very much? It is another source of extreme suffering for me, for I simply cannot fathom how men could do what they are doing to each other, and when I walk through Birmingham or Sheffield or even parts of Leeds my heart sinks and becomes as heavy as lead, and I can hardly bear to think that I belong to a service that is doing the same thing to Germany; in fact my faith in our cause is shaken and I even have temptations that in conscience I ought not to undertake it (i.e. a pilot's course).

Of course these are nothing short of temptations, and are allowed by God I know; but again it is hard for me to see it that way.

By the way, in my last letter there was no 'implicit rebuke'! – I remember far too well our busy days at Cotton, and how welcome a letter can be. I have quite a lot of time compared to you, I bet, though I have not too much.

Well, we are leaving here tomorrow (Sat) for a place near Manchester, from where I hope to get an embarkation leave and perhaps see you all.

Will you please not forget to say an extra prayer now and again especially for my spiritual welfare, which is in great need of fresh support, and I will certainly try my best to pray more for you, and at least offer up my work as one long prayer for these things not forgetting your sister Mary who has chosen a path which is perhaps far harder than she yet realises, and for your family too.

Cheerio and best wishes
Yipe

PS I see I have dwelt at length on my own troubles, and not said anything about you – rather selfish I know, but please excuse for the moment and I will perhaps give you more 'gen' a little later.

PPS. In case you don't know 'gen' is an RAF expression for 'LOWDOWN'

1354399 Sgt. Hermolle
c/o Sergeants Mess
5 A.O.S.
R.A.F.
Jurby
Isle of Man
February 1942

Dear Gargoil,

It is rather a long time since last I wrote you isn't it? In fact I think it was when I was at Yeadon just before I left England. Things have moved since then, I have lost friends and found new ones, and seen many new and different peoples, a vast new country, I have also had my little hazards and excitements and had a glimpse in the very midst of all the terrific strain of war of the joys and pleasures of peace, with freedom from blackouts, rationing and the sights of torn buildings and houses.

For in Canada now, especially in the towns such as Montreal, Winnipeg, Calgary and etc. there is no trace of war, no gas masks; people go about enjoying themselves in a land of plenty. There is no restriction on things you can buy; luxurious and large super–streamlined limousines flash by undeterred by the fact that petrol – or 'gasoline' as they call it – is so urgently needed for the war. In fact, Montreal and Calgary, as I saw them basking in such terrific heat from the sun which had the whole blue sky to itself, were more like an English seaside resort, with people going carefree down to the beach in their light summer apparel in days of peace. And I remember thinking when I was in Montreal – such a beautiful and colourful city – how unreal and unnatural it seemed, and what many an Englishman and many a European would give to spend a day in this city and its carefree spirit.

I compared Birmingham with its smoking factories, and humming machines, its devastation, its lack of food, where people had to work too hard to allow such time for frivolity, where already twilight would be enveloping it, and its citizens might have to expect almost anything to happen – with this, Canada's second city, and could hardly believe my surroundings, when I thought of all my relatives and friends in such hard circumstances.

When I saw newspaper men holding out thick 40 page midday papers, some from Montreal, some from New York, with terrific headlines of typical American papers that 'R.A.F bash Berliners for hours in stupendous Offensive' I wondered how many of those gay and pleasure seeking people realised all that words like that meant.

Personally I was always looking forward to getting back to the 'Beleaguered Britain', as the Canadian and American papers always referred to us, and always used to feel too secure in Canada when things are so hard in England.

Yes it was a wonderful experience going right over to another continent and catching a glimpse of people on the other side of the Atlantic, and there is some remarkable country as well, but being so long away from one's own country also makes one far more appreciative of its qualities and virtues, things that perhaps would otherwise pass unnoticed. For instance I think that it is a remarkable thing that the general moral standard is much higher in our own country than in Canada and America, especially in regard to censorship of periodicals and magazines. The people there are also far more addicted to luxury and pleasure seeking and to a lazy life than we English; in most of the towns especially (and certainly at Medicine Hat where our station was) there was very little family life or discipline; it appeared as though a house was merely a place where most of the occupants returned at late night or early morning and left it again when they were forced to get up. The café was the general place for meals; young girls were apparently allowed out at all times and it seemed that their parents did not bother to watch them or restrain them in any way.

Of course I'm not going to say that this was all universal there, but on the other hand it was far more marked than it has ever been in England, and even most English chaps didn't like it either.

And of course it would be very unfair if I did not make allowances for countries like Canada and America, or if I was blinded to their better elements. I could see plainly that the lack of discipline sprung partly from the fact that they are a much newer race, and have a great sense of freedom from the spaciousness and wild beauty of their country; but it seems to me that their sense of freedom has not been tempered by experience in the harsh realities of life, as has ones in England, with the result that they do not know when to set limits and restraints. Then of course there is not the same snobbery or class distinction over there, and they do not set half so much store by our typically English formalities and etc. which are things in their balance.

I also notice that if there is a laxity over there in censorship etc., there is a very vigorous and fairly successful opposition from a specially organised Catholic organisation, which has also typically American and original ways in its counter propaganda. Some of this Catholic propaganda would I think sometimes make an English Catholic frown, for there is a Hollywood ring about it! However when I started to think of it, and the people to whom it was directed, I could not help rather admiring it, and I think they enter into difficulties of young people in a very sensible and practical way. There is no doubt that I have discovered a far greater appreciation of American outlook and ways now than before I went to Canada. They are as different from Englishmen and Frenchmen are, in fact I often used to wonder if there wasn't more in common with the whole of Europe and England, than England and America. However there is no doubt that all America has been more captured by the British stand last winter than any of the terrific German achievements.

Well I don't know whether all this is very interesting to you but I don't know whether there is very much for me to say. I haven't as yet told you that I am flying Blenheims and Ansons here for training our future gunners and observers. I am very pleased that I am not on bombing operations, but will take a chance at night fighting or coastal command if ever the chance comes along.

We have several Polish pilots here, not to mention others from every part of the Empire and one or two from the U.S.A., and we all get on very well together, except that the Poles 'No speak English' or 'No understand' when there are any dirty jobs to be done! But then you cannot blame them can you! It is all taken in good part and more often than not they will come back and do their full share. They are very interesting to talk to, and there is not a chap about at all who will ever try to deny that they are anything but the best of pilots, and if an English airman will say that about a foreigner you can rest assured it must be true. The Poles enjoy a wonderful reputation for flying. Only the other day a Polish crew landed here in a Wellington bomber when I was Duty Pilot, and the Captain told me that in the last war he fought for the Russians against Germany as an infantry soldier when he was made a prisoner of war; he then fought for the Russians against Germany as an infantry soldier in the Polish war of independence; after which he joined the Polish air force in which he has been ever since. He fought in Poland, France, and now in this very Wellington bomber had made 27 trips over Germany. He was Squadron leader.

And now I wonder about you all at Oscott. Are you still quite ok? How is your sister Mary finding her new life? As for me I am still unsettled as ever and though I pray and pray and pray for so many helps, I do not seem to get any definite answer at all; I am at the moment very sorry because I know that I am not making the most of my chances in the R.A.F., and am certainly not outspoken enough – I often try but I'm afraid courage is lacking, so for some time now I have launched what I call 'a mighty offensive' of prayer for a number of intentions, of which this is one of the most important, 'courage'. I always treat my spiritual life in terms of armed strategy and try and direct a campaign as a Commander in Chief would against the titanic forces of evil.

Well I must conclude now sending you all my very best wishes and prayers,

From Yours Sincerely
Philip

1354399 Sgt. P.J.Hermolle
Sergeants Mess
5 A.O.S. R.A.F.
19th March 1942

Dear Gargoil,

Your letter arrived here this evening and its reading gave me great pleasure. If it was spontaneous then I can guess it was also sincere. I also often have the same feeling, that I write a lot of tripe, but then I reflect that it only helps others to see me as I really am, and not as I simply appear.

Most of what you say in regard to the Priesthood and preparations for it, I agree with, but I do feel strongly on other aspects as well which I noticed you disagreed with, at Christmas when I was talking to you. As a matter of fact, in response to requests from Tony, I have given him most of my views. In the main they are that Priests should translate their sermons into ACTION and DEED – that their people might listen to them; that all a Priest's actions and all his work should be wholly unselfish; that he should not be content with being the servant of the flock, but should set out to be their absolute SLAVE! He should anticipate their thoughts study their difficulties. He should literally fly to minister ANY spiritual help – even if he is kept waiting an extra ten minutes (an annoyance that would be far more profitable to all concerned if he strove to be polite the more he was kept waiting). Yes, I think a Priest should be more than human in his consideration of others and in his allowances for human frailty, but he can treat himself as a very devil! Anyway I will not bore you by a further peroration on the subject.

You pay me rather lavish compliments in thinking that I am one whom you would rather like to see become a Priest, but it does not give me much more confidence – somehow I feel paralysed in this respect, and I am only immediately concerned to do all that I can in the present, and I am trying to view the future as entirely in the hands of God, for then I cannot go far wrong. To tell you the truth my whole inclination to that vocation seems to have been deadened, but nevertheless I am far from dismayed, and my spirits are high and gay, and I still enjoy life immensely.

There is so much beauty in human life and in our surroundings which never ceases to fill me with 'joie de vivre', whether I see it in the frolics of sheep in the fields, or in the rhythmical continuity of vales and hills, the deep tranquillity – or perhaps the awe inspiring wrath of the mighty sea, or, that which I love to see more than anything else, in the actions and nature of all our neighbours who are continually reflecting the infinite goodness and greatness of their creator though they know it not, and though on occasion they seem so wayward. To witness the love of a mother for her child, and then compare it with what gifts some of our 'great' men are going to give the world such as Stalin and his materialistic prosperity or Hitler and his New Order. Our greatest genius has yet to produce anything at all that can even begin to compare with those great gifts from God which we all have and enjoy so freely, such as love as it exists in every family, the gift of children to parents, and the gift of parents to children, the gift of husband to wife, and wife to husband, the gift of thought and of sight, of speech and of touch – I often wonder why, when people have been given so much, that they even want more, for what is your motor car by comparison to all those things?

So you see that though I have my problems and that though the future has no clear horizon, yet nevertheless I find much to be thankful for, and I certainly find plenty to think about, and alas there is plenty in the garden to be put right. Of my soul I might say with Hamlet 'Tis an unweeded garden . . .and things rank and gross in nature possess it merely'. I can also ask with Hamlet Why I am so slow to act and do those things which I should and which I want to do for 'What is a man. . .If his chief good and market of his time, Be but to sleep and feed? A beast, no more. Sure, he that made us with such large discourse, Looking before and after, gave us not That capability and god–like reason To fust in us unused'

Hamlet goes on to analyse his feelings and sentiments as 'A thought which, quartered, hath but one part wisdom. And ever these parts coward'.

And then he goes on to ask

'I do not know, why yet I live to say This things to do'; 'Sith I have cause and will and strength to do't. Examples gross as Earth exhort me!'

Now you will probably remember Hamlet's comparison, but then what of my own particular responsibility? I cannot even say as he did, that my inaction has one part wisdom, for it has none, but it has all parts coward. Yes that is exactly my position, for I am a miserable failure and lack all courage. I don't wish simply to guard my own battlements, I should be sallying forth with counter blows, perhaps even with counter offensives; I should fight as our pilots did in the Battle of Britain without thought of failure or retreat, satisfied with nothing but victory no matter what the cost. My enthusiasm should be dynamic and forge through hardest rock and toughest granite, my will and determination should be adamant. This, Gargoil, is what I am continually seeking for in my prayers day in day out and I even ask that 'I may fight as a British fighter pilot'. I will go on asking and am yet supremely confident that I will get what I want even though for the present I often wonder whether I am becoming yet weaker and more infirm of purpose. It is at this point that I wish to ask you to rally to my side by augmenting my prayers with some of yours, because I must do something; in return I will pray, or try to, even harder for you for your intentions and for Mary, your sister, as you ask. I have offered all my flying hours as special prayers with special intentions – I shall join those of yours to them as well, (just to make certain you are not forgotten nor Mary).

By the way, I hope to be coming home on the 5th May on my next leave. We are now living back at our 'old house'. However I never regard the future as entirely settled these days – one cannot in this job – we get a number of casualties at times that you cannot put it entirely in the background, and it is very distressing to see those chaps you have spoken with and joked with, who have continually laughed through life's storms and scorned difficulties, who had perhaps on occasion been a little more keen on the beer, but who were nevertheless very good at heart. It is very sad, as I say, to see them suddenly wrenched from before you, and the question is inevitably 'Who is the next on the list?' with the realisation 'There is no reason why it shouldn't be me'. For their sakes at home, I hope I shall be okay.

For the present then, I think I will bid you adieu, sending you all my very best wishes and etc.

From one who is striving to fight with his back to the wall but could do with a spot of lease–lend supplies – so how about it!

Yours sincerely

Yipe

1354399
Sergeants Mess
R.A.F.
South Cerney
Gloucestershire
Tuesday evening
Late 1942/Early 1943

Dear Gargoil,

Thanks for your letter which I received on Saturday evening. As usual it was both interesting and welcome. There is far too much that I would like to talk to you about to fit into this letter in the limited time at my disposal, but I shall do what I can.

Behind your few remarks as to my recent misfortunes I don't suppose that you have even the vaguest idea of all that it has cost me, Only one thing I will tell you, and that is that never in my whole life have I had such a disappointment or felt so low. There was one consolation when I was in Brighton – and I needed all of it – and that was for a long period I was able to assist at Daily Mass and Holy Communion, with the other facilities of a church being handy. It would take me far too long to give you all my reasons and the way it affected me so at this point I will not attempt it.

By a miracle – for I can think of no other reason, save the prayers of St. Theresa – I am back on flying once more, and I am hoping that from now onwards things will be better, and I shall be able to go forward to do my duty as best I can.

I have lately been doing quite a bit of writing to Thornton, who knows most of the history of the last few months.

Yes it was simply wonderful meeting Bill Murtagh down at Brighton – we both appreciated meeting another Cottonian in such circumstances, and I think the spirits of both of us soared after that Benediction! I introduced him to the C.W.L. canteen down there – and incidentally to a charming helper there of the name of Dorothy, with whom I formed a very happy friendship during the last period of my stay there. To her also I owe much, for she did much to keep my spirits a little higher. Bill agrees with me that she is a very nice girl, so you can take it for granted that she is!

I had heard of Jenning Grove from Bill Murtagh! As a matter of fact I was not very surprised. The few times I had been up to Oscott, I could detect that all was not well with Jenning and I think for most of his time at Oscott, he has been battling hard with himself – in fact I wouldn't be surprised if he had a pretty hard time during the last two years at Cotton. I hope that he will soon settle down now that the decision has been made, and make great progress along another road which is equally important in these days. If you could give me his address I would like to write him, for it may be that I can help him in what must be an awkward period of his life.

As regards myself, I think that at last I am beginning to see the way a little clearer – in fact I think I am almost certain of my way. But it will, I fear, cause you a little disappointment for I do not think I shall be returning to Oscott or any other seminary. I feel certain that, if I come through this war ok, my road will pass through the gateway of matrimony – it may not be long before I can tell you much more definitely about this. I have been thinking lately what a good opportunity there lies ahead, for three old friends to join hands and form a centre, as it were, for some sort of lay organisation sponsored mainly by Cottonians in some field or other of Catholic Action. I have been thinking of course of Bill Murtagh, Bill (Jenning?) Grove and myself. After all, united we might stand, while divided our strength is at least very dissipated. I have mentioned this aspect to no one yet but you, but ever since I have left Cotton I have often thought that some such combined action might prove very beneficial and invigorating to our diocese. What do you think?

Gargoil, thanks for your views expressed in your last letter which always make me ponder. I think that I can see the point of what you are driving at better than many people would, because it is one that has always had great appeal to me, and had I gone through to Oscott to study as you are, it would have an even stronger appeal – but if you will permit me to add what I think is a word of caution, and which in your surroundings wouldn't come so obviously to you – it would be this, 'Don't forget the human element'.

After all to make great spiritual advancement there is no need to soar above the visions of your people; and though for yourself it is always a good thing to study and peer into the finer points of God's love, and so appreciate him the more, you will have to descend to their level in mind when you talk to them; you will have to have the simplicity and clarity and untarnished view of a child. You will have to increase their devotion by very gradual steps, and in ways which will appeal to them rather than to yourself. After all, isn't this exactly what Christ did? Were not his parables of the lilies of the field and the birds of the air? Were not his illustrations taken from the most commonplace things such as food and drink? Were not his miracles and good works of a nature that had a special appeal to the people, such as at the wedding feast or when he raised from the dead the only son of his mother, a widow? In short, didn't he entirely forget himself in his continual work for others, even if it was only a word of good cheer, or a conversation about the harvest? I quote all these instances quickly and at random for I haven't much time, and I also wish to do it with due modesty and humility, knowing that you have these things at least far more intensely than I.

Well I shall now conclude wishing you all the best, and offering up my prayers for you, thanks for yours.

Yours sincerely
Philip (or Yipe!)

P.S. Pleased to hear about Mary – I think you have a wonderful sister in her, and shall pray that she may bring you all many joys and consolations.

APPENDIX 4

A letter from an RAF pal:

Officers Mess
No. 5 A.O.S.
Jurby
22.7.43

My dear Philip,

Thank you ever so much for the nice long letter I received from you this evening. I was ever so interested in all the news you gave me of all your doings. I was interested to hear of Duft and Thompson. Did I ever tell you I met Jenkins who used to sleep over me at Med. Hut one day when I went to Madley to take Bond when he was posted. He was flying w/opps round in Proctors and was he CHEESED!! It was a pity you would not land here but perhaps someday somewhere we will meet again.

Yes!! Jurby is a very different place these days. The new C.O. has made a lot of difference too. But the only trouble is that one does not get anywhere. The old trips are just the same except for the Saturday ones.

Next Saturday we hope to do a 1000 mile trip landing at different dromes for lunch and tea. This makes a change but it means we don't get a day off. However why worry.

We have got an Avro Tutor now here now, it is a hot plane rather like a glorified Tiger Moth. I have spent a couple of hair raising hours in it. After an Anson it is so light that I don't know when it leaves or comes to rest on the ground. My first shot at aerobatics almost made me sick. The second effort was much better and I enjoyed it a lot. Some change after 'stooging' on new trips for so long!!

I don't know if when I last wrote to you had started on what I call my night circus. That is going round as check pilot with all the people who have not done solo at night on the station. It is some game and I have to do it every other week. Believe me! It is one thing flying yourself, and quite another being taken round at night by some of the Poles we have here circuit after circuit.

Now to give you the gen on some of the postings, Morrison has been posted to Bicester, and a short time ago Austin went to Grantham. I have lost Badlan as he has got his opps posting to coastal (the lucky man) I wish I were in his shoes. When my turn comes I think people here will do what they can to get me onto coastal so I hope for the best. Badlan became a proud father shortly before he left here. The baby was a large daughter and he was most thrilled when he came back from seeing his wife. He had done just over 1000 hours when he left and was a long way ahead of the others on the course he went on when he left here.

There is a C.O's parade this morning but as I am on night flying tonight I need not attend much to my joy. Yesterday we were to have done a 1000 mile trip but the weather did not play so we had to be content with a shorter trip. We had lunch at Montrose which was very pleasant place, though I did not think much of the drome itself. The Mess was in an old house well away from the drome and we spent quite a time after lunch lying in the sun on the lawn. My room looks onto the square and I have just seen them all march on and apart from the Canadians they all looked very smart.

On re–reading your letter I see you say they pushed you off without much ado on the Bostons. Lately we have had two Wellingtons crash land here and the lack of 'gen' those poor chaps had was sad to see, and also the lack of interest their OTUs took in them. Here we get all there is that can help us and when we get to OTU we will know what to ask for if we don't get it.

All sorts of people enquire after you quite regularly, in fact you would be surprised if you remembered them all.

The last few months I have not been doing as much flying as I should like to have but this month I am well over the 80 and if things go on as well as they have so far I should not do so badly.

The night before Badlan went away we went down to Smokey Joe's and had a feast then we went to the Imperial and had a few drinks. We gave Joe the latest 'gen' on you as it was some time since we had been in. These days we have a seven day night flying week followed at once by day flying so we only get one day off in fourteen days. As I usually do a long trip that day I just never seem to get a day off. In fact I have been meaning to go down to Ramsey to get a pair of shoes for six weeks now.

I am posting this to your home address so it can be forwarded. If you go abroad don't forget to drop me a line sometime.

Yours with all good wishes
Bill

APPENDIX 5

LETTERS OF REFERENCE BY HEADMASTERS

From the Headmaster
Very Rev. B. Manion, M.A.
Cotton College
North Staffordshire
September 1939

To whom it may concern

Mr. Philip Hermolle was a student in this School from September 1933 until July 1939. During those years he studied Latin, Greek, French, English Literature, Mathematics and History with the usual English subjects. He gained his School Certificate of the Oxford and Cambridge Joint Board and after two years in the Sixth gained his Higher Certificate.

He has good ability and is a conscientious and careful worker.

On the playing fields too he showed outstanding ability at Rugger Cricket and Hockey, representing the School in each game. He was also Prefect of the School and took a prominent part in the social life of the School. I can recommend him as thoroughly trustworthy in every way.

From the Headmaster
(Rev.) F. V. Reade M.A.Cantab.
The Oratory
St. Philip's Grammar School
Hagley Road
Birmingham 16
December 29th 1939

Mr. Philip Hermolle was my pupil for a year at St. Philip's Grammar School, Edgbaston, and I have been in constant touch with him since then. I have formed a very high opinion of the abilities and character of this young man, and he is one in whom I should be inclined to place implicit trust. I may add that his family has been also known to me for many years, and so I am able to speak of Mr. Philip Hermolle with more than ordinary confidence.

GLOSSARY

A.C.A.C.	Air Crew Allocation Centre
A.C.W.	Air Control Wing
A.F.S.	Auxiliary Fire Service
A.F.U.	Advanced Flying Unit
A.O.C.	Air Officer Commanding
A.O.N.S.	Air Observers Navigation School
A.O.S.	Air Observer School
A.R.P.	Air Raid Precautions
A.T.A.	Air Transport Auxiliary
A.T.C.	Air Traffic Control
A.T.S.	Auxiliary Territorial Service
C.E.G.	Catholic Evidence Guild
C.O.	Commanding Officer
C.W.L.	Catholic Women's League
C.Y.M.S.	Catholic Young Men's Society
D.F.M.	Distinguished Flying Medal
D.R.O.	Daily Routine Orders
E.F.T.S.	Elementary Training Flying School
E.N.S.A.	Entertainments National Service Association
H.E.	High Explosive
Jerry	German (WW2 slang)
Ities	Italians (WW2 slang)
I.T.W.	Initial Training Wings
I.O.M.	Isle of Man
L.A.C.	Leading aircraftman
Ops.	Operators
M.O.	Medical officer
N.C.O.	Non Commissioned Officer
O.C.	Officer Commanding
O.T.	Officer Training
O.T.U.	Operational Training Unit
P.T. Instructor	Physical Training Instructor
R.A.F.	Royal Air Force
R.C.	Roman Catholic
R.T.O.	Railway Transport Officer
S.F.T.S.	Service Flying Training School
S.H.Q.	Station Headquarters
S.W.O.	Station Warrant Officer
Tommy	British soldier (WW2 slang)
U.T.	Under Training
V.R.	Volunteer Reserves
W/opp *or* W.O.P.s	Wireless Operator/s
W.A.A.F.	Women's Auxiliary Air Force
ZZ Blind approaches	Aircraft landing method to assist the pilot to land in bad visibility, using a series of radio bearings.